Credit Unions in a Changing World

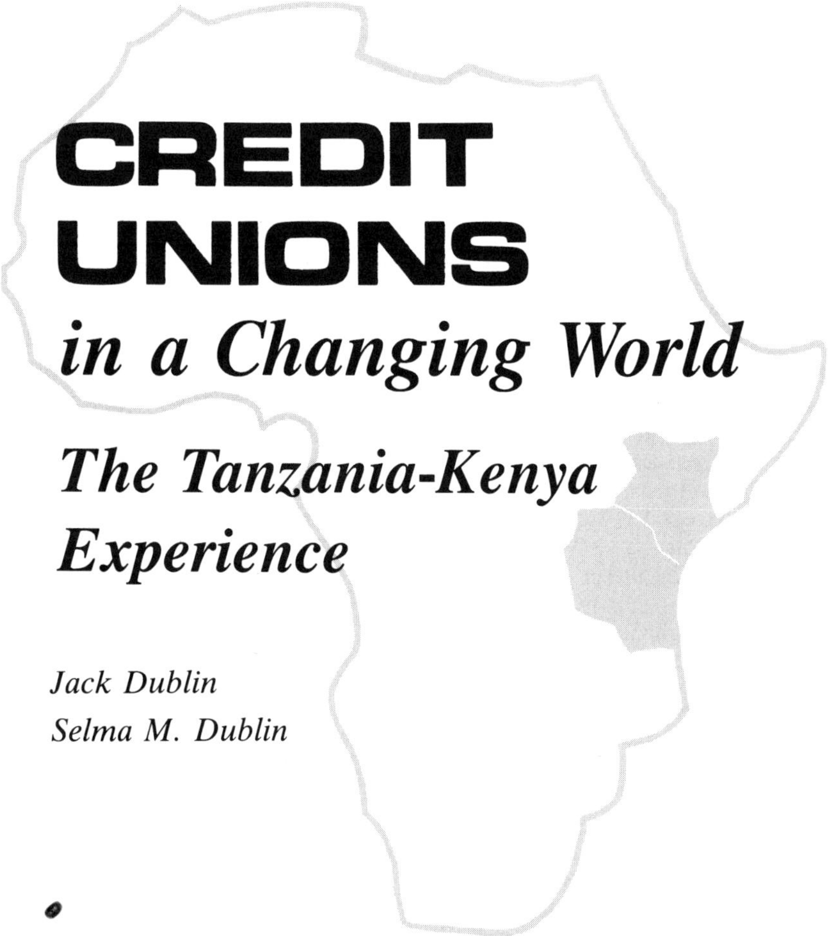

CREDIT UNIONS

in a Changing World

The Tanzania-Kenya Experience

Jack Dublin

Selma M. Dublin

Wayne State University Press *Detroit 1983*

Library of Congress Cataloging in Publication Data

Dublin, Jack.
Credit unions in a changing world.

Bibliography: p.
Includes index.
1. Credit unions—Tanzania—History. 2. Credit unions—Kenya—History. I. Dublin, Selma M., 1918– II. Title.
HG2039.T37D8 1983 334'.22'096762 83-1353
ISBN: 0-8143-1742-1
ISBN: 0-8143-1743-X (pbk.)

Grateful acknowledgment is made to the Michigan Credit Union League Foundation, the Canadian Co-operative Credit Society Limited, the Saskatchewan Co-operative Credit Society Limited, the British Columbia Central Credit Union, the Pennsylvania Credit Union League, PACUL Services, Inc., and the World Council of Credit Unions.

Contents

Preface

We first became involved with African credit union activities in Tanzania, Kenya, and Uganda, three newly independent countries known collectively as East Africa, through our part in a people-to-people effort—the Tanganyika Project—that was sponsored and funded by credit unions of Saskatchewan and Michigan. This led to the continuation of our work under joint credit union–U.S. government sponsorship. Living and working in East Africa in the 1960s (particularly with the Tanzanians), we became imbued with the fervor of their independence objectives and hoped that credit unions might contribute to their political and economic freedom.

Had it not been for the good friends we made in those years, we never could have gained access to the facts that have become part of this record. Fortunately, we had saved a diary and personal files that portray Tanzania and Kenya in the earliest days of their independence. We have relied on this background information to help explain past and current events in both countries that cannot be fully documented in research literature, periodicals, or newspapers.

We have tried to report accurately the facts of our field research and to interpret these facts objectively. Since we were personally involved, our construction of events is not only obviously colored by our feelings but also by hindsight. Certain passages set off in the text reflect Jack's recollections and personal experiences and are necessarily recounted in the first person.

The timing of our research study (Tanzania, December 11, 1977 to March 4, 1978, and Kenya, March 6 to April 23, 1978) was not the best for either country. Tanzania was just undergoing a major shift in co-operative policy and Kenya was in the process of melding several foreign assistance programs into a unified approach to rural and urban co-operative finance and credit. However, both governments not only gave us research clearance, but provided us with invaluable assistance after we arrived, and we are most grateful.

Political conditions in Uganda prevented us from entering that country and including Uganda co-operative savings and credit societies within our research.

In both Tanzania and Kenya the government and league offices gave us what little statistical data they had, but their records were very limited so we went out into the field to get what facts we could from in-depth interviews. Printed questionnaires were not used, nor did we rely on tape recordings, but rather, with a firm outline in mind, we encouraged a free flow of information, sharing ideas in exchange for the privilege of asking questions and taking notes. Being well aware of the Africans' feelings about sensationalism, we were not seeking quotable statements and we tried to avoid any discussions that would place us under obligations of confidentiality.

Many people helped us in personal ways that went far beyond their professional interests and job assignments. To each of them we say thank you.

We were encouraged to embark on the project by George S. May and A. A. "Paddy" Bailey who, with their broad interests in the changing credit union scene, shared our vision of an entirely different kind of credit union book.

John M. Lubuva, manager of the Savings and Credit Union League of Tanganyika, organized our entire stay in Tanzania, and we are totally indebted to him and to the executive committee of the league for the loan of a Land Rover that made our Tanzania field trip possible. We extend our thanks also to the officials of the Kenya Union of Savings and Credit Co-operatives and to their former secretary manager, J. N. Otido.

To the officers and members of the savings and credit societies, to the other financial institutions whose personnel we interviewed, to the people of the rural savings schemes, co-operative unions, and village settlements, we are most grateful for providing us with the core information for this study.

To Stanislaus Msongo who made our safari such an adventure and to our government escorts and the league fieldmen who took daily responsibility for us, we say *asanti sana* (thanks very much).

Bart E. Quainoo, then executive secretary of the Africa Co-operative Savings and Credit Association, took time from his demanding schedule to share unpublished information on the international aspects of our study and encouraged us to write a full and frank account of our findings. We are indebted to the association's former eastern region manager and training officer, A. S. "Steve" Matoyo, one of Jack's government counterparts in Tanzania, for an illuminating briefing, comprehensive source materials, and companionship during our week of travel with him in Kenya.

Representatives of the Danish International Development Agency, the Nordic Project for Co-operative Assistance to Kenya, the Konrad Adenauer Foundation, the Netherlands RABOBANK, and the International Co-operative Alliance assisted us with discussions, staff papers, and reports. Some of these documents are among the most important of our source materials. We appreciate their personal courtesies, goodwill, and understanding.

A panel of distinguished Australian, Canadian, and United States thinkers responded to our invitation to present their views on the economic, political, and social importance of credit unions in their respective countries. In Chapter 20 of "Reflections," we have tried to absorb their thinking into a composite essay that speaks to the three-dimensional thesis of this book. Our heartfelt thanks go to Australia's S. F. Arneil, Reg Elliott, Ken Miller, Les Robinson, and Dr. Neil Runcie; to Canada's Norman Bromberger, G. A. "Al" Charbonneau, Dr. J. C. Craig, George S. May, Dr. Rosario Tremblay, and the late Dr. A. F. Laidlaw; and to Dr. John T. Croteau, Robert L. Curry, J. Deane Gannon, Mandie R. Hellie, Henry L. Peterson, Jerry Voorhis, and Herb Wegner of the United States. We consulted frequently with A. Rod Glen, Canadian world citizen, our friend and colleague of many years who died before the manuscript was completed.

J. Scott MacCready made an invaluable library search and brought us pertinent data and readings from the vast resources of the University of Washington libraries. Mary Jean McGrath, director of the University Center for Co-operatives, University of Wisconsin, and Jerry Burns, historical librarian of the Credit Union National Association, gave generously of their time and resources to provide us with valuable reference works.

We have been sustained by the confidence shown in us by the Worldwide Credit Union Foundation, the Canadian Co-operative Credit Society, the Ontario Credit Union League, and the Michigan Credit Union Foundation, and we thank them for helping us to bring this work to publication.

Explanatory Notes

The term "credit union" is used interchangeably with "co-operative savings and credit society" throughout Tanzania and Kenya. These organizations were known officially in Tanzania first as credit unions, later as savings and credit societies, and since 1974, as co-operative savings and credit societies, which has always been the Kenya designation.

The name "Tanganyika" is used when the events described took place prior to October, 1964, at which time the popularized name of that nation became Tanzania.

The currency in Tanzania and Kenya, respectively, is the Tanzania shilling (Tsh) and the Kenya shilling (Ksh), both written with a slash to separate shillings from cents, viz., Tshs 100/25. The two currencies have maintained a relatively stable official exchange ratio to the U.S. dollar, ranging from seven shillings at the beginning of the 1960s to slightly over eight shillings in the late 1970s.

Since the use of acronyms is necessary in the interests of conserving space, a full glossary is provided.

Glossary

ACOSCA	Africa Co-operative Savings and Credit Association
AFCUL	Australian Federation of Credit Union Leagues
AID	Agency for International Development
ARUCDO	Assistant Regional Ujamaa and Co-operative Development Officer
BCCCU	British Columbia Central Credit Union
CCCS	Canadian Co-operative Credit Society
CDD	Co-operative Development Department
CEC	Co-operative Education Centre
CCM	Chama Cha Mapinduzi (Revolutionary Party of Tanzania)
CIDA	Canadian International Development Agency
CLF	Central Liquidity Fund
CPCS	Co-operative Production Credit Scheme
CRS	Catholic Relief Services
CUNA	Credit Union National Association
CUT	Co-operative Union of Tanzania
DANIDA	Danish International Development Agency
EAC	East African Community
FISS	Farm Inputs Supply Scheme
IADP	Integrated Agricultural Development Program
ICA	International Co-operative Alliance
ILO	International Labor Office
KAF	Konrad Adenauer Foundation
KNCU	Kilimanjaro Native Co-operative Union
KNFC	Kenya National Federation of Co-operatives, Ltd.
KNPC	Kenya National Promotion Committee
KUSCCO	Kenya Union of Savings and Credit Co-operatives, Ltd.
MCUL	Michigan Credit Union League
NACCU	National Association of Canadian Credit Unions
NAFCU	National Association of Federal Credit Unions

NBC	National Bank of Commerce
NCCB	National Consumer Co-operative Bank
NCUA	National Credit Union Administration
NIC	National Insurance Corporation
N.I.E.O.	New International Economic Order
OAU	Organization for African Unity
POSB	Post Office Savings Bank
PRSS	Pilot Rural Savings Scheme
RDD	Regional Development Director
RUCDO	Regional Ujamaa and Co-operative Development Officer
RSA	Republic of South Africa
SCUL	Saskatchewan Credit Union League
SCULT	Savings and Credit Union League of Tanganyika, Ltd.
SIDA	Swedish International Development Agency
SIDO	Small Industries Development Organization
SPSCP	Smallholder Production Saving and Credit Program
STC	Social Training Centre
TANU	Tanganyika African National Union
THB	Tanzania Housing Bank
TRDB	Tanzania Rural Development Bank
UCDD	Ujamaa and Co-operative Development Department
UCDO	Ujamaa and Co-operative Development Officer
UCS	Union of Co-operative Societies
UNDP	United Nations Development Program
UTW	Union of Tanzania Workers
UWT	Umoja Wanawaka Tanzania (Union of Tanzania Women)
VFCU	Victoria Federation of Co-operative Unions
VRSCS	Village Rural Savings and Credit Scheme
WED	World Extension Division (of CUNA)
WOCCU	World Council of Credit Unions

Introduction

We live in an era in which Americans are beginning to feel as powerless as Tanzanians and Kenyans do about exercising any control over their economy—or their survival. Raising a family, feeding and clothing them, and providing for their education concern us—as they do the Africans—more than the big issues of disarmament and the energy crisis. We may worry about the threat of a nuclear war that could destroy our entire civilization, but we are more afraid of inflation, unemployment, and falling crop prices—just as they are. And yet, despite these fears, there are Americans and Africans who share a measure of optimism in their belief that they can help themselves and possibly others in the world by belonging to credit unions.

Credit unions that started by serving poor people in Canada and the United States in the early 1900s are today the newest "near banks" of 45 million middle and low income North American members who believe in saving and making loans co-operatively. With over $78 billion in assets these financial co-operatives have become an industry to be reckoned with by their banking competitors. But in their rise to affluence, they have had relatively few successes in reaching the poor and underprivileged in their own home towns. Except for the community/housing financing ventures of some Canadian credit unions and caisses populaires, most credit unions are concerned with consumer credit. They have had little impact as development institutions. Ironically, the more they have succeeded in the financial marketplace, the less their success or apparent interest in using their considerable resources to change the basic conditions of life for the less affluent Americans who are outside the orbit of credit union services.

This is not to say that credit unions' rise to affluence and growth into an industry has entirely changed the crusading spirit of their leaders. Like most believers, they have tried at times to share their ideas with others, especially the minorities and economically disadvantaged, and they have had some successes but more failures.

However, Canadian and American credit union leaders have not allowed themselves to be frustrated by their inability to change conditions at home. They have poured their energies and money into overseas development activities. And they have done this quite selflessly. The emergence of credit unions in the other regions of the world, with the help of North American credit unions, especially during the last thirty years, owes much to this altruistic drive. An international credit union network, comprising some 52 million credit union members with total resources of nearly $82 billion in 1981, now embraces people in some of the poorest countries of the world, including Tanzania and Kenya (see Appendix).

Credit unions of the United States and English-speaking Canada originated from the Caisses Populaires Desjardins of Quebec, which in turn were modeled on the German Raiffeisen Societies and other European savings and loan societies. The credit union idea has been adapted from these European and North American models by countless countries of Africa, Asia, and Latin America, and by Australia, the Caribbean, and the Pacific Islands. Although they must conform to the laws and customs of their environment, credit unions of the various regions of the world are much alike.

As member-owned-and-operated co-operatives, they specialize in mobilizing savings from their members, making loans to them, and sometimes engaging in related co-operative activities. Membership is limited to some kind of identifiable and cohesive group of employees, community residents, church parishioners, or others having a "common bond" of employment, residence, or association. Members join and save together in order to create a pool of money that will be available for making provident or productive loans at reasonable rates of interest. The size, stability, and income level of the group usually determines the size, maturity, and type of loans made, but for the most part loans are small and short-term.

Specific enabling legislation is considered desirable but not essential for optimum efficiency and protection of the societies and their members, and usually, but not invariably, credit unions' income is not taxed as long as they confine their services to members. Until recently most credit unions have operated on a minimal margin. However the effects of revolutionary changes in legally permitted interest rates on loans and deposits, to enable competition with others in the market for funds, are sweeping away most of the traditional concepts about low-cost lending and limited returns on savings. Dependency on the use of borrowed funds has become noticeably greater, markedly so among the larger credit unions in the more advanced countries. They are taking on more of the characteristics of a financial industry while tending to lose their co-operative characteristics. Notwithstanding, even the largest of the multimillion dollar organizations are directed by volunteer elected officials who oversee the work of managers and staff.

It is not uncommon for governments to encourage the promotion of credit unions in their infancy and to help with the education of their officials, along with supervision and auditing. Employers or other sponsors often provide payroll deductions (check-off), office space, and clerical help in return for credit union services which eliminate payday loans and help to stabilize the work force by providing solutions to employees' financial problems. Organizations of credit unions exist for legislative protection and educational, promotional, and financial interaction. Within the affiliated movement these organizations are known as state or provincial leagues and national associations.

Some differences in this description may be noted from one country or locality to another but, as we shall see, it is because most credit unions are small organizations, run by volunteers on a part-time basis, that they seemed to be feasible for the two developing countries of our study.

Many questions as to the viability of African credit union development arose when the prospects of an East African extension program first surfaced. True, similar questions had been raised earlier in the planning for programs in other regions of the world, especially Latin America, but Africa was different. Much less was known about the African continent than other regions of the world, and what most Americans could recall from sensational newspaper or periodical headlines had to suffice for current information about African people or their individual countries.

No wonder that today some of the questions seem naive, but even now there are valid doubts to be resolved. The answers are not all that clear. Some of them depend on events still in the making. For instance:

- What services can a credit union perform in a poor African country whose people are mostly subsistence farmers?
- After the teachers and advisers have departed, will the credit union as an institution live, die, or be transformed into another institution specifically adapted to the African environment?
- How can the credit union, a democratic institution of the Western world, adapt to the African political scene, especially to countries such as Tanzania and Kenya with single-party political systems?

- Can Africans find volunteer leaders or paid staff with the education and/or business experience needed to manage their credit unions?
- What possibilities exist for self-supported associations of credit unions in Africa?

To develop the answers to these and other questions, we undertook our study. Based on our personal experiences, research, and observations from 1962 to the present time, we have tried to capture something of the total political, social, and economic atmosphere in which Tanzanian and Kenyan development has evolved, including the sensitive issues—economic exploitation, social racism, political nonalignment, and African socialism—that are rarely addressed in credit union literature.

Most of the text relates to our 1977–78 field research in the two countries. Each country is examined on its own. Since we know of no accepted criteria for judging success or failure in a credit union movement, we make no such comparisons between Kenya and Tanzania. At the end of the book, however, we offer a sweeping view of the Canadian, United States, and Australian credit unions whose experiences in adjusting to change may offer some insights (or speculations) into the shape of things to come for the Africans.

PART I

African Overview

1. Understanding Africa

Many of us in the United States have a dim view of Africa that is warped by the persistent myths about African backwardness and savagery and by antiblack racism. Up until the 1960s, when more and more adventurous people began to leave home for volunteer work in African countries, most of our contacts with African people were through missionaries or through the pages of novelists like Edgar Rice Burroughs who had never been in that part of the world. In a recent television series "Black Man's Land" the African view was expressed thus:

> For centuries, the world has looked upon Africa as a thief looks upon treasure: it is there to be plundered. Our forefathers were stolen in millions during the slave trade, and our minerals have fed the industries of the West. Our traditional cultures were suppressed and their artifacts stolen to fill the museums of Europe and America. Our land was occupied by strangers and our people confined to reserves.[1]

Comparatively little background material on Africa was available to the general public in the early 1960s. Ordinary citizens could hardly have been expected to take any serious interest in Africa when the U.S. government was just beginning to face up to the momentous issues of giving full constitutional rights to black Americans. Africa was looked upon as a European political and economic preserve, so much so that many Americans were as outraged as their British, Belgian, French, and Portuguese counterparts when, soon after taking office, Assistant Secretary of State G. Mennen Williams, with the backing of President John F. Kennedy, made his astonishing reference to "Africa for the Africans." In credit union circles few of us had ever dreamed of traveling to Africa, and fewer still expected to see a credit union organized among African people.

The emergence of credit unions throughout Africa is only one of the remarkable changes which make for a new relationship with Africa in the 1980s. Thousands of non-Africans have studied, lived, worked with Africans, and identified with their aspirations.

In today's history books and political science texts, African heroes like Tanzania's Julius Kambarage Nyerere and Kenya's Jomo Kenyatta, Kwame Nkrumah of Ghana, Léopold Senghor of Senegal, Sékou Touré of Guinea, and Patrice Lumumba of Congo (Zaire) are upstaging the places once reserved for the great British explorers, Livingston, Burton, and Speke, and the famous American, Henry Morton Stanley.

Guided by a new breed of African game rangers who have taken over from the "great white hunters," tourists from all over the world, armed only with cameras, tour the Serengeti and other famed wildlife parks now closed to the hunting safaris of the past. And scientists studying the beginnings of civilization make their way to the Olduvai Gorge in northern Tanzania where Kenyan scientists, the late Louis B. Leakey, his wife, Mary, and their son Richard, have been conducting research that indicates that East Africa may be the birthplace of man.

On the other hand, some things never change, as the editor of *Harper's* magazine observed:

> The American press reports news from Africa that deals with disputes between whites and blacks; only large-scale civil wars between armies of blacks deserve mention in the dispatches, and then only if the Russians agree to sponsor one of the contenders.[2]

The continent of Africa is so vast, and in many ways so mysterious, that it defies comparison with other parts of the world. Stretching 5,000 miles from north to south and 4,600 miles from east to west, it encompasses 22 percent of the world's land area—some 12 million square miles of desert, savanna, jungle, and luxuriant tropical gardens. Most of its 435 million people are black descendants of the Bantu tribes that started to migrate across the African continent before the Iron Age, and they live mainly south of the Sahara Desert (which is almost as large as the entire United States) in climates of extreme heat, rain, or drought. Most of them are subsistence farmers, and most of the 51 independent countries are poor.

Yet Africa the continent is rich. Ninety-eight percent of the world's diamonds, 70 percent of its cobalt, 67 percent of its gold, 45 percent of its chrome, 23 percent of its copper, 32 percent of its antimony, 25 percent of its phosphates, and 22 percent of its manganese are in African countries, according to some authorities. Others place the known reserves of rare minerals in Africa still higher, adding to the list nearly half of the world's platinum, one-third of the bauxite, and one-third or more of the Western bloc's supply of uranium reserves.

Today's energy crisis underscores the importance of Africa's having an estimated 10 percent of the world's oil supply, nearly 10 percent of the coal, and almost 15 percent of the natural gas; added to this is possibly the world's biggest hydroelectric power potential from some of the greatest rivers on the earth.

Getting access to this mineral wealth and/or denying it to the USSR has become a cornerstone of U.S. foreign policy and a reliable source of flammable news whenever the cold war shows signs of cooling off. The news media curiously play down the competition for Africa's resources that also goes on between the U.S. and other Western bloc nations, but history records that the "scramble for Africa" and its partition among European nations a hundred years ago were among the causes of the First World War. One of Britain's victory prizes was its seizure from Germany of the mainland territory and offshore islands which are today the United Republic of Tanzania.

Although less than 1 percent of the United States's total imports come from Africa, 38 percent or more of U.S. oil imports are from Nigeria, Angola, and Guinea-Bissau. These oil imports have weighed heavily in the changing balance of U.S. trade with African countries: in 1976 exports to Africa were $5.2 billion while imports were $12.6 billion. United States investments in Africa rose from $600 million in 1960 to $4.9 billion in 1975. One-third of this, however, was in the Republic of South Africa (RSA) whose apartheid policies and illegal occupation of Namibia are anathema to the other African countries.

It was South Africa's armed intervention in newly independent Angola, according to some observers, that triggered the decision of the Angolans to invite in the Russian-backed Cuban soldiers, doctors, and technicians whose continuing presence in southern Africa is now a sore point in U.S.-Cuban and U.S.-Russian relations. This has created a major dilemma for the U.S., which would like to protect its huge high-yielding investments and the friendship of a strategically powerful South Africa without sacrificing its African sources of oil and its African political interests.

Although the United States has not been significantly involved in Africa until recently, these conflicting considerations, compounded by the pressures of black U.S. voters, have forced a rethinking of Africa's importance and the formulation of a new U.S.-African policy.

While black Americans are searching for their "roots" in Africa, their blood brothers and sisters in the African countries seem less interested in historical relationships than in the power politics of getting "nonaligned" development assistance and armaments by playing off the East-West forces against each other.

When President Jimmy Carter went to Nigeria in 1978 (the first state visit of a U.S. president to an African country) the Nigerians did not want to talk about America's displeasure with the Cubans. They made one thing clear: Nigeria would not hesitate to use its oil as bargaining leverage in support of the Tanzania-led Front Line Nations (Angola, Botswana, Mozambique, Tanzania, and Zambia), which were demanding a new election in Zimbabwe (formerly Rhodesia) to include the freedom fighters and an end to covert U.S. support of Ian Smith's "White Supremacists" in the southern Africa border warfare.

United States and British pressures and the Cuban presence in Africa brought Smith to the bargaining table, and in 1980 Zimbabwe won recognition as an independent nation under Robert Mugabe's "pragmatic socialist," black majority government. The implications for Namibia and the Republic of South Africa itself are not lost on the Africans, or the rest of the world. Former Secretary of State Cyrus Vance has said:

> We can no more stop change [in the Third World] than Canute could still the waters. We cannot let ourselves be diverted by the myth that if we encourage change or deal with the forces of change we only encourage radicalism. . . . Our strengths and our principles can help us promote peaceful change and orderly reform that strengthen the ties between government and people. For once such ties are broken, and a government has lost its legitimacy in the eyes of the people, no amount of outside intervention can secure its long-term survival. It is profoundly in our national interest, therefore, that *we support constructive change* before such ties erode and the alternatives of radicalism or repression drive out moderate solutions.[3]

One should not read into this statement the inference that Americans are agreed on an Africa-for-Africans policy. There are those who want to support constructive change. But a more militaristic U.S. foreign policy is in the making in response to Soviet aggressions. In Kenya, for instance, U.S.-Kenya agreements have been concluded for maintaining an American naval base at Mombasa, a controversial decision that could add to Kenya's problems at home and abroad while seeming to alleviate some of her economic woes. America's "moralistic" African policies, which were given new emphasis under the Carter administration, have been further eroded by pressure from business interests and hardline anti-Communists who hold that U.S. self-interest in the status quo of Southern Africa must take precedence.

Although African nations comprise one-third of the entire membership of the United Nations and tend to vote together (with other underdeveloped countries) in support of their Third World interests, they are equally inclined to disunity. In the United Nations and even more in their Organization for African Unity (OAU) they have railed against white economic imperialism and South African racism, but, with few exceptions (such as Tanzania), they have found ways of doing business with the Republic of South Africa, and they have turned a blind eye to such African despots as Idi Amin. It was Tanzania's Nyerere who alone spoke up in the OAU against Amin's mass murders, butcheries, and torture that so revolted the civilized world, and it was the Tanzanian army that drove him out of Uganda.

Culturally it is much the same story, and economically even more so. The individual African countries are tied to their economic trading partners, most of whom are the European nations who were their colonial masters. Africans share no common language that could help restore their cultural ties with each other. An authentically Pan-African language equivalent to Swahili, the lingua franca of East Africa, has yet to be accepted. Mail, telephone and telegraph lines, and a zigzag pattern of airplane flights between European and African airports connect African educators, businessmen, and artists with European capitals far more directly than with the more remote areas in their own countries.

Political changes, uneven economic growth, and social revolution have marked the course of the African independence movements since the "Wind of Change" began to blow south with Libya's independence in 1961. Over forty new nations have been created, Tanzania and Kenya among them. Many of the original constitutional democracies have been overthrown by military coups. National boundaries, capriciously gerrymandered by the European colonial powers, remain a constant source of border wars.

Most of these African countries—Tanzania and Kenya included—remain among the poorest countries in the world. Africans have reacted to their unchanging poverty with a growing resentment against the industrialized countries that continue to take their raw materials at low prices in trade for the expensive manufactured goods, industrial equipment, foodstuffs, medicines, and technology Africans need for their economic development. The nationalism that came with independence once gave rise to hopes of economic freedom in the new nations, but the realities of continued economic dependence have crushed these hopes. Idealistic nationalism has been replaced by antagonism to "neocolonialism." A best-seller in

Tanzania is Walter Rodney's book *How Europe Underdeveloped Africa,* which argues that the rich nations (notably the United States and the former colonial powers) use their economic advantages to subjugate the new African countries which they are unable to control politically. Although the African and other poor countries are determined "to recover and control their natural resources, wealth and the means for economic development" by the establishment of a New International Economic Order (N.I.E.O.), as expressed in UN Resolution 3200 (s–vi) of the General Assembly on April 30, 1974, pragmatism dictates their partners and terms of trade, economic development, and military assistance. Hopes and dreams of a naturally interdependent United States of Africa, expressed as a long-range goal by Nkrumah and Nyerere, have had to be set aside as the individual countries bargain as best they can for trade and aid to speed their own development.

In the 1960s Tanzania, Kenya, and Uganda dreamed of creating the East African Federation and managed to establish an economic predecessor—the East African Community (EAC)—which lasted until 1977. By that time the countries had become hopelessly divided by their individual trade and political interests. Negotiations have been continuing fitfully toward a new co-operation but with little real progress.

Tanzania and Kenya have worked out their individual strategies for advancing their respective political and economic interests. As much as both nations resemble each other in having been born out of European colonialism from as far back as the partition of East Africa by the British and Germans in the 1880s, they came to independence and have conducted themselves since then quite differently.

Tanzania, including the islands of Zanzibar and Pemba (see map), covers about 362,800 square miles composed of 6 percent inland water, 15 percent cultivated land, 31 percent grassland, and 48 percent bush forest or woodland; on the islands 40 percent of the land is cultivated. Tanzania's population in July, 1978, was 16,838,000, of which 99 percent was native Africans of over 100 tribes; the remaining 1 percent was Asian, European, and Arab. Forty percent of the population is Animist, 30 percent Christian, and 30 percent Muslim. Swahili and English are the official languages.

The country's main exports include coffee, cotton, sisal, cashew nuts, meat, diamonds, cloves, tobacco, and tea. The major industries are primarily agricultural, although Tanzania processes sugar, makes beer, cigarettes, sisal twine, shoes, cement, textiles, and wood products, mines diamonds and refines oil. Tanzania imports manufactured goods, machinery and transport equipment, cotton piece goods, crude oil, and foodstuffs. Its major trade partners for exports are China, the United Kingdom, Hong Kong, India, and the United States; for imports, the United Kingdom, China, West Germany, the United States, and Japan.

Tanzania entered statehood on December 9, 1961, under the leadership of Nyerere (Tanzania's first and only president) in a peaceful transition from British Territorial Status. Bloodshed was avoided, probably because Tanzania's arable lands had not proved inviting to large numbers of European settlers and her mineral resources were not considered worth fighting for.

Kenya (see map) covers about 225,000 square miles of which 21 percent is forest and woodland, 13 percent is suitable for agriculture, and 66 percent is mainly grassland adequate for grazing. The population of 14,837,000 is 97 percent native African, 2 percent Asian, and 1 percent European, Arab, and others. Religious affiliations are 56 percent Christian, 36 percent Animist, 7 percent Muslim, and 1 percent Hindu.

The main cash crops are coffee, sisal, tea, pyrethrum, cotton, livestock, corn, wheat, rice, cassava. The major industries are small-scale consumer goods (plastics, furniture, batteries, textiles, soap, agricultural processing, cigarettes, flour), oil refining, and cement. Most of Kenya's imports are machinery, transport equipment, crude oil, paper and paper products, and textiles. Its major trade partners are the United Kingdom and the European Economic Community, Uganda, and Tanzania.

Kenya's rich highlands and excellent climate brought a large influx of British settlers who displaced the native Kenyans from their lands and exploited them as cheap labor. To rectify these injustices, Kenyatta (as early as 1928) and other patriots attempted to gain support at home and abroad. Their inability to prevail by democratic means led to civil disobedience and ultimately to terrorism and oath taking (commonly known as Mau Mau) after British military forces went into action.

Although current research has debunked much of the Mau Mau hysteria that was propagated by the British, it is known that thousands of Kenyans died before their country became independent on December 12, 1963. After Kenya became a republic on December 12, 1964, Kenyatta served as president until his death in August, 1978, when he was succeeded by President Daniel arap Moi, who had been vice-president.

Today Kenya has its closest ties with Britain and is an active member of the British Commonwealth of Nations. Tanzania, also a commonwealth member, maintains a more noticeable distance and an internationally independent course.

From their birth as free nations, both countries have espoused African Socialism in general terms and have experimented with it, but the two countries have arrived at different systems. Similarly, both countries are experimenting with credit unions and are adapting them to meet their individual needs.[4]

2. *African Socialism*

African Socialism is an evolving concept that first gained prominence during the turbulent years of the struggle for independence throughout the African continent. African Socialism has provided leaders with a doctrine to use in bringing their people from the hopes, ambitions, and dreams of a new life after independence face to face with the realities of the continuing battle for economic development. Each citizen is being called upon to participate with hard work and dedication in the present for a better life in the future. The change from colonialism to independence has brought to the masses less wealth and more responsibility than they, in their visions of independence, had ever considered.

With independence, "anticolonialism" was no longer usable as a call to action and "nationalism" alone could not inspire the dedication necessary to the struggle for development because the boundaries inherited by many of the new nations were artificial, engineered by the colonial powers to serve their own needs for raw materials and markets, and had little regard for tribal links and historic trade and communication patterns. "Pan-Africanism" (one Africa) was too difficult an idea to promote in countries which had just achieved their own nationhood. A uniquely African ideology had to be developed as a rallying cry to unite Africans behind their new leaders.

The African Socialism of the late 1950s and early 1960s was not a unified theory, but a reflection of the thinking of the leaders of various countries as they spoke out for the necessity of change in Africa. Among them were Nkrumah of Ghana, Senghor of Senegal, Touré of Guinea, Tom Mboya and Kenyatta of Kenya, and especially Nyerere of Tanzania. These leaders were concerned with problems of land ownership, of the development of classless societies, of transferring the traditional elements of co-operation in African life into co-operation for nation building.

Further, there was a deep felt need to create a sociopolitical format that would permit African leaders to make clear their separation from the machinations and cold war activities of both the East and the West. African Socialism became the statement of neutralism and nonalignment for societies based primarily on self-reliance but with the willingness to accept help from either East or West, or both, if such help would forward national plans and designs.

In their excellent study of African Socialism, upon which much of the information in this chapter is based, Friedland and Rosberg describe this socioeconomic arrangement as forming a necessary framework for a mixed society with emphasis on both agriculture and industry. In this socialist society the public sector and public planning would predominate. There would be less individual economic freedom than had been anticipated in order that economic equality as well as political equality might accrue to each citizen and the spread between rich and poor Africans would not be increased.

The term African Socialism also signified that this form of socialism grew out of different needs and conditions than, say, European socialism—it grew out of the African problems of colonialism and exploitation of resources. It was not the result of the class struggle between workers and owners. Rather, it developed out of the African struggle to prevent imperialism and capitalism with all their attendant problems from becoming the way of life of the new nations. It was designed to solve the peculiar social, economic, and political problems caused by imperialism and colonialism in Africa. Thus African Socialism set forth a doctrine that was not only interested in the ethics of distribution of goods, services, and rewards but also provided a framework within which to work against colonialism and capitalism. It also gave Africans a means of expressing their feelings against racism and white arrogance. Karioki has divided African Socialism into three concepts:

- Afro-Marxists for whom Nkrumah might have been considered the leading ideologist, who believe, overly simplified, that African Socialism should be built on realism and unity with the emphasis on industrialization and with very little attention to the significance of so-called values of traditional African society.
- Welfare Statists exemplified and articulated by Kenyatta and Mboya, who emphasized the middle ground between traditionalism and modern socialism with a concentration on a mixed economy of public and private sectors, and a dedication to continuation of individual property ownership.
- Humanist Socialists, most notably Senghor and Nyerere, who extol the human values of African traditionalism plus a touch of

spiritualism. Nyerere's philosophy of the primacy of man and his right to equality, freedom, and unity with his fellow man, speaks especially to this definition of African Socialism.

African Socialism in Tanzania

In his earliest thinking President Nyerere, the foremost scholar and writer on African Socialism, described the concept as an "attitude of mind." Over the years he has evolved a plan of action, using the two instruments necessary for establishing a true socialist society—the co-operative movement and the government itself.

African Socialism received its fullest and most clearly defined expression in the Arusha Declaration, 1967. It was accepted by Tanzania's ruling political party, the Tanganyika African National Union (TANU), as the working definition of Tanzanian African Socialism: to bring about a way of life in which traditional African ideas of community sharing and mutual support would be updated, and imported ideas, first brought in by the colonialists and then by the experts of the modern industrial countries, would be modified. The main responsibility for such reeducation would rest with the political party. This "blueprint for socialism" stressed the importance of self-reliance and co-operation, of a mixed economy of farmers and workers, of the need for the nation's major means of production to be in the hands of the people, of a population with no masters and no servants.

Not only did the Arusha Declaration define what socialism was but also how it was to be practiced. In a series of resolutions, the government leaders accepted special responsibilities and agreed to special limitations on their activities and ways of life that would show by daily example the true meaning of self-reliance. The Arusha Declaration was reaffirmed in February, 1977, by the reorganized national ruling party, Chama Cha Mapinduzi (CCM)—the Revolutionary Party (an amalgamation of TANU and the Zanzibari Afro-Shirazi Party).

The ideas of socialist leaders from all parts of the world contributed to Nyerere's thinking but his adviser, René Dumont, was probably especially influential in his determination that a massive effort must be made by the peasants, the majority of the population, to bring themselves out of stagnation to start accelerated development. Dumont, known as a critic of much of what the modern African elite stands for (as expressed in his book *False Start in Africa*), has exposed the new privileged class who exploit their own poor. He has also warned against the reliance by developing countries on foreign aid, especially of the wrong kind, which, he feels, is just as deplorable as the overvaluation placed on the need for industrialization as a prelude to development. Above all, Dumont stresses the overwhelming importance of collective self-reliance.

Even though President Nyerere fully understood the necessity of building co-operative enterprises from the bottom up, building slowly and concentrating on member education before embarking on implementation, he was under severe political pressure to "show some action," and hopefully some results. This led to the opening of consumers co-operative shops[1] with imported management (namely the Israelis) and to experimenting with various settlement programs such as the Ujamaa Village program. These settlement schemes proved to be exceedingly expensive because they were equipped with sophisticated machinery, managed by high-paid non-African experts, and given special social services (schools, clinics, roads), all of which benefited only a few hundred people. A very few Ujamaa Villages, organized in stable villages with dedicated party leadership and educated to understand the intertwined relationship of social and economic factors that is the basis of the Ujamaa philosophy, did prosper and became the inspiration for the commitment in the Arusha Declaration to *Ujamaa Vijijini*—the spread of voluntary, co-operative, productive activities throughout the countryside.

Meanwhile, the major thrust to achieve socialism was being made through organizing co-operative marketing societies in local areas and bringing the primary societies together into co-operative unions in order to eliminate the "profiteering non-African middlemen" who had collected and sold the crops before independence. This national concentration on co-operative development was emphasized by John S. Malecela, a longtime political leader and cabinet member, who, in a 1970 speech to co-operative senior officers, said:

> I am sure I will not be accused of exaggeration if I say that the Co-operative Movement in Tanzania is the most well organised Co-operative Movement in Black Africa, to the extent that today the Co-operative Movement is one of the strongest instruments that will lead us to the goal of socialism.
>
> It is absolutely important that Ujamaa Villages in Tanzania do succeed because it is the structure on which true socialism in Tanzania can be built. It is therefore very important that the structure be strong and solid. It is only the Co-operative Movement which can ensure the success of Ujamaa Villages because the Ujamaa Villages are mainly agricultural.

> It is true that in the future the government may introduce small scale industries but at the present moment it is by and large true that the preponderance of Ujamaa Villages will be on a "do it yourself" basis rather than [dependent on] the introduction of another bureaucracy.[2]

From the earliest days of independence Nyerere urged that Tanzanians move gradually from being a nation of individual peasant producers, who were adopting the incentives and ethics of the capitalist system, to become a nation of Ujamaa Villages where the people would co-operate directly in small groups and where these small groups would then co-operate together for joint enterprises. By 1975 the government had come to the conclusion that the country's plan of people coming together to live and work in village communities could only be achieved if the force of law was put behind it. Persuasion, planning, and incentives had failed to move the rural population quickly enough or far enough on the path to rural transformation and African Socialism. In July, 1975, the Act to Provide for the Registration of Villages, the Administration of Registered Villages, and Designation of Ujamaa Villages was enacted and was signed by President Nyerere on August 12, 1975.

Under this act all people living in rural areas must become residents of a registered village. The village and its organs are required to perform their functions as if the village were a multipurpose co-operative society, and no other co-operative society registered under the Co-operative Societies Act of 1968 is to continue to operate in the village. Every village assembly and village council performs its functions under the auspices of the party. When the regional executive committee of the party is satisfied that a substantial portion of the economic activities of a village are being undertaken and carried out on a communal basis, the committee may recommend that the village be designated an "Ujamaa Village." Today over 13,065,000 people are living together in some 8,000 villages of between 250 and 600 families each.

The Urban Wards Administration Act, 1976, attempted to abolish city council government and organize city dwellers on the pattern of co-operative villages, and, in so doing it sought to carry out the final phase of the decentralization of government administration begun in 1972. But the act never became operative.

Tanzania has been known for its willingness to experiment drastically with its major institutions, including co-operatives, in pursuing its socialistic goals. The leading studies on these experiments are presented fully in the two volumes of *Socialism in Tanzania* by Cliffe and Saul.

Whereas co-operatives in general and agricultural marketing

co-operatives in particular were the backbone of development policy from independence to the mid-1970s, by 1975 the commitment was mostly lip service. In 1975 the government abolished the system of primary co-operative societies in the rural areas and substituted in their place the communal villages to be organized as multipurpose co-operatives. In 1976 all of the co-operative marketing unions, having lost their primary society members, were dissolved and their functions transferred to state corporations.

However, co-operative enterprises such as savings and credit societies, consumer shops, small industries production, and handicrafts were being encouraged as part of party policy.

African Socialism in Kenya

African Socialism in Kenya may be described as a doctrine of "economic pragmatism" which requires no major sociopolitical changes from the heritage of the colonial, preindependence days. The only difference is that Africans, not Europeans or Asians, will benefit from the economic growth of the country. While recognizing the great need for better living standards for everyone, including the rural and urban poor, Kenya has accepted the idea of "economic growth" as the best way to bring about improved conditions for all its people. In Kenya the goal of African Socialism is "Equality of Opportunity" for all.

The shape of the Kenyan economy had been so firmly set along capitalist lines in its development as a strong and prosperous British colony that no reversal of the trend toward individual rewards for individual initiative could be effected by an indigenous government with any hope of that government staying in power. By the time Kenyans had won their independence the leaders who had come to power in the new government had been exposed to the "good life" as exemplified by the white settlers. They determined that Kenya could create a prosperous country more easily by democratizing and Africanizing the established positions of privilege than by eliminating them.

In 1965, *Sessional Paper No. 10,* "African Socialism and Its Application to Planning in Kenya" became the definitive document in its development plan. According to Mboya, author of the paper and then minister for economic planning and development, the principal guideline followed in formulating these policies was that Kenya must direct and focus its energies on achieving a rapid rate of growth. The paper declared, "Kenya is already committed to high and growing per capita incomes equitably distributed . . . and to a wages incomes policy that recognizes the need for differential incentives as well as an equitable distribution of income."[3]

Kenya's leaders were somewhat divided in their approach to the implementation of African Socialism, and their differences culminated in personal contests for power between President Kenyatta and his followers, mostly of the predominant Kikuyu tribe, occupying the central area, and the opposition led by Oginga Odinga, representing mainly the Luo tribe living in the western section of the country. In some ways the struggle may also be described as a confrontation between the economic interests of the rapidly rising elitists who were taking over the economic position and wealth of the outgoing settlers and the aspirations of the landless poor. Cold war forces obviously pitted them against each other, with the United States giving unlimited support to President Kenyatta and the Soviet Union providing cash and weapons to Odinga. In winning the struggle for control of the nation, the Kenyatta government settled down to make Kenya a free enterprise African democracy.

Since the first decade of Kenya's independence was one of political stability and marked economic growth, the country became the beneficiary not only of investment and skilled non-Africans, but also of many in-depth studies of its economy to extract lessons for development the world over. Two prestigious and impressive studies—one by the World Bank, the other by the International Labor Office (ILO)—have given excellent information on Kenya development with recommendations for its future economic and social planning. The World Bank document reviews Kenya's development very favorably: "There is no doubt that Kenya's performance in mobilizing resources for growth has been impressive by any standard."[4] The ILO report criticizes Kenya for its failure to ensure that the benefits of development are distributed equitably among all her people.

The agricultural sector in which most Kenyans live and work has not shown the anticipated economic growth. Twin problems of growing unemployment and the continuing poverty of the "working poor" plague the country. A new emphasis is now being put on increasing agricultural production with special attention to developing a smallholder service system providing extension, credit, inputs, and marketing. The major strategy in Kenya's Fourth National Development Plan was devised on a basic needs approach to the alleviation of poverty: special concern for nutrition, housing, health, education and training, and water supply problems.

Theoretically, the economic objective of the Kenyan government remains the achievement of high and growing per capita incomes so that all Kenyans can live without want, disease, or exploitation, and all will be guaranteed political equality, social justice, human dignity, and equal opportunities as well. The particular blend of policies put forward to secure these objectives, including the development of a mixed economy in which co-operatives can offer a parallel to the individual enterprise system, draws upon African tribal tradition in combination with a pragmatic capitalism to develop a unique Kenyan approach to African Socialism. So far the plans and policies have not achieved the desired results. Kenya's economy has produced comparative affluence only for the growing middle class and an elitist wealthy class which live in the cities where they attempt to insulate themselves from the poverty of the landless, the small farmers, and the unemployed.

It is against these two different socioeconomic designs of Tanzania and Kenya, both known as African Socialism, that credit union development in the two countries will be viewed.

3. *Historical Background of Credit Unions in Africa*

Preindependence

Social Importance of Traditional Associations

African society has always emphasized the importance of family and community, and this tradition has characterized the historical methods of savings and credit from the time of the barter economies when goods and crops were stored, exchanged, and used in community activities. The extended family compound was in itself a communal system to which one contributed for as long as he was able, and if he was disabled, from which he accepted (and expected) help without any idea of repayment.

With the coming of the money economy a variety of informal savings and credit associations, clubs, or mutual aid societies were developed to help their members in times of emergencies such as sickness and death; to pay fines or overdue taxes; to pay for education, house, repairs, and construction; and also to foster ideas of community responsibility and good citizenship among them. Feelings of solidarity and social responsibility were as much a part of the benefits of these societies as the monetary assistance they provided. The loans given by these societies were productive in the sense that they strengthened the family and the community.

Studies show that even today these informal savings and lending institutions are to be found in their traditional form in almost half of the countries of Africa. They are known by different names in different countries: *isusu, osusu,* or *esusu* (Nigeria); *ndonju* (Benin); *djanggi* (Cameroon); *tontine* (French-speaking countries); *ekub* (Ethiopia); *sanduk* (Sudan); *gameya* (Egypt); *chilemba* or *kwegatta* (Uganda).

These societies are generally of two different types: fixed fund associations that are somewhat akin to banks of the formal sector (or credit unions) and rotating funds or rotating savings/credit associations of which innumerable variations exist. In most of these rotating plans each participant contributes to a fund that is then given to one member each time the group meets until the collection has been made available to everyone in the group. Some groups operate both a fixed fund and a rotating fund. Required savings range from a penny a day to as much as $1,600 a month. Loans are usually made without collateral, although guarantors may be required, and there is little paperwork. Interest rates vary from zero to as high as 360 percent. Members obtain loans for the individual purposes described above or as a group to purchase grain-grinding mills, agricultural machinery, or transport vehicles. Special funds and earnings from these activities are sometimes used for community projects such as building a school or an access road.

Colonial Savings and Credit Facilities

Great emphasis was placed on the importance of savings in the institutions that were created under foreigners' sponsorship in the colonial era, and money saved was not to be withdrawn easily. Typically a saver could withdraw only up to seventy-five percent of his own savings. The colonial savings schemes required centralization of control, which was consistent with colonial administrative practices that confined most Africans and their traditions to restricted areas or "reserves." Meetings and group discussions so much a part of the traditional savings societies were minimized in the colonial organizations.

Post Office Savings Banks (POSB) operated by the government became the main depository for those Africans who chose to save in the colonial savings institutions; and post office branches enabled the transfer of money to families and relatives in other localities. But the POSB offered no credit and made withdrawals difficult by requiring savers to send their passbooks to the headquarters office for dividend entries and certification of account balances. Africans tended to use the POSB only for limited amounts of their savings and to regard it as another colonial institution over which they had no control, individually or as a group.

Credit was discouraged except for "productive" purposes specifically related to increased farm production for the colonial agricultural export system. This type of production credit was made available by government and the commercial banks to the settler-farmers and much later to African smallholders on a limited scale, mostly through the government's various agricultural financing agencies. Ministries and departments sometimes helped their African employees to conduct revolving credit schemes whereby repayments of loans were made by salary deductions, and to the extent that Africans were involved as participating members these helped to carry over some of the social advantages of the traditional societies into the colonial monetary economy.

But for the average African who had money to save and wanted to join with others in pooling some of it for personal benefits or for social and community purposes, there was little incentive to use the colonial financial institutions. To understand how alienated Africans were from the commercial banks and other finance agencies in the colonial era it may be useful to look briefly at the history of money and banking in East Africa.

East Africa Money and Banking History

Money has been used in the East African coastal areas of Tanzania and Kenya since Roman times, and evidence of this exists in the coins found along the coast. Roman coins, and Arab, Portuguese, Persian, and Chinese coins dating from the Middle Ages have been found. Local currency was first minted in the thirteenth century by the sultan of Kilwa.

Money, however, had only limited circulation in East Africa until the advent of commercial banking in the late 1800s and early 1900s by British and German banking houses. The first commercial bank in Dar es Salaam, Tanganyika, a branch of the Deutsch-Ostafrikanische Bank of Berlin, opened in 1905. In Kenya the National Bank of India (a British enterprise which later changed its name to National & Grindlays Bank) opened its offices in Mombasa in 1896. Together with Barclays Bank D.C.O. and Standard Bank Limited, National & Grindlays Bank dominated commercial banking in Tanzania until 1967 when all three banks were nationalized. The British banks are still the mainstay of commercial banking in Kenya.

In colonial days the commercial banks concentrated their activities on financing foreign trade although, in the late 1950s and markedly in the years just preceding the independence of Tanganyika and Kenya, some attempts were made to mobilize local savings and invest them in local development, with indifferent results. The relatively little money that began to circulate in the local economies was collected in bank deposits and invested mainly by the banks in European money markets. Local capital was drained out of the African economy and exported, largely to London. Africans were unable to get loans from the banks except in rare instances, and even the colonial settlers and businessmen were cut off from bank financing except when it contributed to the main export-import colonial strategy, which according to one school of thought was calculated to exploit the African people and their resources. More charitable explanations of the low levels of local investment by the banks are that inappropriate British standards of credit worthiness were applied (requiring the mortgaging of farmers' land which was not mortgageable since African land was held in communal ownership subject to individual use) and that the banks lacked a branch network.

The East African Currency Board was created in 1919 as an essential link in the exportation of capital to the Sterling Bloc. The EACB discouraged any incentive on the part of the banks to explore local investment opportunities seriously by minimizing losses from the exchange of currency between African banks and British banks, thereby maximizing profits from the foreign investment of local funds. (The ratio of local bank earning assets to total assets in East Africa was only thirty-nine percent in 1938, and as the costs of World War II drained every British resource, declined to ten percent in 1945.) Other important financial institutions—the insurance companies, POSB, building societies, and hire purchase (finance) companies—generally followed bank policies in their investment of funds overseas.

While the POSB, as part of the post office system with its numerous branches, attracted the greatest number of African customers, the bank's largest accounts were held by Asians and Europeans. Except for saving in the POSB, which provided much-needed services in both the rural and urban areas, Africans had good reasons to avoid contact with other financial institutions. Anyone who needed a loan was required by the Credit to Natives (Restriction) Ordinance of 1931 to seek the permission of the district commissioner before he could even apply for credit. (Similar regulatory restrictions made it difficult for an African to obtain life insurance.) Those who were poorest found their way to the pawnbrokers and the local moneylenders who typically collected double or more the amount loaned.

East African building (savings and loan) societies, which held some Africans' savings in both Kenya and Tanzania prior to independence, very rarely made a loan to an African to buy a home and proved to be a shaky place for Africans to save. The building societies suffered an almost complete collapse in 1960 when non-Africans, anticipating the end of colonial rule, besieged the societies as well as the POSB with frantic withdrawal requests and transferred their savings to British institutions. The building societies were saved by huge injections of money from the British and East African governments and some private institutions, but the flight of capital in that crisis marked the beginning of the end of the colonial era in East African monetary institutions. The POSB, as a government agency, was relatively stronger than the building societies, and despite severe losses, weathered the storm.

Institutional credit was practically unknown among the great multitude of Africans who were small farmers or farm laborers. Either they were squatters on settler-owned lands or they had no title to their farms because of the tribal land tenure systems. They owned nothing which could be pledged as security for bank loans.

But, as the potential of the marketing co-operatives became recognized and as financing became an essential element of the colonial marketing system, more Africans, especially those who were members of marketing co-operatives, could get the production loans that were parceled out either directly by government agricultural lending organizations or indirectly through co-operative marketing societies to which some farmers belonged. Acting like plantation overseers of African laborers, agricultural administrators determined what cash crops should be raised by African farmers in various areas and used every inducement to get voluntary acceptance of the decisions handed down. (The Germans had relied on whips and forced labor.) To assure optimum production of the designated crops, the necessary fertilizer, insecticide, and seed inputs were predetermined with little consultation with the local farmers and production loans were provided to them in kind, along with minimal cash for hiring labor in the planting seasons. The farmers, skeptical of outsiders' advice and looking for some tangible return on their taxes, all too often tended to regard the entire process as a government handout primarily for the benefit of the government.

When crop prices were good they paid their loans, but excuses to delay payment were not hard to find, especially when prices fell. Although they were required to pledge their crops to the repayment of these loans and were supposed to market their crops only through the marketing co-operatives or other government-supervised crop purchasers that would collect the loans out of the crop payments, the farmers managed to escape these restrictions. And they often found ways of converting the farm supplies loaned to them into cash which they used for household expenses, school fees, and other purposes not considered productive. The entire system (which continued after independence in both Tanzania and Kenya with few changes) became increasingly vulnerable to losses and delayed collections arising from crop failures, evasions of production credit rules, illegal crop sales, falling markets, and political expediency.

As independence drew near farmers who participated in the marketing co-operatives had high hopes of improving their status—educationally, economically, and politically—as all types of co-operatives gained success and popularity. But there was little understanding of how to extend credit or collect loans other than through the mechanistic production loan apparatus which left most African farmers with little disposable cash and even less experience in handling money.

The social and economic restrictions that barred most Africans from participating in the formal money economy in the rural areas also worked to discourage them from acquiring useful experience in granting and collecting loans in the towns and cities. Most of their mutual aid societies were limited to accepting savings. However, the Ismaili communities, made up of Indian followers of the Aga Khan, organized co-operative societies as early as 1937–38 in Moshi and Dar es Salaam through which Ismailis could save, earn dividends on their shares, and lend money to each other.

African laborers rarely had access or the inclination to approach the formal institutions that made loans—it was better to get a payday advance from the white *bwana* (master). African civil servants, teachers, and clerks were not much better off if they needed a salary advance for an emergency. Some of them were so resentful of the Credit to Natives Ordinance that they avoided making any requests if they could find another way. Personal loans or advances from non-African supervisors were sometimes the answer, and often were conveniently forgotten, a practice demeaning to both the forgetful borrower and the resentful lender, and a sore point sure to be raised in any discussion of the prospects for organizing a credit union among Africans.

Nevertheless, in the preindependence years a few registered co-operative loan societies (some of them organized along tribal lines) were functioning and several credit union study clubs were quietly being organized in Tanzania and Kenya by priests and native leaders. Their members were usually small farmers, teachers who depended on farming to augment their modest salaries, and low-ranking civil servants trying to make the adjustment to living in the cities. Perhaps the Africans saw in the credit union plan an institution which could bridge the gap between the social values of the barter society around them and the economic advantages of the monetary society in which they confidently expected to play a larger role with the coming of independence.

The Early Postindependence Years

Conditions were ripe for savings and credit societies in Tanzania and Kenya in the first five years following independence. In the towns and cities Africans were moving into jobs vacated by departing British civil servants and into new posts created by their governments' ambitious educational, health, agricultural, and commercial development programs. Africanization policies, notably in Kenya, also caused an exodus of Indian and other non-Africans from service and clerical jobs that were then filled by black Kenyans. Less conspicuously, a rising number of business entrepreneurs bought out or, in the case of large corporations, bought into Indian- and British-owned enterprises with governmental assistance. In Tanzania similar job changes took effect, but government ownership of major lines of business, through parastatal (quasi-governmental) organizations, took precedence over Africanization and opened up new civil service-type jobs for Tanzanians regardless of their race or color.

Africans began to experience both the satisfaction of having money to spend and save and a growing need for credit to satisfy their yearnings for a higher standard of living. The POSB's activity picked up substantially as did saving for homes in the building associations. In Kenya a new type of land-buying co-operative was being organized and was gaining popularity as the best way to buy farmland, the most prized purchase of all. In Nairobi the East Africa Building Association opened its doors to prospective African home buyers. Commercial banks shared in the overall growth, but more from the increased financial activity that coursed through the banking system than from a conscious effort to mobilize local savings or to make loans and create a local money market into which they could channel their deposits for local development.

For most Africans, however, independence made it no easier to get a loan. Credit was still not to be had from commercial lenders and money borrowed from a *rafiki* (friend) had to be paid back on the next payday. In government jobs Africans inherited their predecessors' eligibility for government loans on which they paid little or no interest. But these government loans were only for buying transport vehicles and other job-connected necessities—they were not for school fees, clothing, household goods, or the other expenses the workers were encountering in their new jobs.

As keen as they were on saving, the departing British civil servants had themselves not been inclined to use personal credit except what they got from shopkeepers or tradesmen who rarely carried African accounts. None of the institutions they left behind seem to have had the will or the ability to fill the growing need for an African-owned and -managed savings and lending organization, an indigenous institution that could draw on the traditional lending practices of the informal African societies. In fact, consumer credit was generally frowned upon in Britain and most European countries. The credit unions gave the upcoming African civil servants, who comprised most of the wage earners of both nations, a modern financial institution that linked their traditional group savings and credit activities with the respectability and also the prestige of a bank-type noncolonial organization.

There was another area of unfilled savings and credit needs affecting far more people. The farmers whose crops fed the nations and earned the bulk of the precious foreign exchange also needed financial help. Representing almost the entire working population, most of them were illiterate, and a good half of them were not accustomed to using money. After independence the governments were immediately faced with the necessity—most urgently in Kenya—of returning the native people to the lands taken from them by settlers and plantation operators, and bringing them into the money economy. Farmers had to be encouraged, assisted, and even coerced into increasing their crop production or getting into new and different cultivation schemes that would result in increased production. Massive inputs of seed, fertilizers, insecticides, credit, and agricultural expertise were being lined up to help them expand the farmlands already under cultivation or to be opened up in new development programs.

Co-operative Banks

Co-operatives became one of the instrumentalities of both governments for distributing this small farmer assistance, and eventually they were to be given the responsibility for establishing their own savings and credit systems. The magnitude and complexity of providing banking and credit for the marketing of coffee, cotton, and other cash crops discouraged any thinking of a shift from the established banking connections for crop financing, but both countries moved ahead cautiously to organize co-operative banks that could eventually undertake the important role of becoming bankers to their co-ops.

Tanzania's National Co-operative Bank was formed in 1964 and in 1971 was amalgamated with the National Bank of Commerce (NBC). Kenya's Co-operative Bank was approved in 1965, became operative in 1968, and is still functioning. The co-operative banks were visualized as the central organizations in a rural financing system which would be owned by the farmers. Savings from their crop proceeds would be collected in savings accounts maintained by their marketing co-operatives from which the money would flow into the co-operative banks to be invested in rural development.

Multipurpose Co-operatives

The logic of mobilizing savings in an existing co-operative needed no elaboration in these countries where capital, literacy, and leadership were in short supply. However, there were already rumblings from dissatisfied farmers who complained of mismanagement, corruption, and inefficiency in their marketing co-operatives. It was questionable whether these organizations could be converted into viable multipurpose co-operatives. All of the advantages of such co-operatives—their efficiency in putting money to work, their ability to get acceptance of agricultural extension programs and thereby intensify the modernizing of traditional agrarian societies—would depend on their ability to attract honest, competent managers and a steady, strong, continuing flow of governmental assistance. Revolutionizing a backward, poverty-stricken, subsistence peasantry into modern, productive, agriculturalists cannot happen without government intervention on a large, expensive, and long-term scale. And elected leadership must give way to bureaucratic management that hopefully will be more efficient and progressive than local leaders.

Tanzania and Kenya had to decide whether they wanted to commit more of their economic resources and political capital to perpetuate the colonial legacy of top-down co-operation, or whether they should begin to take seriously their own exhortations about self-reliance so often couched in terms of African Socialism. The introduction of credit unions provided an opportunity for experimentation.

Credit unions were rapidly gaining popularity because they were much more of a grassroots co-operative, but they would be slow to develop and more likely to reinforce local initiatives or contentment with the status quo with whatever capital they might have. They might bring up new leadership, or they might siphon off the relatively few literate leaders who were needed in the marketing co-operatives. Their sponsorship had come from capitalistic North America and their image was that of a consumer credit institution not well adapted to the production credit needs of the rural sector or, for that matter, of a basically agricultural, African Socialist country.

But African Socialism allows for a wide variety of interpretations, and with surprisingly little change, credit unions adapted themselves to the differing African Socialist philosophies of Tanzania and Kenya.[1]

PART II

History of Credit Union Development in East Africa

4. Introduction of Credit Unions

As the countries in Africa came to independence, most of their people were poor, illiterate, and lacking medical care. Colonialism had consigned millions of human beings to being near-slaves, taken their land, and destroyed their self-respect. The new governments had to assume responsibility for finding answers to the most pressing problems of poverty, disease, and ignorance while reorganizing their economies to meet the high expectations of the people.

Their leaders were quick to recognize the value and necessity of stimulating economic development and urged their people to contribute individually through the mobilizing of local savings. These savings were not kept in banks—the total amount of money hidden away, unused, was considered, in Tanganyika for instance, to be in the millions of shillings. Much publicity was given to the risks of holding savings in traditional hiding places in the ground, in the thatch of the roof, in food containers, in the mattress—currency notes decay, are eaten by termites, destroyed by fire, lost, stolen. Stress was placed on the new idea that money needs to be put to work; money buried in a tin or hidden in the roof serves no useful purpose.

The government of Tanganyika, through newspaper editorials, meetings, and radio messages, sought to encourage the people to take their money from the secret hiding places and put it into savings bonds, banks, and postal savings. But for thousands of rural people, banks were unavailable, trips to a post office were long and arduous, and suspicions were not alleviated by the release of coin in hand for a piece of paper in return. Access to the deposited money was difficult and often involved considerable delay. Also, the burden of taxes falls on known wealth. Why give up the secret hiding places? Even today the axiomatic reply to any question about where people in Tanzania save is "each man knows where his own money is kept"!

In order, then, to mobilize savings and to develop a desire on the part of individuals to share their wealth for their own good and the good of the country, a more suitable method of approach had to be developed. Since the co-operative idea existed in tribal social codes, co-operative savings and credit societies were considered by those who knew of them as viable vehicles for such mobilization of savings.

Savings and credit societies met the tests of government and the citizenry on many important criteria: socially they followed traditional precepts of community action and shared responsibility; economically they appealed to the self-help objectives of mobilizing individual savings for local needs; and politically they promised to become institutions that could provide a moderate approach to socialism.

There was hope that savings and credit societies might induce some of the more progressive farmers to save money instead of measuring their wealth in cattle and to put that money to work in better farming, related businesses, or improved housing and sanitation for their families. It would also remove them from the grip of money lenders who left farmers with little return on the season's harvest when crops or livestock had been pledged for an emergency loan.

"At last we have come to the waterhole," said one farmer at the organization meeting of a savings and credit society in Tanganyika. "We who were poor and in need of money have had to go thirsty. Now we can borrow and at a decent fee." Perhaps the savings and credit society was overly idealized by the first people who joined, but it did provide a tangible expression of what ordinary citizens could do in co-operating with each other and their new governments by saving their money together for loans to themselves.

The successful development of savings and credit societies in African countries, however, was not entirely a spontaneous reaction of African people to the concept that had taken many years to develop in Europe and North America. Rather, it came about largely through patient encouragement by missionaries, non-African technicians, and other individuals who themselves had been credit union members or had learned about credit unions from overseas sources. These people saw credit unions as an excellent institution for nation building. In the development of a successful savings and credit society, it was believed the participants would learn mutual trust, would practice honesty and develop respect for each other's character, and would put in their own savings as the only means of raising capital against which to borrow.

The Catholic clergy particularly recognized that the credit union idea could be an effective tool for helping their parishioners economically, socially, and morally. The Africans who first accepted the idea became the "experts" in their own countries, and working together, they spread the idea of savings and credit societies among their people.

North American Aid

Some of the early African savings and credit societies were helped in the 1950s and 1960s by North American credit unions or credit union leagues answering overseas missionaries' requests for financial assistance. Usually the requests were for small amounts to cover local education and training sessions for interested Africans who showed promise of leadership.

Africans also were sent to Saint Francis Xavier University in Antigonish, Nova Scotia, Canada, for leadership training. While concentrating on techniques of community development, the Antigonish courses also included practical training in the organization and operation of credit unions based on the experiences of the credit unions founded by Father Tompkins and Father Coady. In 1959 the overseas adult training programs of the university were consolidated into the Coady International Institute which to date has provided courses in social development, social leadership, and co-operative studies for over 2,200 people from 100 countries—over 660 of them from Africa. By the mid-1950s these training programs and other initiatives were helping local enthusiasts to create a growing number of credit unions in countries of Latin America, the South Pacific, the Caribbean, Asia, and Africa. Energetic appeals for help were multiplying and were finding a sympathetic response in North American credit unions and religious orders.

Inside of ten years enough savings and credit societies were functioning in Africa to justify an exchange of experiences between those countries of East and West Africa where most savings and credit society development had taken place. The first two African Conferences on Mobilization of Local Savings in Dar es Salaam, Tanganyika, and Lagos, Nigeria, 1963, under the auspices of the Credit Union National Association (CUNA), launched the North American credit union development assistance program in Africa.

Co-operation between U.S. and Canadian credit unions originated from the early work of a Canadian pioneer, Alphonse Desjardins, who is acknowledged as the father of the caisses populaires which flourish among French-speaking Canadians mostly in the province of Quebec. He is also regarded as a key figure in helping U.S. credit unions get started in New Hampshire and Massachusetts.

Canadian credit unions have consistently worked in harmony with credit unions of the United States, first in 1939 through their affiliation with CUNA, which was reorganized as CUNA International in 1964, and since 1970 with the World Council of Credit Unions (WOCCU). Their collaboration in support of overseas credit union development has been one of the strongest links between the two movements. Together they have provided most of the financing, leadership, and technicians for the credit union world extension programs of the past twenty years. Canadian support to Africa has been especially important since 1968 when credit unions and caisses populaires joined with the Canadian International Development Agency (CIDA) to assist the Africa Co-operative Savings and Credit Association (ACOSCA) and to begin a credit union development program in the francophone countries.

As credit unions in developing countries began to take root and attract interest and support from individual North American credit unions and leagues, the idea of helping them gained increasing popularity, and there were discussions at CUNA meetings about the possibilities of extending overseas help more broadly on a systematic basis. Throughout both the United States and Canada, the Marshall Plan for the reconstruction of war-ravaged Europe was being widely publicized. North Americans, after making great personal sacrifices in the winning of World War II, were enjoying the prosperity of an economic boom. Many were in a mood to give help overseas, especially in support of peace.

At the same time, credit union growth was attracting unprecedented opposition from commercial banks, small loan and finance companies. In the United States, credit unions along with other co-operatives were targeted for sensational criticism by the National Tax Equality Association (NTEA) organized and financed by their business competitors. NTEA newspaper advertisements and letters, addressed to the industrial leaders who were encouraging their employees to organize credit unions, raised the question of whether these credit unions were indeed capitalistic, free enterprise institutions or "socialistic tax-evaders" undermining the free enterprise system.

At the February 12, 1953, joint meeting of CUNA, CUNA Mutual Insurance Society, and CUNA Supply Cooperative, Managing Director Doig recommended that

> we vigorously continue to promote the credit union movement as a quasi public service in the mind of the public—through our league meetings, chapter meetings, radio programs, magazine advertisements, etc. We should, through these mediums, always stress service to the member, service to the community, and service to the nation.

At that same meeting CUNA President Marion Gregory had pledged CUNA's support in foreign affairs to Secretary of State John Foster Dulles:

> The Credit Union National Association, Mr. Secretary, is at your service and the service of its country. We believe that in the credit union idea we have an instrument that can save the underprivileged people from Communism.

At their meeting in 1954, answering both the altruistic interests of rank and file credit union leaders in helping to extend the credit union idea overseas and the political need of CUNA for an unusual patriotic gesture, CUNA directors approved a new World Extension Program. As historians Moody and Fite observe:

> The cause of CUNA's entry into activities outside the United States was the cold war. After World War II the nation began competing with the Soviet Union for the allegiance of war-torn countries of Europe and newly emancipated colonial areas of Asia and Africa.[1]

For the first time North American credit unionism was conceived as both a global expression of the highest idealism and a politico-economic weapon in the international arena.

Since most African countries were vehemently opposed to any cold war involvement in the early 1960s when savings and credit societies were new on the scene, it seems evident that the reception of a savings and credit society development program in Tanganyika and Kenya was not greatly influenced by CUNA's international politics. Similarly, credit union leaders at the local levels in North America were for the most part largely unaware of the cold war overtones of the World Extension Program. They were far more interested in sharing their enthusiasm for the credit union idea through overseas extension work.

5. *Development of Credit Unions in Tanganyika*

In Tanganyika the early leaders who introduced the credit union idea came from the Tanganyika Episcopal Conference at Dar es Salaam, a country-wide social service agency operating in the fields of adult education, health, child care, and vocational training; the Nyegezi Social Training Centre (STC) at Mwanza; and individual priests throughout the country who brought the credit union idea to the local village level as well as to the capital city.[1]

The successes of the early training efforts were in large part due to the skill with which these priests selected the villagers to attend the training sessions and the manner in which they themselves withdrew from active direction so that local leaders had to take the responsibility of leadership. The priests, in their day-to-day contacts, were able to recognize the real leaders in a village and provided for their participation both by recommending their applications and by financing their transportation to training centers and seminars.

The Nyegezi STC was founded near Mwanza in 1960 by the White Fathers Missionaries who brought money to build and run it. The White Fathers, from Canada and Europe, were concerned at the social development gap in the education of those Africans who had completed secondary school and were working in their communities. Candidates for study from Tanganyika and the neighboring countries of East and Central Africa were selected on the basis of ability, maturity, and willingness to serve their communities, without consideration of their nationalities, political or religious allegiances.

Norman Riley, a Nova Scotia Credit Union League educator sponsored by Saint Francis Xavier University, was assigned to the staff of the STC for nine months in 1960–61. He taught about credit unions at Nyegezi as the first "imported credit union expert" and also gave an intensive course in credit union principles and organization to fifteen potential savings and credit society leaders in Dar es

Salaam. Riley worked with government officials on setting up by-laws, on evaluating the Tanganyika co-operative law as it applied to savings and credit societies, and on the design of specialized book-keeping forms.

A training program with Michigan credit unions was initiated during a U.S. visit in the late 1950s of Tanganyikan Bishop Rugambwa, who later became Tanzania's first African cardinal. He thought that the credit union format would fit into the African concept of economics. Under this program three Tanganyikans, Father Bamanyisa, Father Mutashoba, and Joseph G. Mutayoba, a social worker for the Tanganyika Episcopal Conference who had become a promoter of credit unions, came to the Michigan Credit Union League (MCUL) for training and also visited Canada for three months of training in the fall of 1962. Mutayoba was later to become the first president of the Savings and Credit Union League of Tanganyika (SCULT) and also the first president of ACOSCA.

The Tanganyika Project

In the summer of 1962 CUNA's World Extension Division (WED) arranged with the Saskatchewan Credit Union League (SCUL) and MCUL for a joint program in support of Tanganyika credit union development. Tanganyika, with seven credit unions already operating, had been identified in a 1962 nine-country Africa survey by Paddy Bailey of WED as the most promising African country for a credit union development program, and its government had expressed interest in a request to CUNA for help. Saskatchewan credit unions decided to celebrate their league's twenty-fifth anniversary in that same year by donating $20,000 to the project. Fund raising was keyed to their publicity about "adopting a new nation" with credit union potential in the hope that twenty-five years later the receiving nation would be in a position to provide help for someone else.

In Michigan, too, there was real interest in building international solidarity. MCUL's leaders had been early supporters of the WED concept and, having already made a commitment to the training of Tanganyika credit union organizers, they were enthused about the possibilities of a joint Tanganyika program with Saskatchewan that would give WED an active role on a scale of support never before attempted.

It was agreed that a technician and his family would be funded to serve for one year in Tanganyika as the CUNA special representative for East Africa. This joint United States-Canadian effort became known as the Tanganyika Project and eventually covered the two years 1963 and 1964.

I heard about the preliminary plans for the new project from Al Charbonneau of SCUL and from Paddy Bailey of CUNA's WED at a CUNA meeting in the summer of 1962 and immediately expressed interest in it. In addition to my ardent interest in credit unions, I had always hoped to devote some part of my working life to international affairs.

When Roy Bergengren urged the CUNA board to create WED in 1954, I heard his speech and was moved to ask him—unsuccessfully—for a place in the new program. When I left a key post with the Bureau of Federal Credit Unions to join MCUL in 1955, it was partly because the league leadership, and particularly its managing director, Albert W. Marble, was identified as having an interest in international relations. The league was already beginning to attract credit union technicians and organizers from other countries for training and consultation.

In the 1940s one of my professors, Lowell Ragatz, who taught a modern European history course at George Washington University, had fired my imagination about the future of Africa on the world scene. Twenty years later, that future had arrived and I wanted to be a part of it. It was fortuitous that top management changes were being made in the MCUL at that particular time and I could conscientiously give the new leadership, and myself, time to decide whether I should remain in an executive position. Selma helped to settle our family apprehensions about the problems of education, health, and daily living in Africa.

SCUL and CUNA encouraged me to request a leave of absence from my MCUL job as director of member services to head up the new project. L. J. Segadelli, managing director, was supportive and the league's board of directors approved a one year leave of absence. In addition, the Michigan Credit Union Foundation authorized a $14,000 grant to the project. Subsequently, a second year of leave was approved with additional foundation funding. In all, the Tanganyika Project was subsidized in the amount of almost $64,000, entirely paid for by credit union members who were attempting to reach out to help people halfway across the world, people with whom they had little or no relationship of any kind.

The Tanganyika Project was an unstructured, altruistic, and idealistic program with no specific goals except those expressed in SCUL's twenty-fifth anniversary publicity. Although centered in

Tanganyika, the project services were also made available to Kenya and Uganda with the recognition that credit union development throughout East Africa would thus be facilitated at a time when those countries were interested in cementing their ties with each other.

Cold war references were singularly lacking in the publicity given to both the Michigan and Saskatchewan fund-raising efforts. But if political anxieties were set aside, not so racial prejudice. Not everyone who read about the project was enthused, either about the donors or the recipients of the help. One reader of a Detroit newspaper wrote to the editor:

> I read, with much amusement and more indignation, of the Dublin family leaving for a year in Tanganyika.
>
> The amusement stems from time spent in East Africa myself and having, therefore, some acquaintance with Africans and their pattern of thinking; I am able to smile at the naivete of the Dublins . . . . They have yet to learn that even the rare African who understands a little English will have such a conveniently one-sided vocabulary that he will readily comprehend if someone wishes to lend him money (he is characteristically in debt to everyone he knows), but be abysmally dull about the fact that he is expected to pay the loan back. . . . I wonder if the Dublins have ever considered that most of the potential customers to whom they hope to lend money "to buy a bag of cement" and for whom "it's simply a matter of helping themselves," wouldn't know what to do with a bag of cement nor would they care. (*News*, Dec. 23, 1962)

Our family began a home training course in Tanganyikan life with Mutayoba as our houseguest for several months prior to departure. We tried to prepare ourselves by contacting other organizations for their African co-operative development experiences. The entire family studied Swahili. A brief visit to Saint Francis Xavier University helped to get details on the STC credit union training project; contacts with U.S. State Department officials and foreign aid staff helped to establish possibilities for working with the U.S. personnel attached to the East African embassies.

Since Israel at that time was recognized as being possibly the most experienced donor nation for African co-operative development foreign assistance, we made arrangements through the embassy of Israel for a ten-day study tour there enroute to Tanganyika. Although Israel's foreign aid technicians candidly expressed serious reservations about the success of the Tanganyika Project, they were co-operative, and Israel's embassy in Dar es Salaam took a continuing friendly interest in the project throughout our stay.

As CUNA's special representative for East Africa, I was accorded recognition as an adviser to the East African governments and was given the freedom to establish and maintain other relationships in line with this governmental advisory role. I was authorized by CUNA to do whatever seemed necessary to help the Tanganyikans (and other East Africans) develop the kind of credit union movement they wanted, at their own pace, and to do this mostly by consultative assistance.

My field assignment from the beginning was broad and flexible, but there was one rule with no exceptions: I did not provide any capital funds. No loans or grants were made for lending or for savings and credit society operations.

I was not tied down to any location so I traveled widely, visiting remote villages as well as urban centers. When I attended conferences in other African countries I tried to bring back relevant African experiences. I was free to concentrate on whatever was immediately important, establishing realistic and constantly reevaluated priorities.

Notwithstanding my relationship to government, the decision was made to place the project headquarters away from the capital city. There was concern that meeting social and professional obligations as members of the international co-operatives advisers' community in Dar es Salaam would become a time-consuming activity in itself with little direct benefit to the project. Also, Dar es Salaam was being well covered for credit union promotion by Mutayoba.

We arrived in Mwanza, our headquarters for the first year, in January, 1963. Mwanza, a port town on Lake Victoria, 1178 kilometers northwest of Dar es Salaam, is the center of a cotton growing area inhabited by the Wasukuma, one of the largest tribes in Tanganyika. The area at that time was a "showcase" for marketing co-ops, which were organized into unions, and even a third-tier organization, the Victoria Federation of Co-operative Unions (VFCU), which could, hopefully, assist in promoting credit unions. Also, only six miles away was the Nyegezi STC which had facilities for residential training courses and seminars. Father John Lavoie, the STC director, had welcomed us most warmly in his correspondence with us prior to our arrival, and we looked forward to working with him and his staff of East African, Canadian, Australian, and British educators.

Although housing, office, and school accommodations for our family were available at Nyegezi, it was decided that the East African credit union movements would best be assisted by separating the project from any religiously funded and oriented institution.

This decision recognized the fact that Tanganyika was determined to establish itself as a government for all its citizens without regard to religious, political, or tribal divisions. While the government acknowledged the great contributions during colonial times of the missionaries who brought education and health care, its policy from the start was for government to provide such services for all its people.

Very early in the development of the Tanganyika credit union movement parish membership was eliminated as a credit union common bond; community savings and credit societies serving all persons living in the area were organized instead. While priests and missionaries continued to promote credit union development, the emphasis was on serving congregants and noncongregants alike and on promoting local leadership to accept responsibility for running the societies even though priests often continued to keep the cash where banks were not available.

As a North American people-to-people endeavor, the Tanganyika Project surmounted many of the obstacles to understanding and acceptance that might have been anticipated from the problems of different societal background, language, economic, and political perceptions of the donors and the recipients of credit union assistance. Since we were stationed in Tanganyika, we benefited greatly from the good relations then existing between the peoples of Tanganyika, Canada, and the United States.

Early in 1963 we were invited to the opening ceremonies for a new consumer co-op shop in Mwanza. The guest of honor was none other than President Nyerere himself. The Tanganyikans and all of us non-Africans were excited, sharing the contagious joy of the Africans who had a genuine affection for their leader. Jack described the occasion in a letter to a friend at MCUL:

> The big day was Wednesday this week, April 10. We joined the crowd that went down to the railroad station to meet the president and his party, to hear the band, and watch the parade. . . .
>
> Later that afternoon we went to the co-op store ceremonies and found ourselves in a small group seated near the president's immediate party. He gave a moderately long speech, in Kiswahili, apparently full of humor and sarcasm aimed at the opponents of the co-ops. (A friend translated part of the speech for us.) One of the big laugh-getters was when he said that although he had been invited to open the new store, some thieves had deprived him of the pleasure by "opening" the place the night before. All too true—earlier that day, the manager, whom we know well, told us ruefully that the place had been ransacked overnight.
>
> After the speech, I decided to approach the President for an interview—tape recorder and all. I introduced myself, and Selma who came

up later, and told him of our assignment. He politely turned away my suggestion for a tape recording, but after that was out of the way, he relaxed completely and for about fifteen minutes talked with us about co-ops and credit unions. He told us that some years ago he and a group had tried to start another consumer co-op store in another town, but the local merchants had put on a price war that killed their new co-op. Now, he said, the government was determined no one was going to kill the co-ops. He believes very much in building co-ops the traditional way, from the bottom up, as we do in credit unions. But time is short, and in the case of the consumer co-ops the decision has been made to build them from the top down, to the extent necessary. He believes one of the big jobs that credit unions can do in Tanganyika is to give the people a real understanding of their responsibilities and opportunities as owners of co-ops, while the government also is trying to show them in practical demonstrations that co-ops can really help them economically.

You have seen pictures of President Nyerere, I'm sure, but it's hard to capture his personal warmth and magnetism in a picture. Unpretentious, but very keen, he radiates enthusiasm backed up by comprehensive knowledge. He took the initiative in asking whether I was receiving full co-operation from government staff and the big co-operative federations. I think we can count on his support.[2]

There were difficulties, of course, but most of them came from the opposition of other foreign technicians. Although they were unfailingly courteous, helpful, and friendly to us personally, they seemed to regard this small-scale project as another front for America's invasion of the Third World with consumer goods and consumer credit. To some of them, credit unions were interlopers in the rural co-operative field which had been reserved to the marketing co-operatives, and they did not take kindly to the government's introduction of savings and credit societies into the rural areas. The attacks started immediately upon the opening of the first conference on the Mobilization of Local Savings in Dar es Salaam held a few days after my arrival in the country.

I went to Dar es Salaam to join Paddy Bailey who was coordinating the conference, and I was anticipating a reasonably warm welcome. Instead I found myself witnessing an unscheduled debate on the merits of multipurpose versus single-purpose co-ops. The most insistent voice raised against the savings and credit societies, and in favor of multipurpose co-ops was that of the ILO co-operative education adviser, U Nyi Nyi, a former Burmese co-operatives registrar. His British associate, Alex Marriott of the United Nations Development Program (UNDP), took the opposite view. (Both of them were later to become my friends and sympathetic confidants.)

Few of the Africans took strong positions one way or another; they gave the impression that little needed to be said in defense of savings and credit societies. But one of the best informed and convinced multipurpose advocates among them was Emmanuel Bomani, manager of the large and prestigious VFCU. Bomani wound up his eloquent case for multipurpose co-operatives by calling for a vote on the question of "single-purpose or multipurpose co-operatives." As he turned expectantly in my direction, I decided a judicious silence was preferable to what might be seen as a self-serving defense . . . my first experience in international diplomacy.

Here I was, my mission not yet begun, and the entire project—albeit requested by the Tanganyika government—was in doubt. But African political adroitness settled the matter firmly and authoritatively. The commissioner for co-operatives, B. M. Juma, quietly observed that all of the arguments pro and con had already been considered by his minister, who was present, and the decision had been made to organize single-purpose savings and credit societies and that decision was not to be reversed. He did not object, however, when the meeting put the question to a vote. The result was overwhelmingly in favor of the program for single-purpose savings and credit societies.

After only a few months' work, it became clear that the Tanganyikan credit union movement would benefit from continued assistance beyond the one-year commitment of the Tanganyika Project and, in co-operation with government officials, Jack tried to develop broader technical support for the fledgling movement. It seemed fairly certain that the Tanganyika Project would provide the practical demonstration to elicit such support, but more time was needed to negotiate for U.S. government and other assistance.

In concurrence with the government of Tanganyika, CUNA requested that the MCUL approve Jack's application for an extended leave of absence. In September, 1963, the league agreed and, with additional funding assured, we began to make plans for the second year, working in another promising rural area.

In December, 1963, the project headquarters was moved to Moshi, about 550 kilometers north of Dar es Salaam, and 350 kilometers south of Nairobi, Kenya. Here at the base of Mount Kilimanjaro was located the Tanganyika Co-operative College, an important adjunct of the co-operative movement. This move enabled a closer working relationship with the college as well as the development of the credit union idea in another heavily populated rural area of the country with a different crop orientation—coffee. The

Kilimanjaro area is the home of the Wachagga, who are known for their business acumen.

Their Kilimanjaro Native Co-operative Union (KNCU) was one of the oldest co-operative strongholds in the country and a likely asset to the project. The Lutheran church, which sponsored many missions and educational activities in this area, was also a potential ally and did indeed become interested in promotion of credit unions.

While it was recognized that the credit union idea should not be promoted exclusively by Lutherans or Catholic missionaries or any other church personnel, it was apparent that in the absence of employee groups (industrial or business) community savings and credit societies were a logical type of credit union to be organized, and churches were often the key to community acceptance. One of the very first savings and credit societies in Tanganyika had been organized in 1961 at Mawella parish on the mountain under the guiding hand of Father Richard LeClair, an American priest from Massachusetts. This society was a working model on which to base further promotion.

Jack personally organized no savings and credit societies but followed the trail of the trainee promoters to reinforce their efforts whenever and wherever he could. The African oral tradition enabled over one hundred promoters—teachers, mission employees, government inspectors—from Tanganyika, Kenya, and Uganda to take the credit union story to their villages, each using his own local idiom.

The independent island of Zanzibar was visited only once by Jack in May, 1963, when he came at the invitation of Sheik Hashil Ryami, the senior co-operative inspector, to discuss credit union possibilities for dock and plantation workers. Raiffeisen-type, unlimited liability, farm co-operatives had been introduced in Zanzibar as early as 1952. However, Zanzibar farmers were extremely poor and savings were almost nonexistent; their attempts to run thrift and loan societies had been unsuccessful. Ryami thought that the townspeople would be little interested in credit unions since living costs were low, education free through grade eight, and health services provided by government.

Zanzibar's revolution in late 1963 ended further consideration of credit union organization. Recently, however, under Revolutionary Council Decree No. 3 (the Co-operative Societies Decree) of 1979, a number of savings and credit societies have been registered with the help of organizers from the savings and credit department of UCS and ACOSCA.

Before the end of 1963, reports began to come in from Tanganyika and Kenya of savings and credit unions organized, members joining, savings developing, and loans being made. In fact, at the end of the first five months of the project Jack reported to MCUL:

> I feel certain now that credit unions will work in Tanganyika. Before the end of this year we will probably have fifteen operating in rural areas for farmers, for teachers, and for government employees. . . . Provisions for sound operations, stability, and safety are of unusual importance here because of the people's unhappy experiences of the past with similar organizations. Doubt, fear, and lack of self-reliance must be replaced by trust and confidence. This will come as the people see tangible evidence of success. We are already within sight of forming a League. Joe Mutayoba is pressing for the organization meeting to be held this year because he feels strongly that the credit unions here must rely mostly on their own resources for training, supervision and auditing. . . . With a government team (assigned) to develop procedures and begin training in the organization and inspection work, we will prepare for the effective use of more outside assistance if it can be had.

Regular expense and progress reports to CUNA and the supporting leagues were accompanied by tape and slide talks to be used in fund-raising work. Educational and promotional materials were created locally and cheaply, even if they required more time and trouble than bringing in imports. Trial and error experience showed that the Tanganyikans preferred materials illustrated with photographs rather than sketches, cartoons, and charts. The photos were also used in slide presentations that allowed Jack's local government counterparts, co-operative officers Yonah Msuya and Vincent Kuba, to do the narration spontaneously in Swahili.

By September, 1963, however, Jack was being asked to send in data to quantify our progress, a setback as far as he was concerned because it meant getting involved in the "numbers game"—so typical of development projects, and so meaningless—but as WED reminded him, so necessary to keep the support funds flowing.

Savings and Credit Union League of Tanganyika

As the Tanganyika Project gained momentum, enthusiasm began to build among the Tanganyikans to form a league which they thought would build solidarity, provide the savings and credit societies with much-needed technical assistance to augment the governmental supervision, give them access to CUNA's services (surety bonds, stabilization, and educational materials), and enable them to obtain

CUNA Mutual's loan protection and life savings insurance for their members.

Any reservations about the wisdom of this undertaking at such an early stage in the existence of Tanganyika's few infant savings and credit societies were swept away by the enthusiasm which all of us felt for the "successes" of the Tanganyika Project.

The Tanganyikan minister for commerce and co-operatives, the Honorable J. S. Kasambala, who opened the SCULT organization meeting, voiced his government's expectations:

> Credit Unions are obviously here to stay, and in our government five-year development plan (1964–1969) we hope to have 400 of them registered throughout the United Republic in order to encourage thrift, to save our buried treasure from *dudus* [insects], and to protect our urban wage earners from the various sharks all too ready to gobble up their meagre earnings.[3]

The Tanganyikan delegation at the Third African Conference on Mobilization of Local Savings in early June, 1964, at Kampala, had introduced for discussion a "Proposal for Organizing a Tanganyika Credit Union League" to be funded initially through CUNA and its affiliates in the Tanganyika Project. This proposal was formally presented at the SCULT organization meeting at Msimbazi Community Centre in Dar es Salaam, June 26–28, 1964.

Transportation and subsistence expenses were provided by the Tanganyika Project for forty-two delegates representing twenty-five of the twenty-seven savings and credit societies in the country at that time. The proceedings were organized by the Tanganyikan leaders and the discussions were conducted in Swahili; the proposed bylaws had been translated into Swahili in advance of the meeting. The delegates' acceptance of the proposal was by no means predictable. A similar meeting of savings and credit society representatives in Ghana had voted to delay the formation of their league.

A unanimous decision to organize SCULT was voted, and all forty-two delegates signed the registration application. Among the other actions taken were the election of a twelve-person board of directors with Mutayoba of Dar es Salaam Society as president; Joseph Hipoliti of Mawella Society as vice-president; Raymond J. Mwaikasu of Dar es Salaam Society as secretary; and John E. Bunga of Polisi Society as treasurer. The senior co-operative officer in charge of savings and credit societies, E. P. Mwasha, and Jack served as advisers to the meeting.

SCULT was authorized to initiate a dues schedule for its member societies as a start toward self-support. The league was officially registered as a co-operative society in August, 1964. It became affiliated with CUNA International on February 12, 1965, and with the Co-operative Union of Tanganyika on January 25, 1967.

From its inception, SCULT received outside financial assistance that enabled it to hire staff, open an office, and provide services that were not fully paid for by the members of the league. No serious analysis of future income possibilities was made nor indeed did anyone suggest using the limited resources of SCULT for theoretical planning. It was predicted (more in hope than on facts) that SCULT would become self-supporting within five years, but overseas support was not predicated on any specific self-support plan. There was work to be done: the organization of new savings and credit societies, the training of bookkeepers and elected officials, the provision of the services being offered by CUNA and CUNA Mutual.

SCULT's take-off as a pioneer African savings and credit society league also helped pave the way for favorable action on the joint CUNA/Agency for International Development (AID) regional credit union proposal that was worked out with the USAID and governmental co-operative offices of Tanganyika, Kenya, and Uganda prior to termination of the Tanganyika Project but was not approved until 1965. The Tanganyikan ministry had signified its approval of both an AID and a Peace Corps project (which came close to implementation but were never activated) as early as May, 1963, when the possibility was first discussed with Minister Kasambala.

By the end of 1964 when the Tanganyika Project was concluded a league (SCULT) had been organized, a regional East African (and possibly Pan-African) CUNA/AID project had been readied for continuing the development work in East Africa, and the foundations had been laid for East African savings and credit societies' support toward the organization of ACOSCA.

Since Jack's leave from the Michigan league had expired and since no one knew for certain when, if ever, the proposed regional program would be implemented, or whether he would be invited to participate, we returned to Michigan in December, 1964.

6. CUNA/AID Programs

Transition to CUNA/AID Programs

The Tanganyika Project's regional approach was working well enough in its first year to suggest that if U.S. government aid could be obtained, it should also be provided regionally, diplomatic relations of the United States with Tanganyika, Kenya, and Uganda permitting. The ability of the East African countries to get along with each other would also be a factor in the participation of their respective USAID missions in a regional program.

Politically there were few problems, but already in 1963 the East African countries were finding it difficult to maintain the economic unity, or the political concord, they had hoped for in the halcyon days of independence when their leaders were speaking as if with one voice for an East African Federation. In making a plea for federation *before* independence, Nyerere prophetically warned of the "balkanization" that would follow separate independence:

> We need no visas to cross our boundaries now. Separate independence will almost inevitably impose visas upon us. Those unfortunate tribes who now find themselves divided by the present boundaries find it very awkward now. But they will find it more awkward, if awkward is the word, in future for separate independence will, internationally, make Tanganyika as foreign to Kenya or Uganda, as China or America is. Their cousins on the other side of the border will be foreigners. We trade now without tariff barriers; separate independence may necessitate such barriers. We have a common currency which could easily lead to a common Central Bank. Separate independence will almost inevitably lead to separate currencies and the establishment of National Central Banks to make separate independence a reality. One could go on *ad infinitum* to show that separate independence will encourage disunity, not unity. Separate independence means in effect that we shall find ourselves less united after colonialism than before colonialism. Independence will have resulted in greater disunity and the more or less permanent balkanization of our region. The irony of separate independence is as stark as that.[1]

Federation was a mutual objective in 1963. It was a distant dream by 1979. In 1963 each country was trying to make the best deals it could for new factories, tourism, and financial and trade advantages for itself; each went its separate way eventually. In 1967 the EAC was formed to strengthen the financial ties between the countries, but by July, 1977, it had collapsed. Tanzania first closed its borders with Kenya in 1974 following a rash of economic disputes; the border was reopened through World Bank intervention, but in 1977, with the collapse of East African Airways and with Kenya's seizure of the jointly owned steamships on Lake Victoria and its nationalization of the East African Harbors Corporation, the border was closed permanently.

Relations between the countries were good in the early 1960s, however, and apparently growing stronger at the time the CUNA/AID regional program was first proposed. Tanganyika's early agreement to it in 1963 seemed to improve the possibilities of getting not only the agreement of the other two countries, but also the approval of AID/Washington and the USAID country missions in Kenya and Uganda as well. A regional strategy was being promoted within AID's Africa Bureau for various reasons, among them the hope of economizing on AID projects while encouraging the countries to co-operate with each other on problems that transcended national boundaries.

A regional credit union program that could build on the existing co-operation among the co-operative departments of Tanganyika, Uganda, and Kenya would combine all the advantages of the oft-described but seldom realized co-operation among co-operators. There was competition between the countries, of course, but it could be turned to their benefit in credit union development. Competition among the individual AID country missions for the best services of the new regional credit union project might cause them to utilize the regional facilities efficiently to the advantage of all the countries, while each country would have the services of its own technician specializing in its unique approach. Sharing the benefits of the Tanganyika Project, each AID mission and its staff could genuinely agree to work together regionally because they were already doing that in a small way without any investment or commitment of their own funds.

However there was another kind of competition which was taken for granted and never openly discussed—the competition between headquarters and field staff, regional missions and country missions—competition that generated all kinds of internal controversies to play havoc with the plans.

Thus regional co-operation was doomed after government funding was introduced by AID, even though the U.S. Department of State had given official recognition to the Tanganyika Project with its East Africa regional outreach:

> It is with pride that I commend the Michigan Credit Union League and the Saskatchewan Credit Union League for their joint effort in extending the credit union movement to Africa. . . . It is indeed a tribute to the farsightedness of the more than a million credit union members and officers whose voluntary contributions are making this effort possible. You are not only supplementing the efforts of our government today; you are sowing seeds which shall grow into living institutions and bear good fruit for generations to come.

This statement to MCUL was made on October 21, 1963, by G. Mennen Williams, assistant secretary of state for African affairs.

CUNA/AID East Africa Regional Credit Union Development Program

In the spring of 1965 the news came to us in Michigan that AID was definitely going to approve an East Africa regional program. Both CUNA and AID wanted Jack to return and head up the program under a CUNA/AID contract, but he was torn between his desire to get back to work with his East African cohorts and his doubts about whether he could fit into such an AID-funded program.

Speaking at the annual membership meeting of SCUL on February 24, 1965, Jack tried to distinguish between the help provided by the Tanganyika Project and that which could be anticipated from the proposed CUNA/AID program:

> I reported to you last year that we had made some progress . . . .
>
> Then, as today, there wasn't money in CUNA's budget to carry on a project like this. So at the beginning of our first year, after we went, when I knew that we must return after just one year, I had to look to other sources of money to continue the work. Part of my time was spent in conferring with the United States Agency for International Development and the United States Peace Corps, trying to get their support for a credit union program in East Africa. As of today it looks as though they will help and it looks as though eventually we shall see a full-fledged development program under the auspices of the United States AID working with CUNA not only in East Africa, but also in other parts of Africa. But I'd like to be quite frank with you about the drawbacks of government programs. Ordinarily they have done things *to* the Africans; nowadays they are doing things *for* them.

> When you sent an American family over there without any government money you sent an unusual kind of aid; a different kind of aid; an offer to do things *with* the Tanganyikans. Many governments have sent goods and materials. We would not be the first private organization to send a book or a typewriter or even to build a building for them. People in Africa are accustomed to getting material things and like all human beings, once they get something material, they expect something else material. When you sent us without any strings attached to your dollars, with an open assignment and with absolute flexibility, you sent the creative power of at least six human beings, and I include the entire family because by the time we had finished every single one of the family had done something for the project.

Little did we realize then how much difference there would be between the Tanganyika Project and government assistance, nor the extent to which we would be involved in the CUNA/AID programs. Before the end of August, 1965, we were back in Tanzania, Jack as the regional director of the CUNA/AID East Africa Regional Credit Union Development Program for the countries of Tanzania, Kenya, and Uganda.

Jack had already served over twenty years with the U.S. government in the first two decades of the federal credit union program and knew something about the constraints of working with government agencies. Prior to his AID appointment he was brought to AID headquarters in Washington to report on the Tanganyika Project. The co-operative specialists there were very supportive, but there was determined opposition evident among other highly placed officials who controlled the budget.

The regional program was really a federated plan which the country missions could choose to join or not to join. It could bring East Africa a unified credit union support system with a qualified technician in each country, or it could fall apart if the missions refused to participate. Still, there was no other way to continue, or so Jack thought, and he set aside most of his doubts. The family agreed we should go. Knowing that this meant pulling up our Michigan roots for an uncertain future—he could not ask the MCUL for another leave of absence—Jack resigned from his position.

It was agreed that the program headquarters should again be in Moshi, Tanzania. Although the Kenyan Co-operative Development Department (CDD) wanted the headquarters to be in Nairobi, the USAID mission there had not indicated any strong interest.

I decided to make a courtesy call on Elton Smith, the food and agriculture officer, when our plane made a stopover in Nairobi on the long trip from Europe to Dar es Salaam. Smith gave unmistakable hints of a changed attitude, with just a shade of hostility. His carefully chosen words signaled that my fears about the fragility of the regional plan and my forebodings about a government-to-government program were all too real, at least insofar as USAID/Kenya was concerned.

Smith's attitude was never fully explained, but in addition to his own professional reservations about the regional program, his new attitude may have reflected some very real problems in his office. For one thing, the mission was probably not as enthused as AID headquarters over the new regional projects concept which would compete for funds and staff with the strongly entrenched country missions and their bilateral programs. For another, USAID/Kenya did not want to get caught in the cross fire of a jurisdictional-funding controversy that had erupted between the Ministry of Agriculture and the Ministry of Commerce and Industry, which had taken over the CDD after it was moved out of Agriculture. A £4 million (US $11.2 million) Scandinavian grant program to assist rural co-operatives had been obtained by the CDD to the chagrin of Agriculture officials who apparently did not agree with the plan. USAID/Kenya did not wish to exacerbate the hostilities even to the extent of adding a small input for savings and credit societies.

Although several on-and-off agreements were made to provide the Kenya credit union technician and although the Swedish co-operative credit expert advising the Kenyan government under a Nordic Project had recommended strong support for co-operative credit societies as separate institutions, the final decision was negative, much to the disappointment of James A. N. Kibue, the Kenya co-operatives commissioner, and Daniel J. Nyanjom, his deputy who had returned from a U.S. tour determined to promote a major credit union program with U.S. assistance.

Jack's personal disappointment in the Kenya situation was only slightly less painfully repeated in Uganda where the USAID mission, initially favorable to the regional plan while Newman Jeffrey was mission director, was now changing its strategy under a new mission director, Will Mueller. While Mueller's style was diplomatic, he and his staff politely but firmly managed to delay calling up a technician, apparently in a joint decision with the Kenya mission to obstruct the regional thrust. (Subsequently, under a bilateral program, a credit union technician was added to another USAID/Uganda co-operative contractor team.)

"Marking time," an old government bureaucratic strategy, eventually spelled the end of the CUNA/AID regional program as far as these two missions were concerned. But harmonious working relationships were established with both Smith and Ned Mason, his counterpart in USAID/Uganda. In the twenty-one-month period that Jack remained as regional director, he was given enough freedom to answer the invitations of the two countries' co-operative commissioners for assistance with their savings and credit society promotional, supervisory, and training efforts. Both USAID missions helped make available overseas credit union training to prepare government and other technicians for promotional and supervisory functions.

USAID/Tanzania held unswervingly to its credit union commitment within the regional program and later in a continued bilateral program under Samuel H. Butterfield, who had moved up from deputy to mission director in the 1963–65 period. Butterfield and John Cooper, the food and agriculture officer (who had just been transferred from USAID/Kenya), helped to get the regional program rolling. They approved the Tanzanian government's request for a country director, cut the AID red tape wherever they could, and gave all the freedom needed to operate effectively.

Ronald D. Madery, who had backstopped the Tanganyika Project as MCUL's public relations director, served from 1966 to 1968 as the first Tanzania country program director, with headquarters in Dar es Salaam. He arrived in May, 1966, and quickly established an excellent personal and professional comradery with Mwasha, his government counterpart.

When Madery and Mwasha visited the rural areas of south and southwest Tanzania in late 1966, Madery reported:

> Wherever we went we were greeted with receptive and enthusiastic support for the Credit Union idea. We visited Credit Unions in the Mtwara, Ruvuma, Iringa, and Mbeya Regions.
>
> It was encouraging to find in the remotest African village that people are available with the necessary talents to organise, run and manage a Credit Union that will provide savings and loan services to its members. In the vast majority of cases, the books were kept in an excellent way; they were current and up to date; there were very few errors and I would say generally that comparing them with Credit Unions of the same age and size in the U.S., the Credit Unions here are in a much better condition. The delinquency is nothing to be alarmed at and the members have a confidence in the Credit Union that is most encouraging. We did find that in those areas that had trained dedicated Credit Union volunteers who were working either part-time or in their spare time in organising and assisting Credit Unions, that these Credit Unions were usually in a much better condition than in those areas that did not have these types of people.

> It was very obvious that where Credit Union Co-operative Inspectors had been stationed and had been working with the Credit Unions, the Credit Unions were well organised and managed. But in those areas where no Credit Union Inspectors had been assigned, the Credit Unions were in a much weaker condition.[2]

Madery was never as closely involved with his other counterpart, John Lubuva, SCULT manager, partly because Lubuva and other league leaders were finding it difficult to simultaneously manage the league as a co-operative under government supervision and as an organization of savings and credit societies with an undefined measure of independence, but supposedly free to counsel with government on behalf of its members.

Within a few months Madery was initiated into Tanzania government-SCULT politics that were responding to American credit union rivalries.

> *From the time of Madery's arrival it had been uncomfortably evident that Mutayoba, the president of the league, was not cooperating with either of us in any way whatsoever. He also made it difficult, if not impossible, for either of us to meet with the league's executive committee or manager. The reasons did not become apparent until the league's annual meeting in November, 1966, when new officers were to be elected, and it was disclosed that Mutayoba had been attempting to obtain a four-year, $40,000 technical assistance grant and a $26,000 building loan from CUNA Mutual Insurance Society. The total amount involved, some $66,000, would have been enough to make the league financially independent of CUNA/AID and, insofar as technical assistance was concerned, independent from the government.*
>
> *These objectives might have been laudable, but nothing had been said to CUNA in the United States or to either of us who represented CUNA in Tanzania. Nor had any of these negotiations been discussed with, let alone cleared by, the government. CUNA Mutual's relationships with CUNA, although supposedly improved in the 1960s, were still not good enough to permit a simple exchange of vital information affecting their mutual interests in helping an overseas league. These events led to a typical Tanzanian government disciplinary solution that greatly weakened the league.*

In an attempt to bring the league into line with government supervisory requirements and to establish a more consultative league relationship, Mwasha, who was present at the league annual meeting both in his supervisory capacity and as a delegate from a member society, accepted election as president of SCULT. This was unprecedented in Jack's experience, but as Mwasha told him, "This is not America, this is Tanzania." The implications of a government takeover were obvious, so much so that the new board of directors became in effect a caretaker government. This had even worse consequences for the government-league relationships, which continued to be marred by conflict caused both by the government's indecision as to the legitimate role of the league and by the inability of the elected league leadership, perhaps because of insurmountable difficulties, to work effectively with government.

In late 1968, when a new senior co-operative officer was assigned, the caretaker government was replaced with a new, elected administration, and the league resumed its quasi-independent role. But there was little rapport with the CUNA/AID technicians. It was always easier for the technicians to relate to the government staff than to the league staff. It was, in fact, almost impossible for them to maintain normal communications with the league manager or the executive committee. There was the problem of physically getting together. The only desk space available to the technician was in the government offices which were located at some distance from the cramped SCULT office. And there was the problem of communications—SCULT meetings were almost always conducted in Swahili, with scant acknowledgment of the language problems of the CUNA/AID advisers.

With the best of intentions as a carry-over of the Tanganyika Project with its people-to-people foundation, the CUNA/AID regional program in Tanzania evolved more and more into a typical government-to-government program. The regional program of 1965–68 centered around organized training programs for credit union officials, government supervisors, and instructors in the field of credit unions. These activities served to energize a concerted effort by the East African governments' trained savings and credit specialists. "All objectives [of the regional program] were attained in Tanzania," according to CUNA's final report, and the program succeeded "to a much lesser degree in Kenya, and not at all in Uganda."

In Tanzania a credit union section was established in the ministry concerned with co-operatives; a credit union course was instituted at the Co-operative College in Moshi; the credit union bookkeeping system was redesigned with Swahili incorporated on all forms; a credit union bookkeeping manual in Swahili was completed; and a government inspection manual and forms were developed for supervision of savings and credit societies in the hope of standardizing credit union examinations throughout the country.

CUNA/AID Tanzania Credit Union Development Program

Two credit union technicians were supplied to Tanzania in the new bilateral CUNA/AID program of 1968–70 that took up from the phased-out regional program in which Madery had served earlier. Kenneth J. Marin was appointed chief of party and SCULT technician. Marin, a past president of CUNA International and MCUL, was recruited from his post as chairman of the Department of Economics and Business Administration at Aquinas College, Grand Rapids, Michigan. He arrived in August, 1968, and was joined in February, 1969, by Roger S. Teasley, a principal examiner of the Bureau of Federal Credit Unions, who was assigned to be the credit union technician attached to the CDD.

The bilateral program in Tanzania aimed to continue the urban/rural expansion of savings and credit societies, to strengthen SCULT with a full range of league services, and to help establish a strong, independent supervisory credit union section within the government. A further goal was to help Tanzania charter 400 societies which, by fiscal year 1970, would serve 75,000 members who would accumulate savings of Tshs 7 million.

Progress was made on each of these goals, most notably in the number of savings and credit societies organized and in increased membership and savings, but little of the numerical progress could be documented because of the inability of the societies to comply with reporting requirements. Another goal that was substantially accomplished soon after if not within the project period was the plan for U.S. training of a team of sixteen savings and credit society specialists which was to become the nucleus of a geographically dispersed cadre serving every region in Tanzania.

Related to the CUNA/AID programs although not directly attributable to them were the U.S. Government/Participant Training Programs that provided credit union training in the United States and Canada for African governmental staff and other technicians. These programs added to the technical competence of the trainees and in some cases opened their thinking to the possibilities of a sizable savings and credit movement in their own countries. They did little, however, to reinforce or broaden concepts of savings and credit societies as rural development organizations. Worker-based credit unions in North America were seen as the successful models from a supervisory standpoint and far easier to emulate than the domestic variety of rural savings and credit societies that were just beginning to succeed in the villages of Tanzania.

The rural savings and credit societies were still growing as the

CUNA/AID program for Tanzania came to an end in 1970, but the rural drive was losing momentum, and as early as 1969 the CUNA/AID technicians were beginning to accept the inevitability of a preponderance of urban savings and credit societies. According to the first six months' progress report to AID,

> some modest decline in the rate of organization of new credit unions has occurred but serious supervisory problems almost certainly would occur in the absence of this organizational slow-down. There has also been a trend toward increasing urbanization among the newer societies. While there is a great need for low-cost credit among these minimum-wage, urban salary earners, our primary goal is still to mobilize rural credit.
>
> In the Tanzanian economy, dedicated to agricultural self-help as its primary socialist goal, the task order technicians intend to continue an emphasis on strengthening the existing village societies, and creating new ones where credit union service does not now exist. These societies, however, are born only with a very substantial "pre-natal" and "mid-wife" attention. In the urban areas, and notably in Dar es Salaam, many of the new credit unions arise almost spontaneously through observation of nearby successes and word-of-mouth publicity. This much greater ease in providing initial chartering guidance, and follow-up supervision, will almost certainly mean a continuation of the decline in the relative role of the rural-based society. This will come about not because of any abandonment of the original task order emphasis, but because of the normal growth pattern of these societies, closely patterning that of other developing countries.[3]

7. Changing Tanzania Registration Policy

If in fact the government was still pursuing its primary goal to mobilize rural credit through savings and credit societies as late as 1969, its enthusiasm had become less than lukewarm by 1970 when the CUNA/AID programs were terminated. Events were already in motion that confirmed the predictions of an urbanization trend in the organization of new societies. Individual society leaders and government savings and credit society specialists could do little to influence, or even discuss, the impending turnaround.

SCULT, the acknowledged spokesman for Tanzania savings and credit societies, was itself becoming increasingly dependent on large and rapidly multiplying urban societies for its failing dues budget. With a limited amount of aid from MCUL, however, it attempted to carry on a combined rural/urban development effort, and in some regions its staff were teaming up with government officers to provide services to rural societies.

The initial government registration policy, starting immediately after independence, had been to encourage savings and credit societies for all Tanzanians everywhere—the farmers and the workers. From the beginning, these societies were found mostly in rural areas because most of the people, by far, were agriculturists. It was hoped that these peasants could be brought into the money economy as they learned to entrust their savings to their own co-operative institutions, since the few commercial banks and the one building association had practically no interest in doing this kind of business with individuals. Neither did the POSB nor the rural credit institutions have much concern over any such competition that might be generated by the new savings and credit societies. These societies had a wide open field in which to grow side by side with other co-operatives and to demonstrate the viability of self-reliant nation-building initiatives. Or so it seemed from research reports, from national education programs, and from policy statements and reports emanating from the government.

The *Report of the Presidential Special Committee of Enquiry into the Co-operative Movement and Marketing Boards,* 1966, noted that

> Credit Unions in Tanganyika, carefully handled, have been a success. At the end of 1965 there were 80 registered credit union societies, of which we have data for 71 . . . with 10,288 members, shares and deposits . . . of . . . Tshs 1,193,846 and . . . outstanding loans of Tshs 897,670. There is a small section of the Co-operative Development Division which works exclusively with credit unions.[1]

As late as 1970, President Nyerere's 1967 TANU speech urging farmers to form savings and credit societies in keeping with the Arusha Declaration was quoted as government policy at a conference of government co-operative officers:

> Organizing one's income properly is, of course, a particular problem for farmers, who receive money only once a year—when the crops are harvested and paid for.
>
> But such people, as well as wage-earners who are trying to buy some more expensive articles, have a solution which they can develop for themselves. The Savings and Credit Societies (Shirika za Akiba) can be of very great service, both to the individual and to his local community. Many of these societies already exist in Tanzania, but new ones should be started for they can help us very much in our individual and national drive towards self-reliance. I hope that all TANU leaders will learn about them and see how and when people in their area can be helped to establish them.[2]

Based on his research in Tanzania from 1968 to 1971, H. H. Binhammer wrote:

> The savings and credit movement appears to offer the best alternative to encourage and mobilize rural savings. Other schemes and institutions which have been introduced in the past for this purpose have been only marginally successful or have ended in failure.[3]

In 1965 Arne Holmberg of Kooperativ Forbundet, Stockholm, the first director of the Co-operative Education Centre (CEC), and Jack collaborated on a four-part credit union series which was translated into Swahili in 1966 and used as the CEC's first combined radio/correspondence course beamed to rural Tanzania. However, pressures were building to keep the single-purpose savings and credit societies out of the rural areas in favor of multipurpose marketing co-operatives that would include a savings and credit function among their services. There were attempts to put the savings and credit societies under the control of the marketing co-operatives even as the agricultural co-ops were fighting a losing battle for survival. The Presidential Special Committee of Enquiry in 1966 had called attention to their already overburdened functions which accounted in part for their poor performance. Embittered farmers had turned against them, claiming that they took too large a share of the proceeds of the crop sales. Charges of personal dishonesty, corruption, and incompetence of co-operative leaders and staff at all levels raised questions, to say the least, about the wisdom of adding savings and credit to their functions.

And yet the principal of the Co-operative College, Fred Howarth, saw no reason for rural credit unions—or for their league. Referring to the committee's report, he made these observations:

> The present national structure of the credit unions needs to be altered so that they are fully integrated into the co-operative movement. They have, unfortunately, been allowed to form their own National League (a League is merely the American name for a union) which has, inevitably, led to petty jealousies and other unnecessary antagonisms between the League and the Co-operative Union of Tanganyika about who is responsible for what. There is no justification for a separate League for credit unions. The credit unions should join the Co-operative Union in exactly the same way as do marketing unions and unaffiliated societies. There should also be a closer liaison at village level so that the credit union activities are governed, wherever possible, by the same committee as is governing the activities of the primary marketing society. There is no economic or social justification for separately constituted credit unions in the rural area.
>
> Credit unions can and should be developed in the urban areas amongst wage and salary earners, and on the estates. As the report says in paragraph 272: "the basic structure of the Agricultural Credit System is sound." This being so, the intrusion of credit unions into the system in rural areas should be prevented.[4]

Although Tanzania's savings and credit cadre succeeded in spearheading the credit union idea into remote areas well into the late 1960s, by 1970 government staff were doing relatively little credit union supervision and were being routinely transferred into other co-operative work.

Ujamaa Village enthusiasts joined forces with non-African experts and International Co-operative Alliance (ICA) representatives to accelerate the move toward the introduction of savings and credit functions into marketing co-operatives and to advocate the abolition of rural savings and credit societies. With the departure of the CUNA/AID technicians in 1970, Tanzania's co-operative staff firmed up their plans to confine credit unions to urban salaried workers. This started with a series of education and training programs co-sponsored with the ICA Regional Office for East and Central Africa that concentrated on teaching about the production credit schemes of Kenya's and Uganda's marketing co-operatives, without any mention of Tanzania's successful rural savings and credit societies. In 1974 the government adopted an official policy restricting savings and credit societies to wage earner groups, primarily in the urban areas,[5] and decided to introduce a rural savings and credit scheme within the marketing unions.

Why the change?

The reasons were both practical and philosophical. They had little or nothing to do, however, with the thinking of the people who would have been expected to have a voice in the decision. To say the least, the government's new policy decision disregarded the wishes of the Tanzanian savings and credit movement.

As a practical matter, the preponderance of wage earner credit unions in North America undoubtedly influenced the Tanzanian government officers who were trained there and consequently were not equipped to work with rural societies. Likewise, all of the technicians of the CUNA/AID programs had worked mostly with employee credit unions in the United States. There was much less demand on government or league personnel to service urban worker societies that were literally organizing themselves. Added to this was the belief that the steady earnings of their members, mobilized through payroll deductions, would become a reliable source of funds.

Another more subtle factor in the shifting emphasis was the government's desire to minimize any divisive forces that could affect the country's development. The majority of rural savings and credit societies had been organized around parish groups, and some of these had developed into successful community institutions. Ideologically, however, sponsorship by missionaries from foreign countries was a disadvantage in that the missionaries, especially in some political circles, were regarded as colonialists. As in the case of mission schools and hospitals, which were put under government direction and control, parish-based community savings and credit societies may have been seen as obstacles to the separation of church and state.

Finally, there were other factors over which the societies had no control. In 1972 a major government reorganization was effected, decentralizing all governmental agencies into administrative regions. This action was aimed at bringing the government closer to the people, but it failed to solve the pervasive problems of inadequate transport, communications, and supplies in the rural areas. Moreover, many key employees declined transfers to new regional headquarters, leaving the work to officers who were untrained in co-operatives. Furthermore, their time was taken up assisting the new villages to develop into multipurpose co-operatives replacing the primary marketing societies. To the ideologists who were concerned with rapid economic gains in the agricultural sector, single-purpose "CUNA-type" consumer-oriented co-operatives were politically unacceptable. They seemed too small, too slow, and too disorganized to answer to the nation's need for centralized, systematic financing of productive development.

In 1975, to implement its decision to add savings functions to the marketing unions, the government selected twenty-two marketing co-operatives (several of them coexisting with savings and credit societies serving the same farmers) in four regions as participants in the Pilot Rural Savings Scheme (PRSS). The PRSS used savings and credit society bookkeeping stationery donated by SCULT. But time was running out on the marketing co-ops. On May 15, 1976, the prime minister announced in a radio address that at an "extraordinary meeting" of TANU's executive committee in Dar es Salaam, a decision had been reached that the co-operative marketing unions had not eliminated middlemen as they were originally expected to do and had no functions to perform as secondary societies since the primary marketing societies which were their members had legally ceased to exist with the passage of the Village Act the year before (see page 31). Therefore, the unions were ordered to be liquidated, and all of their functions were transferred to government or parastatal marketing and trading organizations.

Village Rural Savings and Credit Scheme

Some basic credit union/savings and credit features are now being carried over into the co-operative activities of the new villages in an experimental Village Rural Savings and Credit Scheme (VRSCS). The few villages which have tried the VRSCS include those whose marketing unions were closed shortly after starting the pilot project of "Kenya-type" rural savings schemes. Up to the end of 1980 none of the participating villages had issued any credit, but all had reported some savings. In effect, the VRSCS is only an extension of the NBC where the farmers' savings are deposited.

Meanwhile, savings and credit societies have continued their operations in some rural areas where the autonomous regional authorities have found that they are not infringing on village programs, and also where they can be justified as serving multiple villages in a more satisfactory manner than would be possible if they were liquidated and their services replaced by the VRSCS in individual villages.

Whether the VRSCS can distill the best features of savings and credit societies and combine them with the supposed advantages of multipurpose co-operatives, and whether voluntary participation in the VRSCS can coexist with the compulsory savings of crop proceeds in the villages are questions not answerable from the evidence available through 1980. Most of the people responsible for making the hard decisions in the villages and the regions seem to be taking great care not to abandon the rural savings and credit society alternative, and the authorities do not seem inclined to force the issue.

8. *Development of Credit Unions in Kenya*

In Kenya the credit union movement started later than in Tanzania and became wage earner oriented at a much earlier period in its development. As CUNA's consultant to the Kenyan government, Jack's efforts were aimed primarily at helping local supporters get official recognition of credit unions and a government policy favoring their promotion. During this period (1963–64) the first co-operative savings and credit societies were registered, and standard bylaws and a bookkeeping system were designed. Training of government officers and volunteers was initiated to spearhead the later promotional drives. The early development work in the field was accomplished primarily by Kenyan laypeople and native Catholic priests. Missionaries who were financed and encouraged by foreign religious organizations later helped to spread the credit union idea.

One of Jack's first official duties in January, 1963, was to join Paddy Bailey in a Nairobi meeting with Mboya, a Kenyan trade union leader, to discuss the credit union potential for helping establish workers' credit co-operatives that would lead later to the establishment of a workers' bank. Mboya's interest was helpful, and it opened doors to government officers who took over the co-operative development program from the Ministry of Agriculture after Kenya became independent. Among those who were influential in launching the credit union program were Julius G. Kiano, the minister for commerce and industry, Kibue, Nyanjom, Alick P. H. D'Souza, senior co-operative officer in charge of credit and finance, and also Richard David Wissolik and the Reverend Father Joseph Van den Dries, director of Catholic Relief Services (CRS).

In its first year the independent Kenyan government committed itself to the expansion of co-operatives in industry and agriculture for distribution, marketing, and consumer purposes, and carried out a detailed feasibility study to plan future large-scale co-operative development. At the same time, it also made plans to encourage the formation of credit unions.

The first few savings and credit societies were parish and community-based societies. This type of society had as its forerunners various tribal associations and thrift and savings societies which existed in the colonial period and just after World War II. Most of these were located in Nairobi. Among the first savings and credit societies to be organized in 1964 were the Mwea Tabere Thrift Society for the members of a rice-growing scheme in Kerugoya and the Vya Savings and Credit Society for a community in Machakos. Interest in credit unions was stimulated during a government training seminar in Nairobi during October, 1963, which was also attended by ten participants from Tanganyika.

Minister Kiano took the occasion of the opening of the first parish co-operative credit society at Mariira, Fort Hall, on August 29, 1964, to link the development of such societies with the goal of increasing African participation in the commercial and industrial sector of Kenya's economy. Credit societies, he said, were very helpful in enabling people to save money and meet the country's need to accumulate as much local savings as possible to add to investment funds. Thus Africans could increase their share in the growing national income of the country.

Earlier, in June, 1964, Jan Mohamed, the parliamentary secretary to the Ministry of Commerce and Industry, had announced that credit unions would be introduced in Kenya with the return of two co-operative officers, Benson Mwea and D'Souza, studying in the United States. These statements received feature coverage in the Kenyan press.

Nineteen sixty-five was a banner year for the new program. The Fourth African Conference on the Mobilization of Local Savings was held at the Kenya Institute of Administration in Kabete, near Nairobi. Nyanjom, now the commissioner for co-operative development, in consultation with CRS and the Kenya National Federation of Co-operatives (KNFC), set up the Kenya National Promotion Committee (KNPC) to formulate policies on credit unions in Kenya and to regulate their promotion. As chairman of the committee, Nyanjom named John J. Musundi, the general secretary of KNFC, as secretary and D'Souza and the Reverend Father Van den Dries as members.

Antoinette-Rose Potvin was assigned with CRS funding to become the committee's first field officer. She started her credit union work in 1965 in Mombasa and other areas of the Coast Province, where she helped organize some of the country's most active societies. In 1967 Boniface Machyo, president of the Social Guild of Kenya and a former CDD officer, was hired as a KNPC field officer, and by 1971 KNPC field officers were working in the Western Province, the Coast Province, and Nairobi Province. All were employed through financial assistance from CRS and the Ontario Credit Union League of Canada.

Staff of the CUNA/AID regional program (1966–70) coordinated their efforts in providing consultations and training services to the Kenyan government with the work of CRS, KNPC, and representatives of KNFC. Samuel X. Mitchell, a UNDP technician, also helped, especially as a trainer of bookkeepers and as a troubleshooter.

Kenya Union of Savings and Credit Co-operatives

Together, KNPC and KNFC played the role of a national association until the Kenya Union of Savings and Credit Co-operatives (KUSCCO) was organized in 1973. At a national conference in June, 1972, delegates representing over one hundred active co-operative savings and credit societies discussed two proposals: whether societies should affiliate with KNFC or whether they should form another new apex organization. The delegates gave recognition to the extremely valuable services rendered by KNFC, which had helped to organize and then administer the grants from CRS to finance KNPC, but they were concerned that KNFC would not be the ideal apex organization for savings and credit societies. One disadvantage cited in the discussion was that KNFC catered mainly for marketing societies and acted more like a political wing in which national associations of co-operatives joined together to defend the movement and safeguard co-operative principles. In making the decision to form KUSCCO, the conferees opted for more of a service-type, credit union-oriented organization specializing in education, promotion, technical assistance, centralized accounting, a central fund, stabilization, and insurance, an organization similar to the North American credit union leagues which some of the Kenyans had visited.

Observing that most of the income-producing services had been preempted by KNFC, the Co-operative Bank, and the Kenya National Assurance Company, the meeting decided upon a dues schedule based on a percentage of member societies' gross earnings. There was also the hope that the existence of a legally constituted national union (or league) would attract support from international co-operative organizations through ACOSCA. At the same time, however, societies were warned "that they should only rely upon grants for a short period and make financial provisions from their own resources to diminish the grants in a systematic and controllable manner through their own sacrifices to pay higher dues."[1]

Chapter Unions or a National Association?

Aside from the question of whether to form a new national apex organization or to affiliate with KNFC, another problem was pigeonholed and not solved in the decision to form KUSCCO: how to give resources and recognition to the local leaders who had started to band together in chapter unions, which were the equivalent of the marketing unions for the primary marketing societies in the rural areas. (The "chapter" designation is a credit union term; the "union" designation is commonly used in Kenya to describe any secondary-level organization of co-ops.)

One of the instinctive steps taken by the more successful societies in the two major employment centers, Nairobi and Mombasa, where the societies were most numerous and the meeting conditions most favorable, was to begin an interchange of experience and ideas in chapter unions. The logic and example of Kenya's co-operative organizational structure would have placed the chapter unions as intermediaries between the primary societies and their apex national organization, be it KNFC or KUSCCO. In that position the unions would have money, staff, and offices commensurate with the resources of their member societies plus some hoped-for foreign aid. And (it could be reasoned) well staffed or not, they would still be more accessible to the societies than any national association that the societies could support in the beginning stages of development.

The chapter union concept worked better in Mombasa than it did in Nairobi, where the affiliated societies failed to appreciate the usefulness of their organization. It was especially difficult to raise dues from the powerful and growing nationwide societies. Although the nationwide society leaders included both advocates and opponents of the proposed national union, most were not inclined to affiliate with an association that might be dominated by the more numerous small societies with which they had little in common. (In 1973 there were already 125 societies, only 6 of them with 1,000 or more members.) Nonaffiliation of nationwide societies is a problem for KUSCCO that continues to this day.

In December, 1972, at a meeting of the KNPC, a working committee of twelve was appointed by the chairman, Commissioner J. K. Muthama, to study the feasibility of forming a national credit union body. Government officers participated with representatives from five large societies in different regions and a delegate representing the nationwide societies. Two members of the working committee, the chairman, G. O. Opondo, and J. W. Njoroge, together with Muthama, had recently visited the credit unions of the United States and Canada.

After submitting its report to the commissioner on May 25, 1973, the working committee presented its recommendations to a series of regional delegates' meetings during May and June, preparatory to holding the national conference that led to the signing of KUSCCO's charter on September 27, 1973. Registration soon followed and the new national union began business immediately. C. J. Thiong'o, senior co-operative officer and member of the working committee, was seconded by the CDD to be KUSCCO's secretary/manager until the employment of a permanent official. His replacement, John N. Otido, took office less than a year later in July, 1974. The work of enrolling affiliates continued to be done by KNPC field officers who were paid by external aid.

At the first general meeting of KUSCCO in March, 1975, a management committee was elected with Njoroge as chairman, and among other actions, steps were taken to affiliate with ACOSCA and KNFC. While part of the wide-ranging program of promotion, education, and field service was initiated with the financial assistance of the Ontario Credit Union League, the Konrad Adenauer Foundation (KAF), and the African-American Labor Center, a USAID-funded agency with offices in Nairobi, KUSCCO was also committed to a program of eventual self-support. Funding was to come from the collection of annual dues, revenue from income-producing activities, membership fees, and share subscriptions.

9. *African Conferences on the Mobilization of Local Savings— The Formation of the Africa Co-operative Savings and Credit Association*

African Conferences

The credit union movements in Tanzania and Kenya were continuously stimulated by continental credit union activities, notably the annual African Conferences on the Mobilization of Local Savings, referred to only briefly heretofore. These conferences were inaugurated as an outgrowth of changing U.S. policy and CUNA/WED's efforts at broadening its scope of activities. With several successful CUNA/AID programs operative in Latin America and in support of the aims of the United States as stated in the 1962 Humphrey Amendment to the 1961 Act for International Development that "it is declared to be the policy of the U.S. . . . to encourage the development and use of cooperatives, credit unions and savings and loan associations," CUNA/WED sponsored an Africa study trip in 1962 to ascertain the climate for a credit union development program in Africa. Five reasons were given in support of an African program:

1. There is a need for the mobilization of small sums on a broad base, as through credit unions, where self help will cover administrative costs.
2. Local savings are necessary for growth and economic expansion.
3. With independence a vacuum is being created by the withdrawal of skill and capital which must be filled as soon as possible.
4. Credit unions can promote better understanding of local prob-

lems by local people and greater willingness to participate fully and freely in the country's development. If this participation is not arrived at in free and voluntary association, through co-operative effort on the part of the peoples of these countries, the danger of totalitarianism in one or another of its forms is ever present.

5. The philosophy of the credit union movement, which is based on the broader concept of the brotherhood of man, will contribute to better understanding between tribes, races, and countries in Africa.[1]

Knowing of the great need for unsecured credit among the people of the newly independent African states but sensing both the African governments' distrust of the word "credit" and their deep respect for the idea of "saving," CUNA/WED embarked on a series of ten International African Conferences on the Mobilization of Local Savings in the years from 1963 to 1972. Eight African governments acted as cosponsors and helped to spread the good word about credit unions over the entire African continent. In January, 1963, the first meeting was held in Dar es Salaam for East Africans; in February, 1963, West Africans met in Lagos for the second conference.

The conclusions drawn by the participants from their discussions in the first Dar es Salaam conference emphasized the expectations of the early credit union leaders in East and West Africa:

1. Credit for both the production and consumer sectors of the economy can be made available by credit unions.
2. Credit unions can be accepted and put to use wherever people live and work, in both urban and rural areas, but there are realities to be faced in East Africa such as
   a. widespread suspicion, which brings about a lack of mutual confidence,
   b. the difficulty of obtaining leaders, especially in the rural areas where a large proportion of the people are untrained,
   c. the difficulty of communication, and
   d. the insufficiency of income.
3. One reason for the lack of local savings is the absence of local facilities in which the farmer has sufficient trust as to the security of his funds and the secrecy of his transactions.
4. To attain economic independence, which is a necessary concomitant of political independence and national sovereignty, there must be an increase of internal capital mobilization over

wide areas in order to provide the capital assets necessary to increase production and reduce the dependence on capital from external sources.

Participants in the Lagos conference broadened the incentives for credit union development to include the following:

5. The introduction of credit unions is desirable to mobilize local savings in rural areas for meeting the local credit needs of petty traders and artisans as well as food crop producers.
6. The present economic trend in West Africa, in which the pattern of living now involves an increase in town dwellers who have a greater need for money and a greater demand for credit to meet their needs, requires that credit unions should be stimulated in the towns.
7. Since the conservative policies of the thrift and loan societies, which allowed their members to borrow only a proportion of their savings, were not successful and because credit unions are more liberal in their loan policies, attempts should be continued to convert these societies into credit unions.
8. As credit unions are an attractive feature of the co-operative development program, attempts should be made to separate credit from marketing and to encourage the farmers to form credit unions to achieve a well-controlled and specialized credit system. It is felt that to encourage credit unions consisting of members of different occupations, whose credit requirements do not arise at the same time, would also be an additional advantage.
9. Credit unions should seek to obtain the security, bonding, and savings and loan protection insurance services which have contributed to the success of the credit union movement in the United States, Canada, and other countries.

Starting with the third annual conference, all the meetings were conducted on a continental basis. The governments of Lesotho in the south, Tunisia in the north, Tanzania, Cameroon, Ethiopia, Ghana, Kenya, and Uganda joined with CUNA/WED in sponsoring these conferences to promote the credit union idea and to encourage a Pan-African credit union movement. The third, fourth, and fifth conferences were held in East Africa where credit union development was being spearheaded first by the Tanganyika Project and then by the CUNA/AID East Africa Regional Program: in Kampala, Uganda, in 1964; in Nairobi in 1965; and at the University of East Africa in Dar es Salaam in January, 1967. Funding and/or facilities were provided out of the project by CUNA/WED and by the host country government. Travel money for delegates came from donations of other agencies such as Misereor and CRS.

Credit union delegates and government representatives came to these meetings from all over Africa, as did representatives of the international organizations in the financial, religious, and developmental fields. Enthusiasm mounted as reports of successful experiences, growing out of their day-to-day credit union activities, were cited by the often evangelical African credit unionists and by the officials presenting the reports of their governments. Every meeting was given excellent mass media coverage—newspaper articles and radio and television interviews (where TV was available)—and the governments, viewing these meetings as prestigious occasions, always provided a social as well as an official welcome.

Although the number of countries involved was but a fraction of the African nations, the new movements cut across geographic, anglophone, and francophone lines. By 1968, when the sixth conference was held in Lesotho, twelve African countries had burgeoning savings and credit society programs and were trying to follow the CUNA pattern for the organization of national leagues similar to the state and provincial leagues of the United States and Canada. Encouraged by their growing circle of donor agencies, these national leagues wanted to organize a Pan-African association. The conference adopted the Tanzania delegation's resolution to that effect.

Few of the conferees knew that the historic Lesotho conference they were attending had come close to being canceled when South African immigration officials tried to block a meeting I had arranged in February, 1967, with Father Joseph Brossard, a Canadian priest working with the Lesotho credit union pioneers.

From Dar es Salaam, I had applied through the United States embassy for a South African visa that would permit me to drive with Father Brossard from the Johannesburg Airport through the RSA to Lesotho's capital, Maseru, where we would meet with officials of the Lesotho government. Since tiny Lesotho is completely surrounded by the RSA, this permission was essential and getting it seemed routine. However, a surprise was in store for me. Americans were not welcome in the RSA at that time. As I learned later at the Johannesburg Airport, a diplomatic squabble had erupted between the United States and the RSA. It had been customary for the U.S. fleet to put in at RSA ports on their voyages around the Cape of Good Hope, and U.S. sailors were expected to comply with RSA segregation policies while on shore leave. But there had been violent demonstrations in the United States protesting these and other segregation policies. To signify official U.S. displeasure with South Africa's racist practices, the U.S. fleet was ordered to omit these visits. The RSA retaliated in various ways.

In my case, immigration officials sent word that my application had been approved, but omitted noting that the approval was explicitly limited: I must transit from Johannesburg Airport via charter flight to the Lesotho airport in Maseru.

Flights to Maseru from Johannesburg were extremely limited and at that time of year were somewhat dangerous. All of this I learned after making the long flight from Nairobi to Johannesburg where I was handed the visa in a sealed envelope. After dinner and an overnight rest in Johannesburg's simple but comfortable airport hotel, to which I was politely confined, I was permitted to arrange for the chartered flight. After circling the area for almost an hour, the pilot pointed to the threatening thunderheads around us and brought the ship down, explaining that without radar or good radio reports the flight was impossible, and he could not predict when the weather would lift. I went back to my room dejected and unable to think of any alternatives.

My depressed mood was lifted shortly thereafter, however, when I was told to report to an airport police office where I was handed a telephone receiver. The caller identified himself as a police lieutenant stationed at the Lesotho border and then went on to relay a message from Father Brossard. A bit tired from the events of the day, I could hardly make out what he was saying, but I thought it was something about Brossard's plans to come get me. But how? No explanation, just a clipped "goodbye," and my mumbled "thanks," and back I went to my room. About midnight, just after I had gone to bed, came a knock on the door. Silhouetted against the frosted glass panel was the towering, gaunt frame of Father Joseph, and when I opened the door there he stood, ashen-faced from exhaustion after driving the three hundred miles nonstop from Maseru. He had come with a letter from the prime minister of Lesotho to the prime minister of the RSA, requesting that my original visa application be approved.

Father Joseph was ready to get on with our return trip then and there, but (fortunately, I felt) the letter could only be delivered to headquarters officials in the morning. After picking up the approval, we also picked up a speeding ticket on our way out of town, and we left Johannesburg for what may have been one of the fastest overland drives ever made to Maseru, driving more often than not on the wrong side of the road to avoid corduroy rutting but miraculously never meeting any oncoming cars in the blind spots of hilltops or curves. (I remember saying my silent prayers and being so grateful to be riding with someone with direct access to the "man upstairs.")

Discussing the projected 1968 conference while enroute to Maseru, we didn't take long to agree on one thing: there couldn't be any risk that any African delegate might be subjected to the treatment I had just experienced. The publicity given to the RSA's treatment of blacks was enough to discourage many Africans from risking indignities—or even physical harm. The host Lesotho government took care of this, just as Father Brossard had assured me they would, and when the conferees came through Johannesburg Airport to the conference in 1968 the South African government literally rolled out the red carpet for them in a display of impeccable courtesy.

The seventh Mobilization of Local Savings conference was held in Accra, Ghana, in 1969; the eighth in Buea, Cameroon, in 1970; the ninth in Addis Ababa, Ethiopia, in 1971; and the tenth and final conference in Tunis, Tunisia, in 1972.

In 1970 CUNA International was reorganized, and support for these African meetings became the responsibility of the newly organized WOCCU, which took over the responsibilities of CUNA International's WED. (Today WOCCU, a member of the ICA, is the apex organization of what is known as the International Credit Union Network, with headquarters in Madison, Wisconsin.)

ACOSCA

To implement the resolution adopted at the Lesotho conference, a steering committee composed of one representative each from CUNA International, SCULT, and CRS was named to work out the details of setting up a Pan-African organization with the support of the KNPC and the Kenya commissioner of co-operatives.

Representatives of thirteen African countries where national associations had been formed or where a national promotion committee existed were invited to a meeting in Nairobi, September 13–16, 1968, where they organized ACOSCA

- to assist these societies with technical assistance,
- to help them gain legal recognition,
- to help them establish national associations,
- to coordinate the activities of these societies, and
- to promote collaboration between them and other sectors of the co-operative movement.

ACOSCA was incorporated under the Societies Act of Kenya as an international, voluntary, nongovernmental, nonprofit organization working for social economic development. Both its first chairman, Mutayoba, and his successor, B. A. Ifunya, came from SCULT. In 1974 the government of Kenya signed an agreement with ACOSCA granting it certain immunities and privileges to enable it to carry out its activities on an international basis from its national headquarters in Nairobi. In 1975 ACOSCA purchased its present headquarters building there, known as ACOSCA House.

As a confederation of twenty-three national associations or national promotion committees, ACOSCA has been operating under a series of plans. The first five-year plan (1968–72) was somewhat expedient in its nature, responding to two main factors: the need for operational programs at the grass roots level and the need to raise funds to carry out the programs. Under an interim plan (1973–75) before a second five-year plan, ACOSCA entered a period of reformulation and consolidation in which Executive Secretary Bart E. Quainoo from Ghana gradually assumed the managerial responsibilities of ACOSCA from Mark Dan Moriarty, the CUNA/AID technician who had served as adviser to the previous acting general manager, John Mascarenhas of the Seychelles. A. P. Amedegnato of Togo, the first delegate from a francophone affiliate, became vice chairman, Mrs. E. Tweh of Liberia became the first female director, and ACOSCA's board chairman, B. N. Mukong of Cameroon, was elected a director of WOCCU.

The second five-year development plan (1976–80) emphasized setting prime strategies for self-sufficiency at national and ACOSCA levels through the increase and improvement of services and for the expansion of ACOSCA's membership to serve newly liberated areas of Africa and North African coast countries. This plan related not only to operational programs and the need to find funds to carry them out but also to organizational structures to foster self-reliance, growth, promotion, and rural development.[2]

ACOSCA has its head office and its Eastern Regional Office in Nairobi. Other regional offices are in Lomé, Togo, and in Maseru. Regional development has been emphasized to mitigate the extensive problems of poor communications. To decentralize activities, regional training centers have been established at Nairobi (using the facilities of the Co-operative College of Kenya); Maseru; Bamenda, Cameroon; Bukavu, Zaire; and Bobo-Dioulasso, Upper Volta.

ACOSCA has also supplemented its education and training programs with the following services:

- Risk Management Program, administered under an agreement with CUNA Mutual Insurance Society;
- Central Financing and Interlending Program, operating at ACOSCA headquarters with the assistance of the Dutch RABOBANK and the KAF of West Germany (still in the initial stages of development);
- Small Farmer Production Credit Program, a joint ACOSCA/CUNA/AID program, operating in Cameroon and Lesotho; and the
- Interpretation and Translation Service (French-English), financially assisted by CCCS/CIDA.

ACOSCA leaders have also considered ways to assist with the development of co-operative housing and to co-operate more fully with the trade union movement.

ACOSCA's need for financial and technical assistance from donor agencies continues to rise as its services to its members and potential members (particularly in promotion and training) increase. In 1975 only 2.9 percent of the total promotion, education, and training budget came from membership dues. Some funding, mainly in the provision of housing, secondment of government fieldmen, and meeting places, came from African sources: governments, intergovernmental agencies, banks, and religious bodies. Subsequent support to ACOSCA from non-African sources was mainly on a project basis. ACOSCA's 1978 income of about $450,000 consisted of revenues from dues, insurance commissions, and the sale of printed materials plus major external assistance from the KAF, CUNA Mutual Insurance Company, CUNA/AID, and CCCS/CIDA (formerly National Association of Canadian Credit Unions [NACCU]/CIDA). Other sources of assistance outside of Africa included WOCCU, co-operative savings and credit organizations in Europe and North America, and church-related, trade union, and intergovernmental bodies.

Since non-African funding continued to be essential to the program requirements of ACOSCA and its affiliates, ACOSCA leaders believed that donor resources should be selectively applied to African needs as seen by ACOSCA's board, management, and affiliates. Projects based on donor perceptions of African needs and requiring donor-approved personnel have been a source of friction. (CUNA/AID has been most difficult to deal with.) ACOSCA management has been handicapped by insufficient funding for its initiation and submission of project proposals, as well as for its management of funded projects. According to ACOSCA leaders and personnel, preparing budgets and establishing long-term plans with ACOSCA's numerous collaborators, each contributing for specific purposes and for limited periods of time, devoured the time and energy of the executive officers and staff, and did not allow them the freedom and flexibility to design and modify their programs in response to needs perceived by themselves and their constituents.

There was deep concern in both Tanzania and Kenya that Africanization of the credit union idea include the provision of African technical assistance and leadership. Leaders at all levels believed that Africans must be able to see the association as their own before they would believe in it enough to support it at whatever level of service they could afford. They felt that for ACOSCA to be effective, it should be able to determine its own needs and fund only those programs it wanted to, with personnel of its own choosing. They saw ACOSCA as having moved beyond a "beggars can't be choosers" role into the status of a recognized Pan-African institution. The prestige of belonging to a worldwide credit union movement has been a convincing reason for league affiliation among the credit union leaders we interviewed, especially those whose societies were current in their league dues. But apparently he who pays the fiddler calls the tune: by 1980 a new ACOSCA executive team was being recruited under an expanded aid program with more non-African personnel.

Part III

Research Study in Tanzania

10. The Social Milieu

From the very moment we arrived at the Kilimanjaro International Airport in December, 1977, to undertake our intensive study of Tanzania's credit unions, we were aware of our need to balance old rosy-tinted memories with the realities of new sights, sounds, and feelings.

Our first several weeks were spent in Dar es Salaam arranging, with the help of SCULT's John Lubuva, to get government clearance for our safari. Dar (as the city is commonly called) is the former capital (still the working capital) and largest city of the country, a dynamic center with an international airport, the headquarters of the TAZARA railway with rail connections to all other parts of Tanzania, and a major seaport on the Indian Ocean.

We noted in Dar (as in the other large towns we visited) that hotels which used to cater exclusively to tourists and non-Africans working in the country were frequented primarily by Africans, and that, in spite of the closure of the border with Kenya and with the exception of the game park lodges, space was scarce. The hotel sleeping space seemed to be filled with personnel of Tanzania government and parastatal organizations or foreign experts and their families waiting for permanent housing. The hotel dining rooms on the weekend and the bars during the week were used almost exclusively by local Tanzanians.

We found the crush for hotel space wherever we traveled. In areas where there was little tourism hotels had not been maintained, but the few rooms available were in great demand. Several times we had to share a single-occupancy room or find space in a hostel. We were unable to visit the savings and credit societies in Njombe, a town in the southern part of the country, because we could find no sleeping accommodations there, and the co-operative officers were uncomfortable with the idea of our sleeping in the Land-Rover.

In Musoma on Lake Victoria, the co-operative officer arranged for us to use the house reserved for the district magistrate as he was not due for court sessions in the week we were there. A new hotel was being built overlooking the lake, and the old Railway Hotel dining room near our lodging had become more a bar than a place to eat. With the continued urbanization of the Tanzanian population, the peasants' social activity of gathering together to drink the local brew (the type depending on the ingredients available locally) has been transferred to town bars, where they drink factory-brewed beer (which is much more expensive than the local brew, as it carries a heavy government tax, but is also much less apt to produce gastric problems).

While food in Dar seemed plentiful, there was a scarcity of fresh vegetables because some of the farm areas which supply the city, such as Lushoto and Morogoro, were quarantined due to a widespread outbreak of cholera. In other regions there were chronic scarcities of cooking oil, kerosene, and flour, as well as meat and fish, attributable mainly to problems of transport. One morning in Bukoba on the western shore of Lake Victoria, our crowded hotel could provide us only tea and sweet crackers for breakfast. But we never went hungry, even on the roads between towns, because we could buy bananas, oranges, mangoes, pineapples, carrots, cucumbers, and tomatoes at local markets, and at local *dukas* (shops) we could get peanut-crunch candy, cashew nuts, and spiced Indian snacks.

Transportation would have been our most difficult problem had it not been for the generous offer of the SCULT executive committee and manager to allow us the use of one of their KAF-supplied Land-Rovers. Most of the visits to societies, to village rural savings and credit schemes, and to training centers would not have been possible without its use. Public transportation (train, bus, plane) would have taken us to main population centers, but there would have been no local transportation to the outlying societies.

The number of government vehicles was severely limited, and use of them was dependent upon the local regional development officer's permission for the co-operative officers accompanying us to use the vehicles—if they were available and not already spoken for by other officers and agencies. In many regions, a good portion of the government fleet was in the shop awaiting repair, which in turn depended on the arrival of parts from abroad. Petrol was expensive and in extremely short supply. The few taxis that were available operated only in main population centers. Buses were so crowded that there was no way of guaranteeing a seat; everyone lined up with his bicycle, baggage, banana stalk, vegetables, and chickens, which were then stuffed into baskets crowding the aisles or stacked on top of the bus.

As petrol stations were scarce in the outlying areas, we carried several extra jerry cans of gas. We had to plan our itinerary carefully, because no petrol was sold from Friday night to Monday morning, and no driving was permitted, other than for emergencies, on Sunday. Our safari was made in the rainy season, which always cripples travel on Tanzania's dirt roads, so we were prepared for the rough 5,600 kilometer trip. But most of the up-country roads seemed in worse condition than we had remembered. The exceptions were in the southwest and northern areas where international commerce or tourism have necessitated improvements. Only the first 196 kilometers of the major route out of Dar es Salaam—a narrow two-lane stretch—has been paved. For the rest of the distance, the road seemed more of a bush trail than a highway, but we made the 479 kilometers to Dodoma in slightly more than six hours. Most of the vehicles using the roads were buses or trucks; Land-Rovers were almost the only private automobiles seen.

While much of our time each day was used in getting to the societies to conduct our interviews in the typically unhurried Tanzanian manner, our evenings were free, allowing us to go over our notes and prepare for the following day's visits. Finding little entertainment, we took advantage of a new development in the country: the existence in each regional headquarters town of a library. We were allowed to check out books upon payment of a deposit (refunded upon their return) equivalent to the cost of the books. Most of the English-language publications came from Great Britain. The range of subject matter was vast. There were books on credit unions, economic development, business administration, co-operatives, the various sciences, as well as history, philosophy, politics, biographies, fiction—all arranged according to the Dewey Decimal System.[1]

In every library there were people of all ages reading; some libraries even had special evening hours. This interest in the printed word was in marked contrast to what we had witnessed in the early 1960s when the main or only library in town was that of the British Council. Then, the largest bookstore in Moshi catered almost exclusively to non-Africans and had very few books in Swahili. The Africans were constantly being told by the English management to "stop handling the books since you are not going to buy." Throughout Tanzanian towns we saw street vendors and stands selling newspapers and magazines in both Swahili and English, especially to people rushing to work in the morning.

We saw young children in schools wherever we went, usually dressed in blue and white uniforms. As we drove along the highways where the new villages were located, we watched groups of children working in the fields, learning and participating in farming activities, playing in school courtyards, and studying in classrooms. As in the earlier years, we found that one of the first joint efforts of the villagers was to build a schoolhouse. When we visited Mwasi Juu village on Mount Kilimanjaro, one of the special items on the agenda was showing us the newly built school, constructed entirely by the village people. These schools accommodated students through standard seven (elementary school) and were very crowded. The children came in shifts so that teachers worked from 7:00 A.M. to 6:00 P.M. Parents and students alike increasingly pressured for higher schooling. While elementary education had become universal, the number of places in government secondary schools was severely limited and granted only on the basis of competitive examinations. Private secondary schools were proliferating rapidly.

The government had committed itself to a program of adult education aimed primarily at reaching the nation's rural population. A variety of institutions, including the Institute of Adult Education, agricultural and technical schools, and folk colleges, were involved. The use of radio as a tool for mass education was given special emphasis. "Plant or Die" was the motto of an intensive radio and newspaper campaign to encourage people to raise food on any available piece of land. And we saw the results. Our first home in 1963 had been an apartment overlooking the Mwanza Club golf course. The Mwanza clubhouse was still in existence, but the golf course was no more—it had become a luxuriant corn field. In Mbeya elected government leaders were observed working their own *shambas* (farms) as an example to their constituents of the importance of raising food. And in Musoma, vegetable gardens rather than flowers surrounded the prison buildings and decorated the grounds.

The nation's adult education programs, the extensive radio campaigns, and the government's literacy efforts seemed to have brought results in the political awareness of the people with whom we talked, in the numbers of people able to read, and in the great dependence upon the radio in outlying areas. However, since the intensive education efforts had been devoted to increasing Swahili literacy, only a limited number of sales clerks, bank tellers, bus drivers, or lower-grade civil servants seemed comfortable speaking English. This contrasted our experience in the 1960s when we could not practice our meager Swahili because all the Tanzanians wanted to practice their beautiful Oxfordian English. In our interviews, the co-operative officers served as translators because our Swahili was limited to the usual polite greetings and to discussions of the savings and credit society forms. In many respects this was not a handicap because it allowed the society members to ask the officer questions about us and our work which he could answer with no embarrassment to either the members or ourselves.

There was no television in mainland Tanzania though there were some privately owned sets which could bring in Kenyan stations. (Color television in Zanzibar was being developed as an educational tool.) The decision to limit mass communication to radio and newspapers was made by the Tanzanian government as it set national priorities to fit national resources.

Increased and upgraded accommodations were by no means limited to tourists; on the contrary, the greatest changes we saw were in the housing of Tanzanians. A major goal of the socialist state has been to improve the quality of life for the people, especially in their housing. The buildings going up in the residential areas around Dar es Salaam were mainly cement construction with *babati* (iron sheeting) roofs. Every savings and credit society reported a substantial number of loans being made to members for upgrading and enlarging houses. Several societies, as part of their new multipurpose activities, were financing brick making and were selling cement and *babati* and also were providing transportation for these supplies to the individual member's plot.

In the countryside, where the villagization program was progressing rapidly, many new houses were being built, most of them of mud brick with iron roofs. As we traveled we saw the results of the government program to bring the widely separated farm families and cattle grazing families together along an existing roadway where the basic services of transportation, water, health care, and schooling could be provided most economically.

The Tanzanian government was making a concerted effort to bring the "good life" to the village—many top level civil servants had been named village managers to serve the eight thousand villages. Senior staff from the parastatal organizations had also been reassigned to the villages as had a number of co-operative officers. Village life could be further enhanced by the return of retired civil servants and parastatal employees. Their retirement pay, we were told, was only enough to keep them comfortable if they returned to their own villages. In fact, many credit union loans were being granted to workers to make their village homes more livable and their family farms more productive, insuring that their approaching retirement years would be pleasant and profitable. On Mount Kilimanjaro some of the new cement block houses were being electrified.

The most spectacular changes we noticed in the major towns

were the increased number of industries: textile, leather, tires, rope and fishnet, beer, shoes. In Dodoma new, small industries such as nails, hinges, brick, wiring, and piping were being set up to make the products that would be needed in building the offices and homes to accommodate the government move to this new capital. Also in Dodoma, a new wine making industry was flourishing with the establishment of vineyards capable of two crops a year.

We must also comment on the Dar es Salaam harbor of the 1960s as compared with the late 1970s. Then, the working boats were mainly fishing boats, few enough in number and small enough in size that pleasure boats could sail at will in the harbor from the boat club (where Africans were rarely seen). By 1977 harbor facilities were being worked twenty-four hours a day. We saw the harbor filled with huge cargo ships from all over the world, creating a brilliant display of lights at night, while twenty or more equally large freighters waited their turn to enter the harbor. There they would be off-loaded with goods for Zambia, Zaire, Burundi, and Tanzania, and reloaded with copper from Zambia that had arrived via the TAZARA railroad.

The daily newspapers regularly carried stories of the problems at the port—of warehouses overflowing with merchandise because the consignees hadn't arranged for pick-up or because railroad cars in Zambia were not being handled efficiently and thus turnaround time was delayed. None of this disturbed the glorious view of the harbor from Dar's major hotels. At dusk and on the weekends unending streams of people walked along the harbor enjoying the beauty and excitement of the busy port.

A Tanzanian problem given much publicity in the press and radio was the prevalent corruption, practically nonexistent in the early days of independence. President Nyerere was quoted as planning to take personal charge of the program to apprehend and punish offenders, be they petty thieves or "big fish" (as pompous and grafting officials are known). However, during the three months of our research stay, we ourselves encountered no requests for *chai* (bribes). We did note premiums being charged on scarce goods which were supposed to be under government price controls. And some officials told us of embezzlements in their own and other credit unions.

The changing role of women had become a major feature in Tanzania's changing world. In the 1960s it was common to see mainly women working in the fields, doing the heavy farm labor. In our study tour we saw village men working alongside the women in the fields. Newspapers carried stories daily of women's success in law and medicine, of women being trained as agronomists, veterinarians, bookkeepers, and store managers. We also met women in the UCDD supervising the operations and bookkeeping of credit unions and co-operative consumer shops. They were also playing a prominent role in politics. We had a productive interview with a young woman serving as a district CCM secretary on Mount Kilimanjaro. In the villages we visited there were women serving on the twenty-five member village councils as a matter of policy.

The employment of women in government had provided some administrative difficulties because married women wanted to live in the towns where their husbands were working. They resisted being posted away from home even though the greatest need of their assistance was in the outlying villages. Single women were also unwilling to work in villages as they thought the villages offered fewer opportunities for finding suitable husbands. These problems were also the problems of young people in general who preferred the life and opportunities of the towns. To keep them in their home areas, the government encouraged village elementary school graduates to enroll in adult education courses that would equip them for jobs such as storekeepers, bookkeepers, and managers of small, local industries.

Women in the villages and towns traditionally have had small businesses on the side to supplement family income, provide clothing for school children, and pay for medical care and school fees. These businesses have included poultry keeping, maintaining small truck gardens, and making *pombe,* the local alcoholic brew. While *pombe* making has been most lucrative (one widow we met was able to finance a new three-room house with her profits), it has compounded the problems of village women who suffer abuses at the hands of drunken husbands.

The economic contribution of women in farming had always been recognized, and Tanzanian women were encouraged to organize themselves into marketing co-operatives to better their incomes. In Musoma there was a concerted effort by the community development officer to organize women who had been working part-time in local tailor shops and women who were sewing at home into a co-operative production unit. The women brought their own sewing machines if they owned them, or they were provided machines out of funds from United Nations Educational, Scientific, and Cultural Organization (UNESCO) and Small Industries Development Organization (SIDO). In a central meeting place, they sewed together, sharing not only clothing patterns, but also ideas for bettering their economic and social status. Twenty percent of the women's profit went to the organization for rent and expenses. Customers who brought their own fabric could purchase a simple garment for about twenty-five shillings (US $3.00). In talking with the women, who came mostly from polygamous families, we learned that it had taken a lot of courage to become part of this organization because the men in the area were very traditional and didn't want any changing roles for their wives. The husband enforced his restrictions by preying upon his wife's fear of being abandoned and having her children's well-being sacrificed if he should favor his other wives and exclude her.

Even among the most dependent wives we found an interest in current styles of clothing (the seamstresses particularly wanted Western pattern books) and in the newest designs and color combinations of *khanga*—a rectangular cotton cloth two meters long that is usually worn draped as a skirt over a simple dress. A matching piece is used to cover the head, carry the baby, or wrap market purchases. We were told that when a new pattern in *khanga* cloth appeared, women made real sacrifices to buy it. A newly designed *khanga* pair was a most appreciated gift from a husband to his wife. Patterns were designed by local Tanzanian designers and woven at the local textile plants in contrast to the early independence years when cotton fiber was exported at low prices to Holland and India, particularly, and the manufactured *khangas* were then imported at high prices.

With independence came an active women's political movement, Umoja Wanawaka Tanzania, which was recognized by CCM when UWT was named one of the five national bodies represented on its executive committee.

All through the country we noted the activities of marching groups of people of both sexes and all ages; we were told that all citizens under age sixty were encouraged to engage in physical exercise and to train for military preparedness. All young Tanzanian men and women, having completed their schooling, must enroll in the National Service for two years.

Our general impressions of Tanzania, reinforced by stories in the daily newspapers, were of a country embattled—tensions on the Kenyan border, on the Ugandan border, on the southern borders—of a country poised for possible military action. But we did not anticipate the march into Uganda in April, 1979; we thought that the country was mobilizing its resources primarily for the struggle in Zimbabwe . . . and ultimately in South Africa.

11. Research Study Findings

Most of the data used in this study were taken from visually verified records in the societies and government offices visited or from statements made by officials and staff of the societies who co-operated in the study. Where inconsistencies have been noted, explanations and reconcilements have been attempted, based on all available information.

Statistics

The compilation of current and valid statistics on Tanzanian savings and credit societies was almost impossible: first, because most societies did not have reasonably current and correct records, and second, because the government in 1972 had decentralized registration and most supervisory functions to regional authorities. As a result, the headquarters office of the commissioner of the UCDD (the recognized repository of government savings and credit society information) had little effective means for compiling nationwide data.

Scope of the Study

We visited thirty-eight societies, including both urban-worker and rural-farmer groups in the ten governmental administrative regions where most of the savings and credit societies were operating. Of our estimated total of 387 registered societies, 290 were located in the regions visited. Nationwide, we estimated that 216 savings and credit societies were doing business as of March, 1978, and 165 of these were in the regions visited (see Appendix).

Upon our arrival at UCDD headquarters offices in Dodoma, we were given copies of their regional lists of registered savings and credit societies as of June 30, 1976. In each region we visited, we checked these lists with the co-operative officer in charge for current information such as which societies in the region were active, which dormant or dead, and which had been transferred to the PRSS.

On these regional lists, inspection dates were to be listed along with the number of members and the amount of shares at the last inspection date. Inspection dates (including dormant societies) varied from 1965 to 1976. (Our regional updates indicated inspection dates of active societies ranging from 1970 to 1977.) Many societies were listed with name and registration date only, others had no figures listed for members, still others had no figures for shares. The central government (headquarters) totals given us on regional activity did not show data for the individual societies.

In correlating the information given by the central government with the information given us on the regional level and with our own findings in six of our ten study regions, we found that, while there were fewer societies by half in operation in 1978, there were more members than those listed in the cumulative figures of June 30, 1976. There was more money in shares, and new societies were being organized in every region. Among the co-operative officers in charge of savings and credit societies there was a feeling that some of the dormant societies could be revived with a little special attention, either from the co-operative officers or SCULT fieldmen.

We were unsuccessful in getting complete, up-to-date, and accurate figures even in the thirty-eight societies we visited. We were shown current balance sheets or financial statements in only five societies; we were given the information on members, shares, and loans orally in eighteen societies and only partial information in thirteen societies. Very few societies gave us any information on reserves or expenses. Though the lack of records presented problems, especially in times of trouble and in large societies, most society secretary/treasurers (volunteer or paid) seemed to know who was saving and how much, who was borrowing and how much, who was repaying and how much, and how much cash was on hand or in the bank.

The reasons for not giving us all the information we sought were varied: all the records were out of the office for audit; the society had no stationery on which to keep financial statements; no current financial statements were being kept by the treasurer and there had been a long delay since the government inspector or league fieldman last brought the records up to date; a traditional reluctance to discuss financial matters with outsiders.

Organization of Savings and Credit Societies

Savings and credit societies are co-operative societies operating under the Co-operative Societies Act of 1968 of the United Republic of Tanzania. Their registration is specifically provided for by Part III, section 4(2) (a) (ii) of the act. (See Chapter 19 for discussions of the act and its application to savings and credit societies.) Standard bylaws issued by the Government Registrar of Co-operative Societies, as revised to December, 1968, limit the field of membership of each savings and credit society to a specific group. The types of groups may generally be characterized as workers' societies usually for employees of a single employer or community societies for residents of a geographically definable rural or urban community. Although societies were at one time registered for groups composed of, or members of, an association, religious faith, or fraternal order, those have either become community societies or have disappeared. When the first societies were organized between 1961 and 1964 and the foundations were being laid for the four hundred savings and credit societies targeted for 1970, government policy was clearly flexible in regard to the type of group that could qualify for registration. Most of the first one hundred societies were for rural communities.

Government had promoted the organization of savings and credit societies since 1963. In a radio talk on International Credit Union Day, October 15, 1964, the minister for commerce and co-operatives said that eventually every citizen of Tanzania would be able to join a credit union. The goal of four hundred had not been achieved by 1978 even though league staff, government officers, AID technicians, the Co-operative College, and the Co-operative Education Centre worked hard at promoting their expansion.

A wide variety of informational sources had introduced the savings and credit society idea to the societies we visited. Most reported that the idea came through a relative who was a society member, through a member of another society, or through someone who had previously had savings and credit society service, reinforcing the universal belief that a satisfied user is the best promoter in any country. Priests, co-operative officers, league representatives, and co-operative college lecturers brought the idea to other groups. One large society of industrial employees was formed as the result of a lecture heard at a political ideology school.

Shares

Total shares and deposits were estimated at Tshs 24.1 million on April 30, 1978, in a SCULT report presented to ACOSCA in August, 1978, but this data could not be verified with government figures. Saving in the societies was voluntary and usually tied to the anticipation of getting a loan, a "personal secret between the member himself and his society." Some societies, by consensus, were requiring minimum monthly savings. Others, even in rural areas where the government's closing of marketing co-ops had tended to discourage savings, succeeded in getting members to save some of their earnings or farm income in larger, lump sum deposits. Teachers in both urban and rural areas were active society savers. Nationally, members' account balances usually ranged from less than one hundred shillings to more than two thousand shillings. Check-off had helped to encourage regular savings, but on the whole savings had not been promoted actively.

Employed women were accustomed to saving in their society with an account in their own names. In rural areas, women saved in the societies out of income they earned by selling eggs, garden produce, handcrafts, and home-brewed beer.

Savings and credit society members also saved in other institutions but especially in the POSB, which catered for small accounts but offered no credit, and in the Tanzania Housing Bank (THB), which made home loans. NBC competition for savings was minimal since the bank did not offer a competing loan service, even to its own employees, who themselves had organized a savings and credit society. NBC's socialist lending policy favored loans to the public sector. Despite the presence of these institutions, however, research by the Bank of Tanzania showed that private savings in the nation equaled more than fifty percent of all savings and circulated among the people without getting into the banking system at all.

Dividends

Dividends were rarely being paid, mostly because bookkeeping was incomplete and/or incorrect, but also because available earnings had not been officially certified by government auditors whose audit program was commonly several years in arrears. The few societies which reported paying dividends usually limited the rate to less than the five percent allowed in the bylaws except where a single dividend was paid for several years in one total payment. In the latter case dividends were not computed separately for each year's business. The shares of the latest year were used since little change had occured in these accounts from one year to another.

In thirteen of the thirty-eight societies, a dividend had been paid one or more times since 1969. Five societies that were being audited expected to pay a dividend for 1977. One society used its undivided profits to buy a corn grinding machine, and the members of one society decided to divide the profits by giving each member fifty shillings.

Loans, Interest Rates, Refunds of Interest

Most savings and credit societies invested eighty to ninety percent of their total assets in loans to members. Many societies had a loans/share ratio of over one hundred percent, indicating the use of retained earnings and reserves to make loans. In the latest SCULT report as of April 30, 1978, total Tanzanian savings and credit society outstanding loans were estimated at Tshs 21.8 million and total accumulated loans granted to that date at Tshs 95.3 million.

Loans were the principal inducement to membership. The manager of a major industry said he could only get an overdraft of up to one month's salary to be repaid by the following payday and that for most people in his circumstances such credit depended on how well one knew the bank manager. Civil servants confirmed reports that in all areas of the country bank credit was unavailable to them. Up until 1976 the government had given loans to its civil service employees for certain household goods and autos with thirty-six-month repayment terms at no interest. Those loans had by 1978 been limited to a very few items such as spectacles and bicycles.

Major loan purposes were for upgrading houses and farms, agricultural inputs, school fees and medical care, home furnishings, including domestic appliances and equipment, dowries, family emergencies, payment of fines, and restoration of items stolen in house break-ins. Urban workers took loans to purchase bicycles while rural workers bought cows both for milk and for manure to fertilize their fields. Most loans averaged from Tshs 200 to Tshs 5,000, although some larger loans had been made for up to Tshs 30,000. Maturity periods usually did not exceed two years but sometimes went as long as six years.

In most societies an effort was being made to increase the savings pool so that more substantial loans could be made for productive purposes. Small loans tended to be frittered away on beer and consumer items because they were not in amounts large enough to meet the members' real needs. One treasurer remarked that in his experience "if the borrower is under thirty years of age, he will probably use the loan for other purposes than for that stated in his request; if over thirty, he probably will use the loan as indicated on the application." A young civil servant told of frequent borrowing to pay off loans from friends for buying rounds of beer when cronies gathered—the application form for such loans often indicating "family emergency" as the purpose of the loan.

Loans were frequently used to help family members become self-supporting rather than having them remain a drain on the major breadwinner. For instance, a longtime savings and credit society member told us that on the death of one of his uncles, he had become responsible for the support of his aunt. After much discussion with her, it was decided that he should apply for a loan to buy her a fishing boat which she could then rent to local fishermen for a fee and/or the price of half the catch of fish. In just a few years she had paid off the cost of the boat while supporting herself, and was totally able to take financial care of herself. In fact, she was considering taking out a loan on her own to buy a second boat.

Interest was usually being charged at the maximum legal rate of one percent per month on the unpaid balance and often paid off on a level payment plan. Refunds of interest (patronage refunds) were rarely paid to borrowers because of the failure to collect interest due and the weaknesses in bookkeeping and auditing. However, patronage refunds had been paid by two societies, one refunded three and a half percent, the other, four percent. Another planned to pay a refund of between twelve and fourteen and a half percent covering a four-year period.

Most loans had been recovered, but delinquency was common, and interest collections not only lagged behind schedule but were also compromised in collection settlements. Most delinquencies among worker societies occurred when employees were moved from one area or government agency to another. Among farmers' societies, there were delinquencies when crops failed or when the marketing unions which had offered loan collection facilities closed.

The commissioner for co-operative development had interceded on behalf of some societies seeking to collect delinquent loans, as had some regional development directors. In other cases, however, regional officers refused to authorize payroll deductions for those employees transferred with unpaid loans negotiated in other regions. A registrar's circular directed societies themselves to take their delinquent loans to their local district courts. A few cases had been taken, but the expense and time involved in getting judgments and collecting on them had proved discouraging.

Losses on loans were not usually charged off to the statutory reserve for that purpose; the accounting procedures for charge-off were not well understood. Losses were said to be minimal, but data on actual losses were not available. Although it was common practice to require that every loan be secured by two guarantors and their share accounts be pledged to the loan repayment, guarantors were rarely called upon to pay when a borrower defaulted. To most members the guarantors were only "friends vouching for each other." Payroll deduction, if available, was commonly considered the real security for loans in workers' societies, although serious delinquencies and losses had resulted when some borrowers attempted to defraud the society by secretly canceling their payroll deduction authorizations after receiving loans. Upon request for assistance one society succeeded in getting the company management to deduct a borrower's loan repayment out of his provident fund account. The legality of a provident fund assignment was not verified. In another society, management paid off the loan of a senior officer.

The only government supervisory restriction on lending to members was the government circular that recommended limiting loans to double the amount of the member's savings. The prime minister's office issued this guideline in February, 1976, when a severe loan delinquency problem surfaced in a large nationwide society covering employees of six government ministries. Much of the money not being repaid was in big loans to a few members. The circular was issued after full discussions between SCULT, government inspectors and officers. Most societies were observing this ruling, but a few permitted loans of up to five times the member's share balance when other factors indicated the need for more flexibility.

The entire loan delinquency problem had also been made worse by the government decentralization program in 1972, the Village Act of 1975 that eliminated primary co-operative societies, the elimination of district and town councils in anticipation of the Urban Wards Act of 1976 that was never signed, and the dissolution of the co-operative unions in mid-1976.

Credit committees were meeting regularly or as often as needed to consider loan applications. With limited lendable funds, committees faced a real dilemma in attempting to satisfy loan requests: should each member get something or should the real needs of fewer borrowers be met? The members of farmer societies seemed to know each other better than employee group members, and their lending activities reflected more concern with the total needs and repayment abilities of the individual than did the workers'. Worker societies relied mostly on payroll deductions and share/loan formulas, and in some, the loan of twice one's shares was considered a right of membership rather than a privilege.

Management, Membership Participation, Bookkeeping, Internal Auditing

Complete bookkeeping systems were almost nonexistent, and few societies could produce a reasonably current financial statement. Without correct records management found themselves crippled, and few management functions were undertaken by the elected board of directors. Elected officials did little directing, planning, controlling, or coordinating. Supervisory committees rarely made internal audits.

The credit committee met regularly in almost all societies, and the board of directors depended on this committee and the secretary/treasurer or clerk to carry out society business. There seemed to be little turnover in board membership. Where it had been made clear by the members that special loan privileges would not be granted to members of the board, there was little competition for the jobs. Early experiences of societies in trouble routinely showed abuse of the loan privileges by board members. Most boards of directors, however, continued to serve to the satisfaction of their members as long as they provided prompt loans and share withdrawals.

Annual Meetings

Membership meetings were being delayed from year to year awaiting official government audits because officers felt they could not answer the questions of their members about the society and their money if they did not have the books in hand. This had been aggravated where books remained with the auditor for several years. Also, incompetent officials were not being removed, and board vacancies were often not filled. Membership meetings, when they were held, were well attended with twenty-five percent to one hundred percent of the membership participating. Only one society reported an entertainment budget to bring members to the annual meeting.

Daily journals, general ledgers, bank records, and reconcilements, as has been previously reported, were routinely removed from the society premises by government officers and auditors for examination at some distant auditing office location. Where hand-posted systems were in use, societies often maintained only the members' individual share and loan ledgers. Computer printouts showing similar information sufficed where computerized payroll deduction systems were utilized. One nationwide civil servants' society with payroll deduction and computerized bookkeeping was wrecked by dishonest officials and employees who took large loans for themselves and looted the funds by fraudulently manipulating the system.

In some of the regions co-operative officers, especially the trained savings and credit specialists, had gotten permission from the regional headquarters to help bring the societies' books up to date and to perform audits, usually without removing the books from the premises. With such an audit that was recognized as "official," the societies could then call an annual meeting and declare a dividend and/or pay an interest refund, if earned, within a reasonable period of time.

Paid Staff, Office Buildings

A managerial class of savings and credit society operators did not seem to be developing in Tanzania. Of the thirty-eight societies studied, fourteen had one or more paid employees but only four were treasurer/managers; the rest were clerks and bookkeepers. Two of these societies had full-time staff members paid by their employer. Among a number of wage earner groups, employees were given time off from their regular jobs to serve the society on company time and company premises. One set of staff employees was being paid out of a church grant; one workers' union representative served as society secretary/treasurer.

Most societies did not have office space of their own: some used space provided by employers, some shared space with CCM staff or with Union of Tanzania Workers (UTW) staff, some had only the desk at which they worked for the company, others worked at home and kept the books with them at all times. The "offices" were typically only one room, furnished with a table, a couple of chairs, and benches along a wall. Most had a cupboard in which officers kept records and supplies, and some had a safe. A few had bulletin boards. The majority did not have any office equipment such as typewriters or adding machines. The certificate of registration was proudly displayed on the wall together with any group photographs that had been taken of board members by visitors. We saw a number of pictures we had taken with our Polaroid camera during the Tanganyika Project and CUNA/AID programs.

Some rural societies acquired their buildings through member subscriptions and donated work time; other societies had purchased their buildings with their undivided earnings. One society rented a part of its building to the NBC; others rented out parts of their buildings for stores and restaurants. These structures were a source of considerable pride, aside from their income potential.

Multipurpose Activities of Savings and Credit Societies

When the savings and credit society was well run, with good management and adequate bookkeeping and controls, multipurpose activities proved viable. Problems arose when management did not have adequate managerial skills and when complete and separate records were not up to date. For instance, in one society where the members contributed voluntarily for the purchase of a building, which included sleeping rooms, bar, and restaurant, as well as office space for the society, the board of directors did not know whether the business activities were profitable or whether the cash they were using for meeting expenses and loan requests represented the liquidation of their inventory. The manager of the business enterprises was also keeping the books of the savings and credit society and was so overworked that she did not collect interest with loan repayments. The employees of the businesses were members of the society and as such had originally been hired at low salaries, but one of the employees sued for a minimum wage and won. The bar did business when it had beer to sell, but when supplies ran out, so did patrons. (All supplies in the country were given first to village consumer shops, then to co-operative businesses, and last to private enterprise.) Teachers in the area made up the field of membership. Problems were intensified because none of them had experience in the hotel business, and the district in which the society was located had no savings and credit specialist assigned to it. The regional savings and credit specialist recognized the society's problems and was seeking ways to assist despite the distance of the district from regional headquarters, the lack of transportation, and his own heavy work load.

Nine societies had undertaken other productive activities, and three were planning such projects. Where buildings were built to house the society offices and provide extra rental space, the financing often came from donations by members of money and labor. In one instance where the building was bought by the society out of its share capital, ten of its farmer members took individual loans to set up a store in the rental section and to install a gas pump on the premises. Within the time limit on loan repayment, the building had been totally paid for and the ten members had paid off their loans.

Ten years later the store was still operating, but gas was no longer being pumped. Some members of this society, located in a small town, borrowed money for a bus, but the project failed because of the difficulties of maintaining the equipment and getting replacement parts. Another society, however, owned shares in a successful bus operation linking a densely populated farming area to a major marketing center. This society also owned a brick-making facility (with records separate from the savings and credit society) that turned a profit in 1976 and 1977. Loans for building inputs were being made in kind (the bricks) and by chits to get roofing at the consumer co-operative store, which was located next to the society office.

In several societies, the co-op consumer shop was financed by special contributions of members or by a company gift and served the same membership as the savings and credit society but kept separate books and paid staff. In one case where the project was not the outgrowth of successful savings and credit society operations but was begun primarily to raise funds to get the society itself going, the business venture failed.

In all societies, the personnel interviewed stressed the importance to them of outside assistance in achieving a successful multipurpose operation, whether from good government supervision and direction, company help, or league advice.

Life Savings and Loan Protection Insurance

Eighteen societies reported that they carried life savings and loan protection insurance through SCULT, which was acting agent for the National Insurance Corporation (NIC), the state-owned and only insurance company in the country. A number of societies admitted they were not current in their premium payments. Where claims had been paid (in four of the societies studied), insurance had become an important selling point to attract both new members and additional savings from old members.

In the larger societies, the benefits of life insurance were well recognized, but in some rural societies the concept was not understood. For example, in one firmly established society the officials were waiting for a claim before they would authorize payment of all the premiums due since the day the society first signed up for the insurance. Some of the large societies felt SCULT premiums were too high; one was planning to contract with the NIC directly; another was arranging to become self-insured.

Government Supervision and Auditing

Government supervision and auditing had weakened measurably since the late 1960s when yearly inspections and audits were a realizable goal. Although there was still a headquarters officer specifically responsible for savings and credit societies, the corps of specially trained inspectors who had been assigned to each of the regions had been broken up in the governmental decentralization.

In some regions the headquarters officers committed to the savings and credit society idea were still helping to maintain strong society growth. A number of the most dedicated and creative officers we met had received training at the Coady International Institute. Some had also been on credit union training visits to the United States.

Likewise, some treasurers who were trained in those early years had developed their managerial competence along with their bookkeeping skills.

It was noticeable that in the outlying districts, isolated because of poor communications and transportation facilities, elected officials were continuing to wait for government officers to help them and were relying on the government's dwindling supervisory program which in the past had provided government staff for management functions.

The combination of these quasi-managerial functions and the minimal training provided to volunteer treasurers, managers, and hired bookkeepers overloaded the few government officers capable of supervising savings and credit societies. This led to the government's increasing pressure on societies to hire competent bookkeepers rather than depend on volunteers.

In addition, supervisory requirements imposed in the early years before there was any experience with savings and credit societies were still in effect. Three rules in particular were not being uniformly enforced because of the lack of staff and transport:

- All checks must be countersigned by a co-operative officer. This was generally honored, but some regional officers permitted the societies to make disbursements in cash to circumvent the issuance of individual checks to members.
- Societies must have their year-end accounts verified by government auditors. This had been sidestepped by permitting government officers who were not designated auditors to make the required audit.
- Each society must submit estimates (or a budget) at the beginning of each year for government approval.

A Three-Way View of Savings and Credit Societies

Problems as Seen by Government Officials

The majority of government officials with whom we spoke felt that the societies offered a much needed service not provided for elsewhere in the economy, that they would continue to grow in number and size, and that they could be run by their members and officers.

Among most of the supervising officers the problems were seen more as a result of difficulties in the UCDD than in the societies themselves. Ill-conceived regulations emanating from uninformed top leadership and vacillating government policy made supervision difficult. Since "word comes down from the top," according to several officers, a special education program was needed for the government and party decision makers to explain savings and credit societies—what they were and how they functioned. The officials also complained of the lack of communication between the central UCDD and the regions and between the regional offices and the districts. There seemed to be no avenue for two-way communication: reports were seldom acknowledged, requests for information and guidance seldom answered. Some officers had given up trying to communicate with the office of the commissioner.

The problem of inadequate staffing was made worse, they stated, by the lack of transportation. The use of officers from a community development or general co-operatives background to supervise savings and credit societies also lessened service to the societies, especially if these officers were not interested in such societies. However, we found one community development officer who was so challenged by the new experience that he revitalized the government's assistance to these societies in his area.

Many officers told us they hesitated to recommend liquidation of any savings and credit society because they felt that with more trained government staff and better transport, these societies could be assisted to function and serve their members once again. The savings and credit specialists felt competent to do the audits themselves and thus hoped to eliminate the long delays. The officers agreed that they could and should use the audits to teach and upgrade the skills of society treasurers and boards of directors. The regional officers were looking forward to having new savings and credit desk officers assigned in each district available at all times to aid treasurers and society officers who would come to the district office for assistance. The societies have to take the initiative in asking for assistance.

The major problems for individual societies were seen as a lack of local leaders, unsuitable board members, and loan delinquency. These problems could, they felt, be mitigated with regular supervision by qualified technicians working with SCULT field staff to provide education and training. Some other solutions included stepped-up training of local leaders in management functions, close supervision of loan practices as part of the audit, and better co-operation by the government in loan collection. Delinquencies occur, for instance, when civil servants and parastatal employees (making up most of the wage earner savings and credit societies) are transferred. Although a government circular had been issued asking each regional development director (RDD) to help collect the outstanding loans of those members transferred to his region, some were not enforcing the directive because they "didn't want to be unpopular."

Another problem seen by government officials was that of establishing a common bond for membership. As long as registration policy limited societies to urban areas and to wage earner groups with check-off provided, the problem of defining the common bond of membership was simple. But there had been rising pressure to provide savings and credit society services among *townspeople in general,* whether in urban or rural areas. Developing an acceptable and definable common bond to cover these people was proving difficult.

Most of the government officials (in all agencies) with whom we spoke were themselves members of savings and credit societies and said candidly that they had nowhere else to go for personal credit. The director of the Manpower Development Administration of the Ministry of Finance insisted that savings and credit societies helped to prevent corruption by meeting some of the needs for credit in the country and provided for the necessities of life as well as for investment in nation building.

The officers with whom we traveled were all savings and credit society enthusiasts. All of them had special training; all of them spent their own time participating in a local society and organizing new societies; and all of them continued to work on behalf of savings and credit societies while being trained and accepting responsiblity for supervising the new VRSCS.

Government Relations from the View of Society Officials

Where there was an active, dedicated, well-trained savings and credit specialist/co-operative officer who had been on the job in the same area for a number of years, the society officials had praise and only the warmest feelings for the government's role in supervision and promotion of their societies. Officials noted that when co-operative officers made the audits the books were only gone a few days; the officers trained treasurers in bookkeeping; they gave much needed advice to elected leaders, especially as the societies tried to take on other multipurpose co-operative activities; and they assisted in collecting bad loans. They also helped societies get rid of incompetent officials in situations where the society felt unable to act.

This last type of assistance was displayed in one society in which the treasurer was a member of a local tribe and related to one of the board members. The society members were having problems getting money and other services from the treasurer but were afraid to move against him. On a routine visit, the co-operative inspector noted the treasurer's laziness, inefficiency, and arrogance in handling members and at the same time found unduly high expenditures in the society. He thereupon instructed the board of directors to discharge the man, thus placing the blame upon the government and not on the elected board of the society.

Where there had been continuous changes of government officers and where officers had been taken away from the area on lengthy training programs, there were complaints. Society officials reported that the government gave no help in bookkeeping or training of officials, and that its audits were slow, often resulting in the societies' books being out of their hands for long periods of time. They also claimed that societies became dormant where there were no government officials around to be helpful.

Savings and Credit Society Problems as Seen by Savings and Credit Society Officials and Members

Almost all societies reported that their priority problem was not having enough money to lend. The need was so great that it was recognized by parent companies, which in some cases donated or loaned funds for relending. This problem was most common in rural areas where there was no regular income. There were exceptions, however. Farmers tended to be savers rather than borrowers so that in some rural societies surplus funds became a problem. One treasurer of a rural society felt his problem was to get the farmer-members to use credit. In another rural area, the treasurer of a teachers' society complained that the loans taken were all very small, and therefore little income was being generated from revolving the available funds.

Loan delinquency was another problem, particularly where government and parastatal employees were transferred. However, with perseverance, the societies managed to locate the defaulters and arrange for them to be put on payroll deduction at their new job site. But where employees of private industry left the field of membership, it was extremely difficult to locate them and collect. One society felt that SCULT should provide this collection service for the local societies since it was a national organization.

Of the three societies reporting embezzlements, two had continued operations and made up the losses. The third was not doing any business while its books were being brought up to date and its members with loans outstanding were being located to arrange for repayment. This society had served several government ministries, but according to its secretary, it will be reorganized to serve only the employees of the original ministry for which it was organized. Other members will have to transfer their membership to the savings and credit societies of the respective ministries in which they are employed, thus making for better management control. The members of this society, even though it was in trouble, did not want to take their shares out because they wanted to be able to make loans as soon as the society was opened for business again.

Another category of problems among volunteer treasurers was the lack of time to maintain the books. They felt that pressure ought to be put upon companies and agencies to give them time off from their regular jobs to do the society bookkeeping because they were relieving management of the numerous, time-consuming requests for salary advances.

Lack of adequate office space with the attendant lack of privacy which interfered seriously with the confidentiality of lending and saving was also an area of difficulty. This secrecy was important in view of the extended family tradition which demanded that every family member share his money with his relatives in need. Members feared questioning by tax authorities about where their savings came from.

Many societies complained about the delays in getting their books audited and some resented its high cost. Getting new stationery was a problem as well as an expense. League representatives kept some stationery supplies on hand, but the materials ordered from headquarters were often delayed because of prepayment requirements and slow mails. Some societies resorted to having their own stationery printed locally (sometimes of their own design) both for cost effectiveness and convenience.

Ordinary thievery was not a problem, but not all thieves were ordinary. In one society a thief stole eight thousand shillings, two thousand of which was recovered when the cash box was found. The police took the cash box and the society's books for evidence, and then the prosecutor, who is now in jail, handled the case by stealing the cash and destroying the society's books.

Some managers and officials discussed at length the inefficiency of boards of directors and claimed that some board members even neglected their societies. The need of training for officials and managers was stressed as being more important than the need for help with bookkeeping. There was a lack of training/education materials at all levels.

A number of societies felt they were unable to get assistance with their problems either from the government officials or from the league staff. Where government officials were available and helpful, the societies could see little need for the league, especially since government services were free of charge. Where there was no government help, the societies turned to the league.

Savings and Credit Society Promotional and Technical Publications

In July, 1967, the CDD produced the *Inspection Manual on Savings and Credit Societies* to assist inspectors in providing more complete and meaningful inspections. In 1972 the CDD produced a bookkeeping manual in Swahili for savings and credit societies (originally developed under the CUNA/AID project) which was being used by a few savings and credit society specialists to help them in their bookkeeping and auditing duties. This manual had been a primary teaching document until the department turned its attention to the development of the PRSS.

Conferences of senior co-operative officers, such as those held at Mwanza in 1969 and Moshi in 1970, had served as training sessions and forums to exchange ideas. The proceedings were published in full and served as educational resource materials for the co-operative officers who were unable to attend.

The Co-operative College in Moshi continued to provide educational opportunities for government and society officials. It offered a three-month specialized course for savings and credit societies and rural savings and credit schemes and a broad, two-year, co-operatives diploma course which included studies equivalent to the three-month course.

The Nyegezi STC provided a two-year diploma course in rural development with a comprehensive co-operative syllabus which included a section on savings and credit societies. This course was primarily for community leaders.

Savings and credit societies and rural savings and credit schemes were also included in the syllabus for the UCDD assistants/home economics course.

SCULT produced posters that appeared on bulletin boards in the offices of some societies. In the government co-operative department offices, many charts and printed materials, including relevant newspaper clippings and posters, were displayed.

SCULT

At the time of our visit SCULT's status was in limbo as a result of the abolition of all second tier organizations in the Tanzanian co-operative movement in 1976. The staff continued to operate from SCULT's headquarters and regional offices, but it was obvious that changes were underway.

The main thrust of the discussions on reorganization was to bring SCULT into the Union of Co-operative Societies (UCS), the new apex organization embracing all co-operatives in the country. Various solutions were being considered to allay SCULT's fears that it might lose its international funding and representation and that it might disappear altogether. SCULT's representatives reported to an ACOSCA meeting in 1978 that:

> Structure changes are on the way and so the League will shadow under the umbrella of Union of Cooperative Societies as an apex organization. The UCS will be the only cooperative association to protect the interest of cooperatives in the nation. SCULT has the role of representing the Savings and Credit Societies in UCS and Government because it has been experienced that SCULT is capable in handling properly the welfare of its members.[1]

From its beginning in 1964, SCULT gave leadership to African savings and credit society development while establishing itself as the specialized organization of savings and credit societies in Tanzania. Its stated aims were to

- further the development of co-operation among people,
- help people understand how to make the best use of their earnings for their own needs and how to give mutual help for the needs of others,
- enable people to combat the social evil of usury,

- provide the most effective methods of promoting the growth of savings and credit societies in the country,
- be ready to give support to any co-operation development.

Membership in SCULT was voluntary. However, some regional officers ruled that the government could and did require societies to join SCULT. SCULT claimed some 282 members (of which 26 societies were not operating) or about seventy-one percent of the registered savings and credit societies in Tanzania. In 1977, when its total income was Tshs 447,406, 60 member societies were current in dues payments amounting to Tshs 59,958, while overseas grants totaled Tshs 375,684, stationery sales, Tshs 8,183, and education contributions, Tshs 3,680. Of the 38 societies studied, 27 reported they were members; 20 of these were current in their dues payments.

Dues income and entrance fees from the member societies, augmented by stationery sales and insurance commissions, had amounted to about half a million shillings in SCULT's fifteen-year history, whereas grants, received mostly from outside the country, had totaled over 1.7 million shillings. Principal donors had been KAF, MCUL, and SCUL.

Personnel had also been seconded by the Tanzanian government (1971–73), the CUNA/AID program (1967–69), and the KAF (1976–79). According to a 1978 SCULT report, meeting facilities had been furnished by various church missions. SCULT had been renting headquarters office space in Co-operative House, the building formerly owned by the Co-operative Union of Tanzania (CUT), at a fifty percent subsidy, and the Tanzanian government had also been providing the league's field officers with office space and field transport whenever possible. However, since field transport was almost nonexistent throughout Tanzania for government co-operative officers, SCULT field representatives had to share their Land-Rovers in the outlying regions with government officers who came to depend upon SCULT vehicles for their own transportation. This led to some difficult situations when the league representative and government officers could not agree on travel priorities.

The morale of SCULT's leaders had been tested repeatedly not so much by financial crises as by their inability to influence the government on savings and credit society policy. In recent years there had been unrelieved tension over the league's role in the co-operative development plans of the country. Throughout the regions visited, leaders of member societies were divided between those who felt that something could be done to preserve their national organization and those who were resigned to a government takeover. Although some societies were lax in paying their dues, a representative number continued to send delegates regularly to SCULT meetings.

Chapters

SCULT's bylaws called for the establishment of ten chapters to conduct educational activities and to provide representation on a geographical basis. While some chapters had met periodically in certain regions, they were not phased into the administration of SCULT's program. Instead a system of zonal offices (each zone covering two regions) was being established to decentralize SCULT's services through the localized work of zonal fieldmen. No role for chapters was described in either the SCULT *Policy Paper* of 1976 or the 1978 SCULT Report to ACOSCA. Two regions, nevertheless, held so-called chapter meetings during the period of this study. In a third region, plans for chapter-type activities were being developed by the government specialist who was encouraging the societies in the region to include costs of transportation and lodging as well as donations to chapter activities within their annual estimates of expenses to be submitted to government for approval.

SCULT's Management

SCULT's last ten-person board of directors was elected in December, 1975, by delegates of member societies meeting in plenary session. The board was to serve a three-year term. At the annual membership meeting in Morogoro in November, 1977, no election was held due to the unsettled co-operatives situation, and the incumbents were authorized to continue to serve. Actually, operations were in the hands of the executive committee. As of August, 1978, SCULT's staff numbered fourteen Tanzanians, eight senior staff and six support staff, plus one non-African KAF technician. Plans for the future elections of board members call for delegates of savings and credit societies to meet within their zones during the SCULT general meeting to select from among themselves a representative and an alternate to serve on the board.

SCULT's principal services had been to provide education and training, technical assistance, provision of bookkeeping stationery, and insurance. Through SCULT's affiliation with CUNA International and subsequently with ACOSCA, and with help from KAF, the NACCU/CIDA program, MCUL, and the Coady International Institute, over 120 participants (most of them government co-op officers) had received specialized savings and credit society training. Originally many of the trainees were schooled in the United States and Canada, but later on more of the training was given in East Africa at Tanzania's Co-operative College, the Kenya Co-operative College, and at ACOSCA, ICA, and SCULT sponsored seminars.

Acting as agent for the NIC, the league had been offering loan protection and life savings insurance to both member and nonmember societies. Up to August, 1978, NIC had collected Tshs 413,800 in premiums and paid Tshs 115,801 in claims. This service was originally introduced by SCULT in co-operation with the CUNA Mutual Insurance Society, which also paid some claims. The NIC agency, which was supposed to yield commissions to SCULT, paid them only once since 1970. Payment was being withheld because there were unresolved questions about the actual amount of paid-for coverage in view of the noncurrent, inaccurate, or incomplete bookkeeping records of the individual societies. Also, NIC itself was said to be understaffed and delinquent in its own record keeping.

A stabilization fund for emergency assistance to societies was introduced by SCULT in 1968 and was funded on a voluntary basis by fifty-two societies. With its limited finances (Tshs 30,000) it had already helped rescue one of the largest societies in Tanzania. An interlending service (central fund) and internal auditing service were being planned for the future.

SCULT's education, training, and information programs attracted visitors and savings and credit society pioneers from other African countries. In 1977 SCULT sponsored visiting leaders of the Zambian movement and took them to see societies in action in a number of Tanzanian regions.

12. Conclusions

Why Savings and Credit Societies Have Survived

The importance of the Tanzanian savings and credit society is in the "miracle" of its survival. It is a money-handling co-operative that has managed to persist, often without good bookkeeping or good management, that has measured its profitability almost totally in terms of member satisfactions, that has adjusted to changing governmental directives about its roles and services—and has emerged with its basic principles intact. It is an organization that in the process of adapting to Tanzania's changing environment has gained enough membership backing to establish itself as a self-supporting, informal auxiliary of the predominant state banks in both the rural and urban areas.

If, judging by conventional standards, Tanzania's few hundred savings and credit societies were found to be small, weak, inefficient institutions for the most part, they were also strikingly relevant to the Tanzanian situation. That is why over half of the societies registered were still alive in their first twenty years as a movement. To describe how they have survived is to describe the survival of Tanzania itself: "this is how we live" says it all. To explain their continuing existence requires some subjective interpretations of the facts already reported. We suggest ten major reasons.

1. The expectations and apprehensions of society members were balanced: they committed enough resources to make their societies work reasonably well, but not enough to risk serious personal losses of money or prestige.

2. Tanzanians were not led to expect too much and they did not risk too much. The societies were introduced as an experiment and not as a part of any "scientific strategy" that guaranteed given results from given inputs as in typical foreign aid programming.

3. Savings and credit societies met essential needs of the

Tanzanian nation and the Tanzanian people in providing savings and loan services for rural production, for education, housing, community projects, and subsistence purchases. Some loans they made helped provide secondary schooling for children who would otherwise be deprived of an education. Most rural communities would have had to wait to a long time for government funding of such things as a bus to carry their people and produce from the local villages to the nearest trading center. Society members managed to get their buses by themselves, in addition to corn grinding mills, hotels (restaurants), and small office buildings. Sometimes a fine had to be paid with a society loan—and a worker was able to hold onto his job.

4. By acting out the Ujamaa nation-building scenario of "small is beautiful" co-operation, savings and credit societies became an indispensable economic convenience to thousands of Tanzanians. In doing this, they helped keep the country going by making life bearable for the people, by conserving the resources of the nation, and by adding to its productivity.

5. They have been effective agents of experimental government policy in testing the possibilities of multipurpose co-operatives.

6. They have helped maintain confidence in co-operatives at a time when (despite government commitment to them) it was found necessary to dismantle Tanzania's world-famous co-operative marketing system.

7. Government policy never went so far as to force the savings and credit societies into the arms of the marketing co-operatives.

8. The leaders of these societies were either unable or disinclined to build a power bloc which could solicit government influence, support, or funding, and which could equally have attracted powerful opposition.

9. Savings and credit societies have had few institutional competitors in the lending area.

10. Decentralization of government permitted the stronger rural savings and credit societies to remain in business while their local regional government officials worked out ways to adapt central office rulings to local situations.

Limitations and Opportunities

In the 1960s and early 1970s, when the hopes and promises of independence were about all the Tanzanians had to show for their newly won political freedom, savings and credit societies multiplied. Savings grew although people had little money to save. The movement as a whole was set back by the exclusion of these societies from the rural sector in the early 1970s, but by the end of the decade, workers' societies had established themselves as the "people's banks." The societies were sometimes the workers' only lifeline to the credit they needed to stay afloat in a sea of inflation.

In the 1980s, another era of privation seems inevitable. Wage earners will be especially hard hit if the government is unable to contain inflation and black-marketing. Consequently, the outlook for cash savings is almost as bleak as it was twenty years ago. Savings and credit societies will have to work hard if they want to grow.

Offsetting these negative factors is the workers' widespread and increasing recognition of savings and credit societies as good places to save, primarily because of the credit services offered and, to a lesser extent, the insurance coverage available to members. These societies appear to be the single most important source of personal credit for workers, teachers, civil service and parastatal employees, including many in middle management and some in executive positions. The potential exists for improvement in savings through check-off both as an incentive for getting larger loans and as a means of providing for life insurance through life savings and loan protection insurance programs.

The urban work force (especially civil servants) may be expected to increase despite all the political rhetoric and economic inducements to keep people on the farms. Consequently, societies' membership should grow, and enough new societies should be organized to more than compensate for the normal mortality of groups that fail or lose interest. However, the government must be willing to encourage their further expansion while seeing that they are spared political over-expectations and excessive supervision.

The movement will become more dynamic when there are more paid managers and staffers with self-interest to motivate them. Also, a new generation of government supervisors from the banking community, although less imbued with co-operative ideals, may be more inclined to let the society managers manage.

Government Registration and Supervision Policy

The decision to restrict societies to the wage earner sector would seem to have been a step backward from a socialistic viewpoint. Instead of equalizing economic opportunities it gives added advantages to the civil servants and others who are at the upper limits of earnings. In so doing, it broadens the gap between the "bureaucratic bourgeoisie" at the top and the people at the bottom.

By making check-off a prerequisite to the registration of a new society, government in effect makes it difficult if not impossible for day laborers, transient workers, and small artisans to organize themselves into savings and credit societies. What may have been a good policy for wage earners' societies, or at least defensible as a mechanistic solution to the problems of those societies, becomes a self-defeating exercise that denies service to those who may need it most.

Some government rules intended to remedy management weaknesses actually appear to have weakened the societies still further. The "estimates" (or budgeting) requirement has merit but is a hindrance when government staff are ill-equipped to make management judgments or unable to find time to approve the estimates. Check countersigning is ordinarily a responsibility of management. The requirement that a government officer must be one of the countersigners has delayed service to the members and has not protected the societies from fraud and embezzlement. Granted that government in Tanzania is respected as the guardian of citizens' welfare, the question remains whether this stricture does more harm than good by counteracting progress toward management responsibility. Although societies may apply for permission to eliminate this requirement, practically none have done so, possibly because Tanzanian co-operators are accustomed to a strong government presence.

Savings and Lending Policies

If societies are to become more than they are today, they will have to reach out into the urban neighborhoods for more savings. They will have to become better known among other than worker groups. Entirely new concepts of service may have to be tried out. If government is willing to officially recognize that the capitalistic notions of interest on loans and dividends on savings are not essential to the savings and credit society concept in Tanzania, these concepts might be eliminated in favor of the no-interest, no-dividend, service fee practices already accepted in some new Islamic banks.

While nonpayment of dividends has certainly not enhanced the societies' reputation as a profitable place to save, it has apparently had little negative effect on the savings habits of members whose principal concern in saving was to get a loan. Although it was not openly discussed, a more likely reason for not saving was the prohibition against business activities on the part of government and parastatal employees of middle rank and above. The need for supplementary income is forcing many workers to hoard their money outside of the savings institutions where their financial transactions might be scrutinized by government.

Importance of Supporting the Development of Rural Co-operative Savings and Credit Societies

Rural Tanzania is changing very slowly. The need for modern Tanzanian institutions which can fit in naturally with traditional rural institutions points to the socioeconomic advantages of savings and credit societies. They have proven themselves in Tanzania to be pliable, readily adaptable to large and small groups, and as co-operatives, they are a logical and politically acceptable social and economic activity at the primary level.

Savings and credit societies could play an auxiliary banking role in rural areas if they were given a blanket exemption from the prohibitions of the Village Act or special permission to operate on a multi-village basis. They might attract savings that are being hidden in the villages as peasants, who are required to open savings accounts in the village savings and credit departments, will be looking for a place to save money which is not village controlled.

SCULT: A Tanzanian and African Resource

SCULT owes its modest successes to the fact that the savings and credit societies needed and wanted its services. Their leaders still believe that sharing knowledge and enthusiasm is important; they are hungry for education and training. Inspired by the ideals of Pan-African and worldwide credit union co-operation, they want to belong to an organization that links them to other credit unionists and the outside world.

With hindsight, it could be said that in making it possible for the Tanzanians to organize their league in 1964, before there were enough savings and credit societies to support a national association, overseas advice and funding made things happen too easily and too early. It might also be agreed that conditions in Tanzania dictated some other approach to the building of a savings and credit society movement—perhaps a slower and more deliberate evolution of numerous small self-funded local associations into one nationwide organization.

Governmental educational, promotional, and technical services could have substituted for SCULT, or, if the government could not afford such a program, foreign aid could have provided it through the Co-operative College, CUT, or some other existing organization. But it should also be admitted that had any of these other alternatives been attempted, the savings and credit societies might have been forced into a losing fight with the politically powerful marketing co-operatives for government assistance and subsidies, and there might not be any semblance of a league in existence today.

Similarly, if there was ever any sense to the original strategy of adopting a dues structure based on expectations of a constantly increasing member society income (as had been done in North America), it did not take account of the problems faced by the infant movement. Bookkeeping inadequacies and the weaknesses of SCULT's untrained management were compounded by governmental supervisory requirements and vacillating directions, not to mention the relatively astronomical amounts that were needed to field a staff of technicians throughout Tanzania's far-flung regions.

The Tanzanians wanted to experiment with other financing devices—investment in a building which could provide rental income, an auditing service to earn fees, a campaign to raise voluntary donations—but all of these ideas died from lack of government or donor support. In the opinion of the government supervisors and foreign advisers, these ideas were no doubt farfetched, but realistic or not they might have forced the financing issue back to the individual members of the societies, and a true, grassroots Tanzanian solution might have emerged. But all of this would have taken time, and Tanzania's savings and credit society leaders were driven by their nation's euphoric expectations of rapid changes for the better.

As the government moved ahead to decentralize its administration and to implement the new village program, it dealt a series of body blows to SCULT. At the time when the societies most needed SCULT as their spokesman to government, the league itself was faced with the question of its own survival. It seemed that the best course of action at the time was not to press for a decision by headquarters but to allow the individual societies to negotiate the terms of their continued operation with their various regional officials. The rural societies, having witnessed the closure of the marketing co-operatives, neither expected nor urged SCULT to act on their behalf. They preferred to take their chances with their local authorities.

In the tension of the times, an unfortunate arm's length relationship between the government and SCULT replaced what had been a candid and mutually supportive alliance. The government's declared policy not to abandon SCULT failed to dispel the league's apprehensions.[1] The entire atmosphere had a paralyzing effect on SCULT: elections were not held, management decisions were not implemented. SCULT lost its momentum and fell back on its foreign donor funding and support to keep itself alive.

It has taken Tanzania over sixteen years of experimentation to arrive at its own individual adaptation of the league concept it had borrowed from North America. SCULT's moderate success has proved that, with allowances for an altogether different relationship with government than was originally contemplated, the league has been effective in achieving its objectives of helping savings and credit societies band together for their mutual benefit in the areas of leadership, education, training, technical advice, and linkage to the worldwide credit union movement.

13. Selected Profiles

A Sampling of Savings and Credit Societies

We tried to visit a cross section of successful and unsuccessful savings and credit societies. The latter had disappeared, so we pieced together the fragmentary evidence of their experiences. Apparently most of them succumbed to their members' lack of interest and support. Some of them became inactive only because they lacked leadership and encouragement. Those that survived had some interesting stories to tell. Some of them had come through almost every conceivable type of setback—embezzlement, theft, fire, crop failures, loss of members transferred to other locations, loss of field of membership—and still they survived.

Before visiting any society, we met at length with the regional co-operative officer who usually introduced us to his RDD, or, if he was not available, to the district development director and to the local CCM secretary. We always showed our letters of official research clearance, and after this formality we outlined the purpose of our visit. These officials were most hospitable and forthcoming. The individual societies visited were selected by the co-operative officer in charge of the societies in his region, after he checked with his district co-operative officer.

Arusha Region

Arusha, the prosperous headquarters city of the Arusha Region, has a superb climate. It is a perfect tourist spot leading to some of the best game parks of Tanzania and always a preferred location for settlement by non-Africans. Arusha had been the headquarters for the dissolved EAC, and the EAC building complex has now become the Arusha International Conference Centre. As a small industries center, Arusha continues to be one of the more developed areas of

Tanzania. It is served by Kilimanjaro International Airport, one of Tanzania's biggest investments in tourism. The hotels, always superior, have been modernized, and the entire hotel business has expanded since our earliest visit in 1963.

In a land of scarcity, Arusha seems to have more of everything than any Tanzanian community we visited in spite of the fact that the EAC is no longer operative. Of the twelve societies registered in this region, five were active, two had become part of the PRSS, and five were dormant. We met with the officers of a number of typical savings and credit societies operating among wage earner groups in the city.

We also visited one of the early community savings and credit societies, the Usa River Savings and Credit Society. This society was organized early in 1964 at the Usa River Mission as a parish society but was now operating within three villages as a community society. It mainly served employed people, most of whom also worked their own small farm plots. The idea of a savings and credit society was originally introduced as a possible solution to the problem of getting money for farm labor and fertilizer to cultivate these farms.

The secretary/treasurer, who was part of the original group of five which formed the society, remembered the first discussions at a meeting held with Father LeClair, Mutayoba, and Jack during the time of the Tanganyika Project and welcomed us warmly. He has been the one and only secretary/treasurer of the society. His training has been limited to attendance at a one-week seminar in 1971 and another in 1974. The chairman has also served for a long time and "knows his job." The society has no problem getting members to serve on committees, and those elected perform their duties regularly and faithfully, according to the secretary. Father LeClair is now the pastor of the Usa River parish and is a member of the society, but he plays no active role in it.

Most of the society's members were employed on the mainly Indian-owned large farms and coffee plantations in the area. Some members who are government/parastatal employees have arranged for payroll deduction with the society. Most members have no source of credit other than the society.

Usa River is on the main road between the Kilimanjaro International Airport and Arusha, where the nearest banks are located. The distance has made supervision and assistance difficult for both the league representative stationed at Moshi eighty-five kilometers away and the government co-operative officer headquarted in Arusha. Thus, government supervision has been sporadic and limited to a few visits from savings and credit officers to help with the bookkeeping. There has been no audit since 1972. The SCULT representative helped the society get check-off privileges for those members who worked for the government and parastatal agencies, but he had not carried out his agreement of six months standing to help with the application to SCULT for life savings and loan protection insurance. The supervisory committee was to meet and decide on follow-up action.

The society at the time of our visit had 216 members out of a potential of 800 families. As of December, 1972, its books showed Tshs 20,935 in shares, Tshs 1,308 in deposits, and Tshs 22,857 in loans. There were no entries in the general ledger accounts after that date. The society's books were current only for the receipts and disbursements. The bank book showed Tshs 5,100/90 in a current (deposit) account. Since most members did not withdraw from their share accounts and members' share payments had been coming in regularly, the treasurer believed that the total shares were now larger than in 1972. Loans were limited to maturities of one year; interest was charged at one percent per month on the unpaid balance; and most payments were made monthly. Loans were made mostly for cultivating coffee *shambas,* both for labor and fertilizers, in amounts usually between Tshs 300 and 500. The largest loan was for Tshs 3,000.

Loan collections usually presented no problem, especially from borrowers who lived close to the society office or from those on payroll deductions. But 1977 was a bad crop year, and many members found it difficult to repay their loans. However, no loans were believed to be uncollectible. There was a problem collecting loan repayments from three members who were formerly employed by the co-operative union and lost their jobs when it closed. The government inspector had sent dunning letters to these borrowers but there had been no response and no other follow-up.

In addition to its regular loan service, the society made fertilizer loans in kind to its members and sold fertilizer to nonmembers for cash at seventy shillings per bag. Most farmers required four bags of fertilizer a year, so the credit terms were an inducement to join the society. Since the village stored its fertilizer supply in the building used by the society, eligible nonmembers were constantly aware of the availability of the society lending option. Cash fertilizer sales were conducted by the society as a service to the village which owns the building and allows the society to use it rent free.

Membership morale was high. The chairman and secretary were serving without pay and were getting good co-operation from other committeemen. The society office was open daily from

3:00 P.M. to 4:00 P.M.; the credit committee met frequently and not only approved loans but also discussed strategies for getting repayment. General membership meetings were held regularly, sometimes even twice a year. Nonmembers also attend, and efforts were made to get them to join the society while they were at the meeting. The society was continually turning down membership applications from persons outside their field of membership who could not find other sources of credit.

The society members had been looking into other activities and were considering either operating a maize mill (to compete with several mills in the area which they felt were charging too much) or getting a small piece of land to farm collectively. They had considered a co-operative consumer shop but decided they did not have a suitable location. The secretary/treasurer said that members felt an acute need for more technical advice before starting any multipurpose activity and recognized that more money would be needed for these types of investment.

The secretary of the society is also a member of the local village council and serves on the transport and building subcommittee. The village had started to build an office building and a school and was planning a house for the use of the members of the UWT. The villagers had discussed the new VRSCS, but hadn't come to any agreement on whether to initiate it. The members, meanwhile, felt secure that their society would continue to operate because it was an employee-based organization, not a village co-operative activity as defined by the law.

The society was a member of SCULT and paid dues since 1965. The secretary once attended an annual meeting of SCULT and recalled receiving good training on the duties and responsibilities of the society committees.

Dar es Salaam Region

The greatest number of savings and credit societies in Tanzania are in the three districts making up the Dar es Salaam Region. The city of Dar es Salaam has been discussed elsewhere in the text as the original capital, the largest city, the busiest port, and the railroad headquarters of the country. According to Dar es Salaam regional records as of December 30, 1977, there were thirty-seven active societies out of the fifty-three originally registered in Ilala District, twenty-one in Temeke District (status of individual societies unknown), and five (all active) in Kinondini District.

Reflecting the early emphasis on rural savings and credit societies, only seven societies were registered in this region between 1961 and 1966. With the introduction of the CUNA/AID program and the assignment of the three North American technicians stationed in Dar es Salaam, the emphasis began to shift to urban worker societies: in 1967–68, nineteen societies were organized; in 1969–71, fourteen were registered; and in 1972–74, thirty were established. With the passage of the Village Act, only one society was registered in 1975. Five more were organized in 1976, but none were listed as registered in 1977 after the passage of the Urban Wards Act.

Of the early societies, only the Polisi Savings and Credit Society registered in 1963 was still active; the three earliest community societies, Akiba Kianga (1961), Dar es Salaam (1962), and Ukutu Youth (1963) were dormant. Most of the societies registered in this region since 1967 have been among government and other employee groups.

These data are taken from three different sources (with sometimes conflicting facts): the national headquarters in Dodoma, the regional headquarters office in Dar, and SCULT files.

As an example of a national credit union operating with branches throughout the country we have selected the Polisi Savings and Credit Society. We visited one of its branch societies in Arusha as well as its central headquarters in Dar es Salaam. The society had some 7,500 members nationally, 465 of whom were members of the Arusha branch and worked in some department of the Ministry of Home Affairs.

We were officially welcomed to a meeting of the staff and board members at headquarters by the chairman of the ministry's CCM unit.

The following history was detailed to us: in 1963 a priest giving religious instruction to police officers in one of the Dar es Salaam police barracks spoke about credit unions and suggested that if the men wanted more information they should contact Mutayoba who could tell them how he organized the Dar es Salaam Savings and Credit Society. Later Mutayoba, accompanied by Bunga (who became the first secretary/treasurer and was named manager of the society in 1978) and Johanus Mweita (who became its first chairman), called on the police commander to explain that credit unions were not political organizations and to get his permission to hold a meeting at the Kilwa Road barracks to discuss credit unions. The commander approved, attended the meeting, and gave not only moral support but also one hundred shillings for the registration fee.

Some members signed up immediately and by August 24, 1963, the society, one of the earliest in the nation, was registered with 210 members.

In 1964 Jack was invited to visit the other barracks in the city to explain the credit union idea. Later that year, Bunga left the country for an extended period to attend a U.S. police training course; while in the United States he studied the credit union serving employees of the U.S. Department of Justice. Although upon his return home Bunga was at first too busy with his police job to resume his society responsibilities, by February, 1978, he had been appointed manager of the society.

It was not until 1966 that the society adopted a resolution to extend its services to ministry employees wherever they were stationed. This resolution became effective in 1969. Julius Nyakuyeye was elected chairman in that year, and he continues to serve in that capacity. He was also elected secretary of SCULT in November, 1973, and was still in that position at the date of our interview in February, 1978.

In the early years, 1964–68, some of the officials of the society took loans without following the proper procedures. When subsequently prosecuted in a court case, these officials avoided conviction on embezzling charges, but each arranged to pay back his loans: one had the loan repayment deducted from his pension fund, another continued to work for the police force and paid by monthly deduction, and the third changed jobs and got funds to repay the loan from his new employer.

In order to reestablish membership confidence after this misuse of power by the elected officials, the police commander in 1968 asked Bunga and Nyakuyeye to bring the books up to date, and the facts of their findings were published in the *Police Gazette*. From that time on, the society has been growing, but due to manpower problems in the police force and lack of staff in the society, it continued to have bookkeeping problems. In 1977 a full complement of staff, capable in finance and management, were assigned to the society and were completing the books for 1974 and 1975. By 1978 the general ledger was up to date for 1977 but not balanced with the individual members' share and loan accounts.

The manager and staff are all members of the police force and are paid by the force. Office space is provided at police headquarters. The society was just going onto a computerized check-off system which was expected to facilitate the bookkeeping in the branch offices and in central headquarters. A duplicate of an individual member's records could be transferred with him as he was moved around the county, while the control records remained at headquarters.

As of October 31, 1977, the society had shares of Tshs 1,202,008, cash in bank of Tshs 631,966, and loans outstanding of Tshs 1,607,359. The treasurer believed that when the final, year-end statement was drawn, there would be Tshs 72,000 with which to pay a dividend.

Loan service could be obtained at any hour. The main purposes for loans were housing, household welfare, education, medical treatment, or emergencies such as paying fines for traffic and other minor offenses. The largest loan of Tshs 30,000 was for a building. For loans over Tshs 15,000 applications had to be submitted three months in advance. The repayment period was up to five or six years depending on the member's shares and salary. Whenever a member was transferred, the police paymaster at the new station was immediately notified and instructed to arrange the proper payroll deductions.

As a member of SCULT the society had taken advantage of its training, consulting, and insurance services. Society management told us they were looking forward to better service, especially to more field visits in the regions, with the contemplated additional SCULT staff.

The branch societies in each region operated quite independently with a local board of directors, audit and credit committees, and a secretary and treasurer who conducted the daily business. Only three regions in the country were without branches. The chairman, secretary, and treasurer of each branch society were salaried members of the police force. At the December, 1977, general membership meeting, it was decided that each of the regional branches had the right to prepare its own financial statement and to declare a dividend. The regional branch we visited maintained its own bank account, banked its own savings, and approved its own loans. However, the headquarters society helped with large loans, which were carefully checked out at both the branch and headquarters. Each branch considered its own loan applications and checked to ascertain whether or not the applicants had adequate share security. If a loan application passed this screening, it was then forwarded to the central headquarters society which sent it to the ministry's central information bureau for a credit check. After this clearance all information was copied into the central records, and the loan was authorized.

Monthly reports of collections and expenditures were sent to headquarters from the branches. On the basis of these reports, twenty-five percent of the interest collection was retained by the central headquarters and seventy-five percent was sent back to the branch society from which it was to pay its own dividend.

Each regional branch selected two delegates, plus political advisers, to attend the annual national membership meeting where the fifteen-member national board was selected, and then that board elected its officers. The regional delegates were encouraged to bring their problems to the annual meeting for full discussion. The actions of the meetings were reported back to the regions and to the UCDD.

The Polisi Savings and Credit Society/Arusha was organized in 1971, and in 1972 the present chairman, the head mechanic for the Arusha force, took office. He has been traveling at his own expense to the various districts of the region to handle problems and promote membership. Most loans were for education, building houses, illness expenses, and traveling to the funerals of parents. In the Arusha branch (and supposedly in all regions) the member paid not only an entry fee but a life insurance fee. The society then paid all premiums for life savings and loan protection insurance.

The headquarters society had also taken on several multipurpose activities, including a *duka* manned by a separate staff which kept their own bookkeeping records but operated under the society's board of directors. The capital grant to open the shop at the barracks in 1976 came from the police commander out of a fund that had accumulated from insurance commissions. This shop operation generated enough money to enable the society to buy an Isuzu seven-ton truck, which was used to deliver the cement sold in the *duka* and was also hired out for a fee. This project was earning about Tshs 1,700 daily. Out of that income, the society was planning to buy a second lorry to work up-country.

The managers of these operations were all paid members of the police force. Another member, attached to the police repair unit, supervised repairs to the lorry.

Dodoma Region

The town of Dodoma was selected to replace Dar es Salaam as the capital of Tanzania in October, 1974. The shift is expected to be completed by 1990. By then the small, poor railroad center should have the facilities available to accommodate the mass influx of people requiring housing and government agencies requiring office space. The infrastructure to support an international center—sewage, electricity, roads, telecommunications, health services—is being established and/or substantially expanded, and a complete range of technicians is being trained.

The choice of centrally located Dodoma, approximately 479 kilometers from the coast, was also intended to stimulate economic development in this backward, resource-poor region. It was here that we met a number of experts from India who were invited by the Tanzanian government to assist with the setting up of small industries to provide the bricks, nails, screws, hinges, and other hardware needed in building the new capital. They were selected because the level of the Indian construction technology was considered more appropriate for Tanzania than the building technologies of the more highly industrialized countries.

A group of priests in the area had discovered that the soil was good for growing grapes and a substantial wine industry was being developed. The white wine was consistently good and hard to find, but the red and rosé wines, the quality of which varied considerably, were sold all over the country. The vineyards were a welcome sight in the arid, always yellow landscape around Dodoma.

The two-lane "washboard" roads leading into the city, especially from the Iringa Region to the south, were very rough and narrow and were made even more dangerous by the piles of gravel stacked to one side, hopefully to be used to resurface the roads if it did not wash away before the scarce and overused road building equipment was available for the job. The car's vibrations were violent enough to snap the ropes holding extra tires and the thick rubber bands holding jerry cans on top of the Land-Rover.

The office of the prime minister, which has as one of its functions supervision of the UCDD, was one of the first government offices to be transferred to Dodoma.

At the time of this study there were fourteen active savings and credit societies in the area, including a branch of the Polisi Savings and Credit Society, and eight dormant societies.

The first society we visited in Tanzania was the Dodoma Comworks Savings and Credit Society, serving the local employees of the Ministry of Public Works. The present chairman had been approached with the credit union idea by the local co-operatives inspector. He then presented it to his fellow workers, and the society was registered in 1967. One hundred percent of the field of membership, 350 people, belonged to the society. All their money was out in loans. The loans were small because members' salaries were small and savings were difficult to accumulate. The largest loan outstanding was for Tshs 14,000, and the woman who borrowed the money had three and a half years to repay, with interest at one percent per month on the check-off system. She had Tshs 7,825 in savings and provided two guarantors for her loan.

Members took out loans for timber and iron sheets for building houses, bicycles, household upkeep, family emergencies, and fines. A number of loans had enabled members who were victims of break-ins to replace stolen household goods quickly.

The treasurer has been paid by the society since she was hired in 1974. She received her training at three SCULT training sessions. The society paid her transportation costs to the classes plus a small amount to the league for her training. She was most anxious to get additional training in savings and credit society bookkeeping and management. She was not getting much help from the co-operative officers in the region or district. However, SCULT was assigning a fieldman to the Dodoma Region who could be helpful.

The books had not yet been audited for 1977. The last annual meeting, which almost all the members attended, was held in October, 1976, at which time a three and a half percent dividend was voted. At the year end 1977, the society had shares of Tshs 697,970/60 and loans of Tshs 524,876/85.

According to the officers, this society needed simple office machines such as a typewriter and an adding machine. Office space was furnished by the ministry at the members' workplace.

In order to get additional income to make larger loans to members, the board of the society was planning to submit a plan to the next annual meeting to build a lodging house which would be rented to provide increased income.

Kagera (West Lake) Region

The Kagera (West Lake) Region, with its regional headquarters in Bukoba, is primarily a coffee-producing area with some cattle raising as well. This has been one of Tanzania's most progressive and prosperous regions; its people are a homogeneous tribal group, the Wahaya, who have had the advantages of early missionary education. Their co-operatives, notably the Bukoba Native Co-operative Union, have been leaders in Tanzania's co-operative movement. The first African Catholic church promoters of savings and credit societies came from this region; one of the first societies to be chartered was located here; and the Kagera credit union movement has provided a number of national credit union leaders.

The RUCDO—the regional ujamaa and co-operative development officer—and his assistant, the ARUCDO, were both old friends. The RUCDO had been a co-operatives officer in Mwanza in 1963 when we first came with the Tanganyika Project. The ARUCDO had been credit union-trained in Tanzania and in the United States. Having been stationed in this region for thirteen years, he had an intimate knowledge of the activities of the societies in his region.

The climate for savings and credit societies was further enhanced by the assignment of a SCULT fieldman with a Land-Rover. Some conflicts had arisen about the use of this vehicle since the government and the fieldman were working with the same groups, and the government officers had very limited transportation.

To the date of our visit, sixty-six savings and credit societies had been registered in the region, fifty rural and sixteen urban. None had been liquidated; thirty were considered to be doing very well. The optimal period of growth was from 1969 to 1971 when government support provided both manpower and vehicles. However, the decentralization of government, the closure of marketing co-operatives, the shared border with Uganda that necessitated the support of armed forces and vigilance against smuggling, the scarcity of supplies due to the elimination of boat transportation between Kagera Region and the rest of Tanzania all had a profound effect on the once-prosperous town of Bukoba. The urban area seemed to be suffering more than the surrounding rural areas, where food was available and daily life seemed to be little changed.

We were able to visit five rural community savings and credit societies (each of which we had visited during the Tanganyika Project and CUNA/AID programs) because the regional office provided the necessary petrol, and we had the use of the SCULT jeep. We were accompanied on all visits by the ARUCDO and the league fieldman.

The Bugandika Savings and Credit Society was reached at the end of a rough mountain road, and the bus from Bukoba made the trip just once a day. We picked up the secretary-treasurer/manager at his home and went to a nearby school to hold our meeting. The manager, a charter member and long-time officer, was getting an allowance of Tshs 250 per month. He told us he kept all his books and records with him and conducted all business from his home or at the area coffee crop center where he collected members' loan repayments when the center gave out its final payment to the farmers.

The society was organized by Mutayoba in this, his own village, in July, 1964, in a meeting with about fifteen people who after much discussion agreed that a society would be a good idea.

The group met regularly thereafter, attracting more members by "preaching about the idea and working hard." As of December 31, 1964, there were 115 members with shares of Tshs 1,555 and loans to eight borrowers of Tshs 815. Thirteen years later, on December 31, 1977, the society had 238 members (out of a potential of 2,000 residents in the area), Tshs 83,090/80 in shares, and Tshs 95,399/80 in outstanding loans. Since organization, the society had made 653 loans totaling Tshs 356,546. A dividend of four and a half percent was paid in 1976. Bugandika was one of the few societies in the study to give us a current and complete financial and statistical report.

According to the manager, the progress of the society has been continuous (as has been the leadership, with some of the same committeemen serving since the first organizing meeting). The manager has submitted yearly his estimates of expense to the government, the estimates were approved promptly, and he has kept within these limits. Government inspectors have come regularly, and the books have been audited regularly. The inspectors have helped the manager keep the books, and he said he could not manage without their aid.

The society was a member of SCULT, was current in its dues payment, carried life savings and loan protection insurance, and has had claims paid under these coverages. SCULT provided the society with stationery and training seminars. The league representative stationed in the region visited them several times and assisted with problems. The manager had attended four SCULT annual meetings. He knew that much of the funding for the league was from foreign donors and felt that if the grants were stopped, it would be the end of the league because the money locally subscribed was too little to run SCULT; indeed, a cut-off of foreign funds might even cause the end of the societies themselves.

The field of membership included all the residents in the area of Bugandika encompassing seven villages, though two were really too far away to participate fully. The manager believed that the individual villages had too few members to operate a society on a single village basis.

Loans were given for whatever purposes members wanted to borrow and, on the whole, they were paid back. The society had very few bad loans and had not charged any loans off to reserves. Most loans were made to upgrade member housing; the second most popular purpose was to purchase cows to provide manure for their farms (a small cow cost Tshs 1,220 to 1,500); the third most popular purpose was to buy another piece of land (an acre of developed land cost about Tshs 30,000). Loans were also made for radios, bicycles, home furnishings, and dowries (an average dowry was Tshs 1,500). Loans were usually small—the largest given by the society was to a woman on the loan committee for Tshs 12,000 to be repaid within five years. The average loan in 1977 was approximately Tshs 1,000, and the average of all loans made since registration was Tshs 546.

The manager said that the biggest problem facing savings and credit societies now was the scarcity of government inspectors to assist them: "The government should increase the number of inspectors because there are too many societies to be serviced properly now."

Kilimanjaro Region

Moshi, the regional headquarters town, had long been a business center for the prosperous farmer-businessmen of the area around Mount Kilimanjaro. Workers (with their produce) descend, mainly by bus, to the city in the morning and return in the evening to take advantage of the comfortable and cool mountain nights. The valley in which Moshi is situated is very hot by comparison.

The Wachagga, the main tribe of the area, have been raising cash crops since colonial times; they have been among the earliest beneficiaries of the missionary educational opportunity. They also have earned an international reputation for their business aptitude. We were told that the Wachagga learned well from Asian businessmen and have taken over as aggressive entrepreneurs. As land for expansion on the mountain has disappeared, they have purchased valley land on which to raise maize and other crops to feed their dairy cattle, which in turn provide manure for fertilizer. Many farmer-businessmen arrange monthly transfers from their current bank accounts to repay savings and credit society loans. Typically they borrow to hire labor to prune the coffee trees and cultivate the land, to rent tractors, and to expand their activities throughout the country.

The Moshi market had been enlarged and remodeled; most of the stalls were under cover, and the entire market was made secure by an encircling fence. The market has served as the center of commercial activity, surrounded by small shops, bars, and eating places. The new YMCA hotel had become a gathering place for travelers from around the world who come to climb Mount Kilimanjaro (5895 meters), the highest peak in Africa. A new international teaching hospital, funded primarily by Lutherans (especially from Germany), had brought in an influx of non-African doctors. An international (privately funded) school was also operating in Moshi.

The few Asian-owned shops remaining in Moshi were no longer filled with goods as they were in the early 1960s. But the Moshi Consumers Co-operative store, which opened in the 1960s with limited stock, now had several branches, each with full shelves though the variety of goods for sale was limited.

There were nineteen active savings and credit societies in the region. One former society had lost its field of membership and fifteen others were dormant—these were mainly community savings and credit societies. However a substantial number of societies continued to flourish in the area and were serving members living in multiple villages.

The regional ujamaa and co-operative office had a savings and credit specialist, but his time was being spent developing and supervising the VRSCS. All assistance to the area savings and credit societies, including auditing, was being left to the SCULT fieldman assigned to the Moshi and Arusha regions. The fieldman was given office space and clerical services in the regional offices, but his motorcycle, salary, and other expenses were paid for by SCULT. He was constantly beset by conflicting demands on his time.

In Moshi itself there were two active community savings and credit societies as well as societies among employee groups. The Moshi Savings and Credit Society served residents of the area whether or not they were on check-off. The Kibo Savings and Credit Society served area residents and government employees who were on check-off. Originally this society was organized to serve the employees of the Lutheran Church of Northern Tanzania who were mainly teachers, but when the government took over all schools in the country, the field of membership was changed.

Before meeting with the manager of the society, we paid our respects to the general secretary of the Lutheran Church of Northern Tanzania who was also serving as Kilimanjaro regional chairman of the CCM. As a party chief, he told us he knew that the CCM was behind workers' savings and credit societies and purposely did not dissolve them with all the other primary societies. It was a conscious decision.

The original Lutheran society was started in 1967 among church employees and had offices in the old church. By 1970 there were 1,200 members and the late Bishop Stefan Moshi felt the society could no longer be managed properly by volunteers. New offices were assigned, and the former volunteer manager, who had also served as education secretary to the church, became the paid manager of the society and the church's promoter of societies.

In 1971 the Lutheran World Federation gave a five-year grant to this society to cover the manager's salary, car, and maintenance. (Two other society employees were being paid by the society itself.) The grant was then extended two years to September, 1978. The federation also paid for the manager's three-month study trip in 1975 to attend the Nineteenth Co-operative Education and Management Seminar at the University of Wisconsin Co-operative Extension Program.

This grant gave rise to bitter feelings among the leaders of other SCULT members who had originally understood that the money would be given to SCULT, which would supervise its distribution. The grant also served to alienate those groups in the area under the influence of the Lutheran church from the other local members of SCULT, which at this time had a working chapter in Moshi. When the manager (who had served as SCULT secretary from 1968 to 1971) was replaced on the chapter and SCULT boards, chapter activity in this region was effectively paralyzed, even though the chairman of SCULT came from a society in this region.

Kibo Savings and Credit Society, according to the manager, did not feel that SCULT had any services the society could use. Even its audit fees were more expensive than the subsidized government audit. Since the league was started from the top, in his view, the individual societies have had no input toward the directions of the program. He felt that if external funds should dry up, a new league of a different type would be formed from the grass roots: "Only Tanzanians can solve problems in Tanzania." He thought regional chapters with a single employee, paid by the societies in the region to supervise services, would be a better idea.

The society also did not feel it needed the league insurance programs because it was self-insured through reserves for bad debts. Loans were given only with security: Tshs 650 in shares would secure a loan of Tshs 1,000 to 3,000; Tshs 1,500 in shares would secure a loan of Tshs 5,000—the maximum allowed to be given by savings and credit society staff. The credit committee had to approve loans above Tshs 5,000. The maximum loan it permitted was Tshs 10,000, and this was usually disbursed in two installments if the loan was for house building. Borrowers had twenty months to repay, and collection difficulty occurred only if the member was fired from his job. Other loan purposes were for marriage expenses, school fees, medical fees, and farming. Every member in the society was required to save Tshs 60 per month.

Approximately seventy-five percent of the members attended the annual meeting, in 1973, and in 1974 Tshs 6,000 were placed in the budget to provide entertainment at the next annual meeting. The society paid a four percent dividend annually but had never paid a patronage refund.

The society had almost three thousand members. Current records for the year end 1977 were not available in February, 1978, because the books were out of the office being audited. We were told, however, that as of January 31, 1976, the society had shares of Tshs 1,363,561, outstanding loans of Tshs 1,473,646, cash on hand of Tshs 78,926, fixed deposits of Tshs 11,025, reserves of Tshs 38,785, undivided earnings of Tshs 54,061, an educational fund of Tshs 28,668, and a building fund of Tshs 66,167. The society planned to build a Tshs 3,000,000 complex starting in September, 1978. The management was trying to get a donation of Tshs 100 from each member, a grant from the Lutheran church, and a loan from the THB for the building.

Mara Region

Musoma, headquarters of the Mara Region, is a small, clean, rural town located on the shores of Lake Victoria about 238 kilometers north of Mwanza. Most supplies had to be brought in by twenty-four railroad cars that were filled and locked at Dar es Salaam and transported by train to Mwanza, where they were loaded on barges for the rest of their trip to Musoma. The Mwanza-Musoma road, which for some distance borders Serengeti National Park, was excellent at the Mwanza end where it serviced the new industrial development sites and poor at the Musoma end, except for the section of road from Musoma to President Nyerere's home village of Butiama. Though remote, Musoma had an active Lions Club, the majority of whose members were Asian businessmen. Otherwise, there were very few foreigners living or working in the area.

The economy of the Mara Region had been dependent on cattle (much of it being rustled across the nearby Kenya border, we were told), some fishing, and some cotton. The cattle raisers were very hesitant to turn their cattle into cash. They did not usually sell their cows, but if necessary they could get Tshs 1,000 for a steer to buy house materials such as timber, nails, and cement. It had been difficult to coordinate farming (farms averaged four acres) and cattle raising which needed so much more land. However, farm income in the area doubled as production rose with the use of fertilizers, insecticides, and oxen-pulled plows—developments resulting from government assistance, according to our government escort.

In Musoma we found evidence of an emerging network of persons who, having benefited from credit union education and services in Dar es Salaam, Dodoma, and elsewhere, were carrying on the idea in this northernmost area. In fact, at central headquarters in Dodoma, the officer acting for the UCDD commissioner had told us that he himself had been responsible for organizing the society of government employees in Musoma.

In this region there were seven active and nine dormant savings and credit societies.

The Mara Teachers Savings and Credit Society was started in 1962 by six teachers who were sent from Nyegina to Nyegezi STC to learn about credit unions on scholarship from Father Robinson, a U.S. Maryknoll missionary, then education secretary of the Musoma diocese. The society when we visited had about 360 active members. Most of them belonged in order to save for the future; they tended to take out only small loans. Tshs 5,000 for three years was the largest loan granted; the average was Tshs 3,500. The loans were usually either for fees to private secondary schools for their children or for building houses in their home villages.

The offices of the society were in a government primary school. An acting treasurer and a full-time typist, both employed by the society, maintained business hours every weekday and Saturday from 7:30 A.M. to 12:30 P.M.

The society had Tshs 428,635 in shares; loans outstanding of Tshs 344,926; a fixed deposit with NBC of Tshs 50,000; Tshs 50,000 invested in the THB. The members were saving regularly from Tshs 10 to 100 per month. Because the society had more than enough money to lend, it was not looking for more income-producing activities. The society's problem was to get the money "out."

The society did not usually lend more than twice a member's savings, but this limit could be adjusted if the board of directors felt the member was trustworthy. The society was on check-off and has had little trouble collecting on loans except from teachers who had been transferred out of the region. Such members were expected to refinance their loans with Compower, the national savings and credit society serving the education ministry and five others.

The Mara teachers' society first started to pay a dividend in 1974–75. The district co-operative officer, who is allowed to do the audit, takes the society books for only two or three days so there is no need to create new books on expensive additional stationery.

In the towns, we were told, many of the teachers were women who were married to men who worked in the town; in the villages most of the teachers were men. The standard of living of teachers had improved since independence and could be seen in their homes and furnishings. Inflation was a real problem, especially for townspeople, as was the acute scarcity of such newly introduced—and highly prized—items as refined sugar and wheat flour. Kerosene stoves, which replaced charcoal ovens, had become everyday necessities, and kerosene was both expensive and difficult to get.

Mbeya Region

Mbeya Region in southern Tanzania is large and diverse. It encompasses very productive agricultural areas with high concentrations of population (in the southern highlands) and very poor, arid areas with sparse population.

Credit union activity in this region, other than missionary endeavors, did not get much attention until 1969 when Mwasha was transferred to the headquarters city, Mbeya, from Dar es Salaam where he had been serving as chief co-operative officer in charge of savings and credit. As the regional co-operative officer, he urged the marketing societies holding member deposits to encourage savers to form savings and credit societies as separate entities operating alongside the marketing societies. At that time several marketing societies were holding up to Tshs 60,000 in idle money. Mwasha was opposed to savings and credit becoming a multipurpose activity of the marketing societies until proper model bylaws protecting the intents and purposes of the savings and credit function could be drawn. Eventually there were fourteen savings and credit societies registered in the Mbeya Region, of which six were active at the time of our visit.

The Tukuyu District of the Mbeya Region has been one of Tanzania's most fertile areas with good rainfall. Mountains cresting at 2961 meters contrast sharply with the low, hot rice fields near Lake Nyasa. Much of the land was formerly farmed by German settlers. The area has been thickly populated and closely cultivated; a good portion of it has been set aside as national forest land, leaving little if any available for new farming. Everything seemed to grow well here, including bananas, coffee, tea, maize, potatoes, and avocados. A farmer could easily get cash for his produce and "always had at least twenty shillings in his pocket," we were told.

Tukuyu, the district headquarters town, was large, and the

farmers in the vicinity did not want it to grow any more because it would use up valuable farm land. The Nyakyusa, a major tribe of this area, along with the Wahaya of the Kagera Region and the Wachagga of the Kilimanjaro Region, benefited disproportionately in comparison to the rest of Tanzania in gaining the educational advantages of early mission schooling. These areas which were the most fertile were also the first to be developed by foreigners.

Apparently savings and credit societies were never organized here because the farmers were prosperous enough to be able to use the commercial banks and the Tanzania Rural Development Bank (TRDB) for credit. Payments for tea had always been paid directly to the farmer's individual account with NBC or one of its predecessor banks; the Tanzania Coffee Authority paid the farmer directly. Loans (presumably from the NBC or TRDB) were for building materials for houses (the average loan was Tshs 500), for salaries of workers to do the building, for purchasing ox plows for cultivation (average loan, Tshs 300), and for fertilizer, bicycles, motorbikes, and weed killers (used especially around the tea plants).

The Upimaji Co-operative Savings and Credit Society was originally organized to serve only the employees of the office of surveys in Mbeya. It was soon found that a potential membership of 60 was too small to do business, so, in February, 1974, the bylaws were changed to allow any of the more than 2,000 civil servants working under the Mbeya RDD to join. By January, 1978, there were 205 members.

The volunteer treasurer who had been serving the society for two years was given special training at the Co-operative College. He had learned about savings and credit societies at a Catholic mission, and his father was a member of a society in Bukoba.

Cited as the biggest problem was the lack of enough funds for lending. The society had never paid a divdend but was expecting to declare one at the annual meeting scheduled for the end of January, 1978, upon completion of the annual audit.

The society was lending up to twice the member's shares at one percent per month interest. Loans of less than Tshs 500 were expected to be repaid at the rate of Tshs 50 per month; if over Tshs 500, at Tshs 100 per month. Payroll deduction was available to members through the computer in Dar es Salaam serving all civil servants. With the approval of the RDD, transferred employees could arrange to continue their payroll deduction payments to the society.

The treasurer had attended SCULT annual meetings, and the society was using SCULT stationery and carrying life savings and loan protection insurances. SCULT dues were scheduled for payment by January 31, 1978. The treasurer felt that SCULT's obligations to assist member societies in the region were being carried out by the government officers, and this would probably continue until SCULT could assign a fieldman. The major government weakness mentioned was the noncurrent and erratic audit program.

Mwanza Region

Mwanza, the headquarters city of the Mwanza Region, is strategically located on the shores of Lake Victoria in the heart of a prosperous cotton-producing area. The city has historically been a trading center, with access by train to the eastern part of the country and by boat to the rich coffee-growing area of the Kagera Region as well as to Uganda and Kenya. However, Kenya, as a result of its many differences with Tanzania in 1976, seized the boats that had been jointly owned by the three East African countries and kept them in its port of Kisumu until May 29, 1978, when they were returned to dock at their home port of Mwanza once more. Mwanza has become an industrial and railroad center with a number of substantial and growing industries such as textiles, boat building, fishnet production, metal box construction, and a large electricity generating facility.

Eighteen savings and credit societies had been registered in the Mwanza Region, of which eleven remained active. The co-operative officer in charge of savings and credit societies was working with an additional eight groups interested in forming societies.

This area has had experience with marketing co-operatives since colonial times; it was also the area in which were centered the first Canadian and U.S. efforts to help introduce the credit union idea.

The Nyanza Savings and Credit Society organized among employees of the once-powerful VFCU, had survived the VFCU's dissolution by government and a series of its own major catastrophes. In 1966 the secretary embezzled Tshs 5,000 and the members of the board, Tshs 40,000. They were removed from office. In 1969 a special meeting replaced the officers of the society, including the secretary/treasurer, who had taken loans and not repaid them. In 1975 the society was reduced from serving members in three regions to serving members in a single region and had to pay off the shares to the members transferred out of their field of membership. In May, 1976, the union that had been their "employer" was dissolved, and finally, in the same year, the society's books were destroyed in a fire and had to be completely reconstructed on the basis of members' passbooks (with help from SCULT's stabilization fund).

Despite such disasters, the current secretary/treasurer and members of the board were able to greet us with the following speech:

> We, the committeemen of Nyanza Savings and Credit Society, Mwanza, are heartily grateful for your visit for you have made a pretty long safari visiting our fellow members who have got a similar society.
>
> Secondly, we are so happy for your coming to see our progress, you as founders of the credit unions. Till now we are following and teaching the same ideas to our fellow members.
>
> This credit union was started in the year 1964, spreading in other two regions, Shinyanga and Mara. The society so far has 1,030 members with total shares of Tshs 2,500,000, and up to now we have managed to give a maximum loan of Tshs 22,000 and a minimum loan of Tshs 1,000.
>
> We are planning for a project of building a guest house, an office, and a store for building materials like cement, corrugated iron sheets, wire nails, and timbers for the members to lend.
>
> As soon as we succeed with these projects then we hope to indulge in the following: one, to buy a lorry for transporting members' building materials, two, to buy a milling and grinding machine. In short these are our plans.

The field of membership has been limited to employees of the Tanzania Cotton Authority and the Regional Trading Company within the Mwanza Region.

Up to 1978 the society had never been able to pay a dividend; in 1978 they expected to have a surplus of about Tshs 10,000 to enable them to declare a dividend. They managed to make enough loans and collect enough interest to help recoup their Tshs 45,000 loss of 1966, which was also partially offset by a recovery of Tshs 7,000 through court action.

Loans were of substantial size by Tanzanian standards, with the minimum loan of Tshs 1,000 being well above the minimum of the majority of Tanzania societies. The largest loans were for house building; big loans were also made for dowries ranging from Tshs 2,500 to Tshs 6,000. Other loans were for school fees and family emergencies. Loans for house building materials were often given in kind from the society's purchases of such materials in large, bulk quantities. The society made loans up to twice a member's shares, to be repaid within three years. All members were on the check-off system.

This society was a member of SCULT, carried life savings and loan protection insurances, and bought stationery from the league. It has regularly sent delegates to the SCULT general meetings, including the last meeting in 1977 in Morogoro, and it was looking forward to electing a new board of directors for SCULT as soon as the government made its recommendations on representation from urban and rural societies. The society committee members wanted to be represented in SCULT as an urban society.

The Nyanza Savings and Credit Society attributed its success in continuing and expanding its operations to the continued interest of the RUCDO in charge of savings and credit societies in the region.

Shinyanga Region

This is a sparsely populated cotton and cattle raising region which has not enjoyed the prosperity of Mwanza, its neighboring region, mainly because there had never been any colonial inputs in Shinyanga, and for many years it was administered as a district of the Mwanza Region. All the major trading was done in Mwanza, 163 kilometers to the north.

Shinyanga was without adequate roads, sewage, and housing—a very poor town with even its market area looking dirty and neglected. The biggest building, which may become the government's regional headquarters office, was the vacant, relatively new, and imposing former home of the dismantled Shinyanga Native Co-operative Union. We saw more bicycles in use here than anywhere else in our travels in the countryside.

The main Dar es Salaam-Mwanza railroad line was just across the road from the new railroad hotel, which replaced the Diamond Field Hotel we knew in 1963. However, there was not enough water pressure to serve the second- and third-floor rooms, and so water was brought up by the bucketful. As in the other railroad hotels in which we stayed, this was the main gathering place for the local populace because it had the best, and sometimes the only, beer in town.

The RUCDO, himself a savings and credit society member and booster, spent several hours of off-duty time with us along with his assistant, who had taken a nine-month community development course at Missouri State University, and with the UCDO in charge of savings and credit societies. This latter officer had been interested in savings and credit societies since his diploma course at the Co-operative College in 1970. For two years prior to his coming to the Shinyanga Region, no one had been assigned there to supervise and to audit society books.

The Shinyanga Savings and Credit Society, one of those audited prior to his coming to Shinyanga, was still awaiting the return of its books and records from final review in Dodoma. The UCDO was using the bookkeeping training manual developed under the CUNA/AID program to assist him in completing his current audits of other societies. But, reflecting the acute problem of limited numbers of trained officers, he was being promoted and transferred to central headquarters at the time we left Tanzania—before being able to complete the audits.

Of seven registered societies in the Shinyanga Region, only four were still active. Two new ones were in the process of being organized. The society serving the employees of the Mwadui Diamond Mines was one of the largest societies in Tanzania. In order to meet with the board of directors and members of this society, the Shinyanga RUCDO had to get clearances for us from Williamson Diamond Mines, Ltd., to enter and stay at the compound.

Mwadui Mines Savings and Credit Society served the employees of Williamson Diamond Mines living at Mwadui. It was registered in October, 1966, as the hundredth savings and credit society in Tanzania. Its original chairman, Paul Ibrahim, was still serving in that capacity. The idea was brought to Ibrahim, the town manager of Mwadui, by his personal secretary who had attended Jack's lecture on credit unions at Kivukoni College, the political education school for adults in Dar es Salaam. The society had many problems in the beginning: first in getting members to join and then in collecting the loans. The society began to grow only after the company offered payroll deduction services in 1971.

The society employed two full-time secretaries to serve the 1,081 members (out of a field of membership of 2,000 employees who support about 14,000 dependents). The board of directors, we were told, met regularly to handle the business of the society, and the treasurer received an honorarium. The chairman, members of the board, and credit and supervisory committee (which included members from management personnel, especially the accounts department), were active in the day-to-day running of the society, assisting the secretaries in collecting cash payments, disbursing funds and balancing the books. The employer provided generous office space and office equipment, including a safe.

Since the books were in the regional headquarters being audited, we were only able to verify that the shares at the last audit (1976) amounted to Tshs 2,225,178. Presumably, the society paid both a dividend and a patronage refund in 1977. We were told that as of July 31, 1977, the society had shares of Tshs 2,205,869/05, Tshs 800,000 in fixed deposits at NBC, and a cash balance of Tshs 39,527/40. A two and a half to five percent dividend was expected in 1978 in addition to a patronage dividend of twelve percent. How to use their remaining surplus funds was a problem.

In this society no one could borrow more than twice his shareholdings nor contract for more than one-quarter of his gross salary per month to be deducted for repayment of the loan. Loans were to be repaid within thirty months, and a one percent fine was imposed for late repayment. The largest single loan given was for Tshs 25,000 to purchase a car. Seventy-five percent of all loans were for purchasing materials and employing labor to build retirement homes on plots outside the Mwadui compound. (When a worker was no longer employed, he had to leave the compound.) A decent, small, three-bedroom house cost from Tshs 100,000 to 150,000. Other loans were for bicycles, education, cultivation of home farms, hospital fees for relatives, the purchase of farms (if they could be found to buy at Tshs 6,000 to 8,000), and domestic purposes. Members also took individual loans to participate in other co-operative activities such as a transportation system. The average loan was Tshs 3,000 to 5,000. One member borrowed Tshs 24,000 to build a home during his work holiday and was killed in a car accident on the way. All the money was recovered because the society carried both life savings and loan protection insurance.

The society had been a member of SCULT but was withholding dues because the society's management was dissatisfied with the league's performance and felt it offered no technical help or other services of value to the society. Even the various insurances, they believed, could be purchased directly. Whatever assistance the society needed had come from the local government co-operative officers. Therefore, the high league dues (since the society is large) and the SCULT bookkeeping forms seemed an unnecessary expense, especially since the stationery took from three to four months to arrive. The society was printing its own stationery instead. It had offered to become a center for distribution of stationery for SCULT, but refused to pay the league the required Tshs 5,000 advance.

For Tanzanians who had lived elsewhere before coming to Mwadui, this was indeed the model town it was meant to be when built by Dr. John T. Williamson, the Canadian who found the diamonds here and ran the mine until his death in 1958. The lowest-paid mine digger earned Tshs 310 per month, but with the "perks" that came from living within the township where health care, housing, subsidized food, entertainment (workers' clubs), and schooling were provided, this equaled about Tshs 1,000 earned on the outside. However, the young people who had known only compound living yearned for the excitement of a free, open living and working situation.

No new jobs were opening up as the company continued to ration production to extend the life of the mine as long as possible. The rock-locked diamonds available were not gem quality, but the mine was making money because of the rise in the price of industrial diamonds.

Part IV

Research Study in Kenya

14. The Social Milieu

We flew to Nairobi from Dar es Salaam by way of Lusaka, Zambia, because there was no way to get across the Tanzania-Kenya border unless one had special Tanzania police permission, reserved for health and/or family emergencies. We remembered earlier times when we used to drive at will among the East African countries. There was a common currency then, and no passes or visas were needed.

Modern Nairobi had spread out in every direction, including up. The world-famous Kenyatta Conference Centre dominated the city's soaring skyline. Factories were seen on the outskirts of the city, and a new international airport was in service. The streets were filled with private autos (many of them luxury models), taxis, buses, trucks—all driven by Africans. In the 1960s only non-Africans would have been seen driving private cars, unless the vehicle had a hired, uniformed driver.

At the hotel we were welcomed by the owners whom we had known before Kenya's independence and by many staff members who had remained in the hotel's employ throughout the years. The front office was manned by Kenyans; the operating manager was Kenyan; and a goodly portion of the guests were African—a marked change from our earliest visits. During the weekends many local people came for tea to the beautiful hotel gardens where Asian, African, and European children played together on the equipment provided by the hotel.

Though we were told of purse snatching by one woman visitor who had been knocked down and injured while shopping in Nairobi and of the theft of a friend's wallet while he was in the park, we had no such bad experiences walking to town from the hotel. We were approached, as we had been years ago, by the young boys known as "parking boys"—children without families—who lived in the city and survived on money they conned by offering to watch your car while it was parked in town. Since there were many stories circulating about car thefts and about autos being stripped, these boys were seldom turned down.

A schoolteacher described Kenyan society as divided into the rich and poor, with no middle class. Much ostentatious wealth was displayed while the slums were so located that they were not evident to the tourists. Nairobi, the magnet city, still lured Kenyans from the countryside to find jobs which often proved nonexistent. The lives of the unemployed sharply contrasted with those of the government officials, company employees, international agency representatives, tourists, or factory workers who could afford the vast array of goods for sale in the many thriving shops. There were no scarcities of foodstuffs or fabrics, autos or artworks, hotel rooms or restaurants in Nairobi.

One of the main national events while we were in the city was the Kenya Safari, a cross-country race for beefed-up stock cars. This race had formerly been the East African Safari with three loops—through Tanzania, Uganda, and Kenya—on the roughest possible roads. The 1978 safari started and ended at the Kenyatta Centre; thousands of people of all ages and economic classes gathered to watch the winning cars come in. The dream, of course, was to have a team of native Kenyan drivers win, and a number of such teams were being sponsored by local businesses to meet the challenge of the professional racing drivers from around the world who have continued to participate.

Nairobi, known as the "jet set conference capital of the world," was offering at comparatively reasonable prices all the amenities of the world's great cities, plus easy access to some of Africa's great game parks. The horse racetrack just outside the city was providing popular entertainment for native Kenyans as well as for the international set; there were also a number of gambling casinos operating. The latest movies from around the world were being shown in the cinemas for very modest prices, usually Kshs 7/50 or less.

African art from all over the continent was being displayed and sold; Tanzanian Makonde wood carvings and batiks by Ugandan artists were featured. Jewelry of gold, silver, and precious stones was plentiful, but ivory and other game trophy items were no longer available. While we were in Kenya the government closed all shops dealing exclusively in these items and confiscated the stock that remained after the deadline date, which had been announced three months before. This action was taken to save the dwindling herds of elephants and other animals that were being decimated by uncontrollable poaching in the national game parks.

There was much talk in Nairobi among the Kenyans, the non-African citizens, and the foreigners with whom we visited about the widespread corruption in the country, especially at top levels of the society, but there did not seem to be any concerted drive to eliminate it. The people, rather, seemed sold on the idea that money would solve all problems—individual and countrywide—and seemed resigned to the prevalent level of corruption. We ourselves were never exposed to it.

The farther west we got from Nairobi, the less frenetic the existence of the people, the friendlier they became, the more conscious they seemed of group goals, and the more realistic they were in terms of the living standards they could achieve through their own industry. Goods were available for sale wherever we went, but there were few displays of strictly luxury items.

Kisumu, the provincial headquarters of the Nyanza Province, was growing with a new luxury tourists' hotel, a remodeled, upgraded, businessmen's hotel for traveling representatives of national and international companies and government officials not stationed permanently in the area, and several modest local hotels. There were also a number of good-sized restaurants available other than at the hotels. There were clothing shops, book shops, and furniture shops. One women's wear store had an attractive window display featuring smartly styled, locally made clothes against background pictures, sketched by a local artist, of Kenya Safari cars. All this commercial activity contrasted with the sleepy little town we had first known in the early 1960s.

We attended a benefit given by the Inner Wheel Club (the women's circle of Rotary International) at which tickets sold for Kshs 50 to 300 (US $6.25 to $37.50). Most of the women running the benefit were Asian, leading us to believe that much of the business in Kisumu was still being run by Asians who may have become Kenyan citizens. Most of the audience were Asian with a sprinkling of Africans and Europeans. The performance of an Asian corps de ballet brought from Nairobi was opened by the African mayor of Kisumu. The tickets, donated by a retail store, advertised the store as the authorized dealer for Akai, Aiwa, and Kenwood hi-fi equipment, the sole distributor for Black & Decker power tools, and also retailer of car supplies, general home appliances, and Lego toys.

Traveling to Kisumu by car on paved two-lane highways, we passed through the Kisii area of tea estates, a most beautiful sight—miles and miles of green tea plants. Good roads persisted on our return trip through the Kenyan sugarcane plantations. Roads have been an important part of Kenya's development effort and have funneled the crops grown in the countryside into the population centers.

We then traveled east from Nairobi to Mombasa by train, an overnight trip. Our European-type, vintage cabin was comfortable with rented, fresh bedding. Full meals were served in the dining car and drinks in the cabins.

Mombasa, the international trading post and the main city serving the resort developments to the north and south along the Indian Ocean coast, has been growing steadily. According to the hotel workers we interviewed, the resort hotels did not stimulate the local economy as much as had been hoped for. Most of the travelers (mainly German and Scandinavian) came on packaged tours paid for at home. With everything provided for them in the trip price, they did not spend money locally. They were poor tippers, did not buy local goods and souvenirs, did not take sightseeing trips, and spent most of their time on the beach or eating at the hotel. Prostitution flourished around the hotel area. During the off-season for tourists, an intensive campaign was underway to entice Kenyans with special tours and reduced rates.

Mombasa reflected the abiding Arab influence of the early traders and residents. Most of the new building was on the shoreline so that the city remained much as we remembered it from our earliest visits—narrow streets crowded with all kinds of small shops and street vendors of native handicrafts.

Although women were active in the job market, especially in the larger cities, their traditional farm labor role had remained relatively unchanged in the countryside. Many male Kenyans who are city residents have at least two wives, one working the family farm and the other living with them in the city. Women owned many businesses and shops in Nairobi, following the example of Mama Ngina, the widow of President Kenyatta. A number of handicraft co-operatives exclusively for women were also being developed in the up-country areas.

A sight sometimes commented upon disapprovingly by our government and KUSCCO escorts in the rural areas were women seen riding bicycles and driving motorcycles. Women throughout the country seemed to prefer westernized dress to wearing the more colorful *khangas*. In Nairobi there were shops catering to tourists which featured stylish dresses made from locally designed cloth.

After the easy informality of the Tanzanians, we found the Kenyans much more formal in their relationship with us. Officers of the various institutions whom we wanted to interview would not see us unless we had a letter of introduction or were brought in personally by someone well known to them. Savings and credit society people seemed to take longer to relax in their conversations with us. Even former colleagues seemed cautious and security conscious. The relationships of the society officials with their government cooperative officers were very correct and reserved; every visit, interview, and document had to be cleared according to the government hierarchy. We were unable to visit as many institutions and societies as we had set aside time for because our KUSCCO hosts and the government officials upon whose assistance we depended told us they were under great pressures to keep up with the demands of their everyday work. These same people were also being called upon to assist in preparations for the ACOSCA Tenth Anniversary Meeting, which was to be held in Nairobi in August, 1978.

15. Research Study Findings

Statistics

Data were becoming available in Kenya although few reports had been published by the government or KUSCCO. Generally good transportation, communications, and other infrastructure were in place so that government inspectors, league fieldmen, and officers of savings and credit societies could be in contact to obtain statistical information. Societies were encouraged to hire trained staff to keep their books and records. KUSCCO was also assisting the smaller societies with a centralized bookkeeping service which was functioning, in its beginning stages, at several locations throughout the country.

Government supervision was highly centralized. A specialized staff in the Ministry of Co-operative Development, working in headquarters and provincial offices, were making all-out efforts to collect reliable data on which to base planning and programming for the ministry.

Notwithstanding these positive factors, the statistics available from the central headquarters contained many estimated figures, and could not be considered totally reliable because audits of some of the societies were as much as four years behind schedule, year-end statements from some societies had never been received, and the books of many societies were not up-to-date (see the table on page 171).

Scope of the Study

The study was conducted in five provinces where most of the savings and credit societies were operating. Selection of the eighteen societies visited was made by the senior co-operative development officer in charge of savings and credit societies in consultation with the manager of KUSCCO. Appointments were made on our behalf through the provincial and district officers.

We met with ministry officials and staff in Nairobi, provincial and district officers assigned to savings and credit societies, and with the staff of the KUSCCO head office (Nairobi) and its branch office in Mombasa. We talked with staff members of the Co-operative College, the Co-operative Bank, the KNFC, the research departments of several banks, building society officials, and University of Nairobi-Institute for Development Studies professors; a cross-section of Kenya workers, farmers, businessmen, and teachers; and staff members of ACOSCA and foreign aid organizations and other international organizations assisting directly or indirectly with the Kenyan savings and credit co-operatives program.

The senior co-operative officer also arranged for us to visit three co-operative marketing unions that had various savings and credit programs: Co-operative Production Credit Scheme (CPCS), Smallholder Production Services and Credit Program (SPSCP), Farm Inputs Supply Scheme (FISS), and Integrated Agricultural Development Program (IADP). This gave us some understanding of other types of credit assistance available to farmers.

Six of the societies we studied operated nationwide, serving government and company employees either directly from the home office or through local branches; eight served workers in local industries or local government; two served sugar plantation workers; and two were rural community savings and credit societies.

The societies studied ranged in asset size from Kshs 25,592 to over Kshs 20 million. The number of members ranged from 42 to 15,128; all but two societies reported growing memberships. The ratio of actual to potential membership was ten to ninety-four percent; half of the societies covered forty-nine percent or more of their membership potential.

Thirteen of the societies we visited were registered before 1972 and reported getting their inspiration from church workers, co-operative officers, trade union officers, members of other societies, management staff, and non-African advisers. For the five registered after 1972, promotion was initiated by company or government managers, KUSSCO, co-operative officers and, in one district, its member of Parliament.

Organization and Registration Policy

Kenya has had a clear-cut organization and registration policy favoring salaried worker savings and credit societies since 1966, but it was first enunciated in the 1970 *Sessional Paper No. 8*, titled "Co-operative Development Policy for Kenya":

> The encouragement of thrift among the salaried community and the accumulation of saving through savings and credit co-operatives can make a significant contribution towards providing local development capital and thereby reduce the need for borrowings from outside the country. Also, these societies provide soft consumer loans to members and help to train them in the basic principles of money and its proper use. The current country-wide programme for the promotion of savings and credit societies among the salaried communities in both the public and private sectors is now being given priority over most other aspects of co-operative development.

Savings and credit societies have become an accepted, preferred, and acclaimed source of credit for urban workers, but not for rural dwellers. Worker-based societies offered government supervisors relatively easy accessibility (plus the operational advantages of steady income and payroll deductions) as compared with the community-type societies which could function in rural areas. These community societies were reputed to take more time to promote, to require greater organizational effort, and to demand more advanced management. The co-operative officers trained in North America were exposed mostly to worker credit unions, which predominate in the United States and Canada. Also, the government's choice of the marketing co-ops as the preferred facilities for co-operative agricultural credit and the Nordic Project input into the development of banking sections for co-operative marketing unions were part of a strategy to prevent rural savings and credit society development. This plan would thus prevent the duplication of services or the competition among farmers seeking credit that might weaken the marketing co-ops.

The first nationwide society, CODEPT Staff Co-operative Savings and Credit Society, was organized in 1969 by the staff of the Ministry of Co-operative Development whose employees, including those in the CDD, were anxious for hands-on experience in order to understand and be prepared to cope with the problems of savings and credit society operation, management, and development. By the early 1970s the government staff were approaching personnel managers of the large businesses, shop stewards of labor unions, and other members of government ministries, urging them to consider credit union services for their employees and members.

The twin-engined promotional drive by government and KUSCCO has proved eminently successful. Unsolicited interest in savings and credit societies also stimulated registration activity. In the eight-year period between 1964 and 1972, 101 societies were registered, while in the next five-year period from 1972 to 1977, 347 were registered, most of them in Kenya's increasingly industrialized urban areas. Nairobi alone produced over 150 applications in 1977, of which only 49 were approved because the CDD did not have the supervisory capacity to handle the large influx of newly registered societies (almost one hundred annually for the past several years). The department's problems were further aggravated by high staff turnover and lack of adequate transportation for staff. Nor was KUSCCO able to provide enough fieldmen to do the necessary promotion and training of the new societies—tasks assigned to it by government.

In 1971 nationwide government workers' societies were given a big boost when the treasury and the director of personnel management in the Office of the President issued instructions and letters encouraging civil servants to participate in the savings and credit societies. Nationwide societies began serving the government ministries and a number of the largest companies in the private sector. The officials of Harambee Co-operative Savings and Credit Society (serving workers in the Office of the President) were the first to negotiate successfully for full payroll deduction facilities for shares and loans.

Asset and membership growth, which had been generally strong, became explosive in the nationwide societies in the years 1972 to 1977. As a group they almost constituted a separate industry, encountering problems of membership control, management, and finance of altogether different dimensions than those of the other societies.

This growth reflected the individualistic emphasis of Kenya's economic policies, as expressed by the minister for finance and economic planning, Mwai Kibaki, at a conference in December, 1977. He stated that the greater social goal must be the sum total of the goals of the individuals of the society; that Kenya would not pursue a policy of social justice at the expense of individual freedom; and that income equality was not a goal because "there is no way economists can prove that a more equitable distribution of incomes could lead to greater economic efficiency and higher production."[1]

Shares

Preliminary estimates by the Ministry of Co-operative Development in early 1978 showed total shares and deposits of saving and credit societies at Kshs 225,277,518 as of December 31, 1977, with 267 out of 448 societies reporting. These statistics were modified slightly downward in an ACOSCA report later in 1978. The table shows the government figures of the development of savings and credit societies from 1972 to 1976.

Data were not available for the societies in Nairobi Province where most government and commercial workers were employed, but in the second most active area, Mombasa District of Coast Province, 69 out of the existing 81 co-operative societies in 1977 were savings and credit societies with an estimated membership of 14,363 and share capital of Kshs 31 million.

The number of savings and credit societies as a whole was believed to have tripled between 1974 and 1977 (155 to 448) when their members totaled 156,443.

Of the 18 societies in the study, half had over one million shillings in shares. One of them (Harambee) claimed to be the largest savings and credit society in Africa with total shares of Kshs 20 million and over 15,000 members, with a potential membership of 60,000. By the way of comparison, private sector savings deposits in commercial banks, according to the Central Bank of Kenya, as of September 30, 1977, were Kshs 1,889.50 million; in private financial institutions, Kshs 299.91 million; and in the POSB, Kshs 181.46 million.

Dividends

Dividends were paid in half the societies studied and ranged in amount from 2 percent to 9 percent (legal limit was 10 percent). In discussions with society officers we learned that the dividends in and of themselves did not seem as important to the members as the opportunity to question the reports on the management and accomplishments of the society and holding elections at membership meetings. The society with the largest individual shares average, Kshs 4,599, was a workers' society and the oldest in our study; the last dividend in that society was paid at 6.7 percent for 1975.

The smallest average individual shareholding was Kshs 128 in a rural community group whose farmers and traders brought in a few shillings at a time and were given a receipt for a share when Kshs 20 had been accumulated. The average savings of individual members in the eighteen societies was Kshs 1,713, with the greatest number having either over Kshs 2,000 or under 1,000.

In addition to saving in their savings and credit societies, Ken-

Kenya Co-operative Savings and Credit Societies (1972–76)

Statistical Items	*1972*	*1973*	*1974*	*1975*	*1976*
No. of societies	101	125	155	230	308
Members at year-end	35,745	51,355	84,322	101,170	129,181
Borrowers at year-end	15,345	29,282	41,115	60,976	67,269
Average savings per member at year-end	Kshs 453	Kshs 523	Kshs 1,062	Kshs 1,158	Kshs 1,340
		(in millions of shillings)			
Members' shares	16.2	32.0	83.9	118.2	173.1
Members' loan balances	10.0	25.3	53.6	87.0	139.1
Total assets	19.0	33.4	84.2	119.5	179.1
Statutory reserves	0.28	0.40	0.64	1.2	2.5
Gross earnings	0.75	1.7	4.4	6.9	13.3
Total expenditures	0.33	0.77	1.0	1.9	3.8
Amount loaned to members during the year	13.9	30.9	60.9	99.6	140.7
Amount loaned to members since registration of societies	27.5	54.0	125.2	187.5	293.9

Source: Ministry of Co-operative Development, Nairobi, Kenya.

yan members also saved in building societies, in the POSB, and in their provident fund (National Social Security Fund). Among many members, saving in and of itself was considered good; payroll deductions made it very easy to put money aside and build a nest egg for retirement.

Although commercial banks were beginning to promote their savings services, savings accounts were not connected to bank credit; few workers could qualify for bank loans, which usually required collateral security. Those with precious land titles were reluctant to put them at any risk whatsoever. Savings and credit societies were almost alone in offering workers a place to accumulate savings for the express purpose of getting loans amounting to several times the amount they had saved. This advantage made the societies most attractive to savers.

Building the general economy of the country was a national goal, and productive loans were getting preferential treatment, so the main emphasis among members of societies was on accumulating large enough savings balances to qualify for sizable income-producing loans. As individual share accounts grew, societies were demonstrating their potential both as mobilizers of local savings and as development institutions.

Loans, Interest Rates, Refunds of Interest

In many societies over eighty percent of the loans went into development purposes such as the purchase of houses to rent, farm improvement, and the purchase or establishment of small businesses. A much smaller percentage of loans went for consumer needs. According to a government report, Kshs 149.7 million were loaned to society members in 1976 and an estimated Kshs 200 million in 1977.

Interest was usually charged at the maximum rate of one percent per month on the unpaid balance; patronage refunds of interest were permitted but rarely, if ever, paid. None of the societies studied had paid a patronage refund.

In addition to providing their members with loans, many societies invested surplus funds in shares of the Co-operative Bank, commercial banks, and building societies.

Even with the inflation, Kenya's urban workers seemed to be earning enough to maintain a rising standard of living. Salaried office staff, especially the higher paid professionals or supervisors, and working couples could often accumulate enough savings to make a down payment on a farm, business, or rental property to generate more income, or get title to a piece of land—the most highly prized possession.

Since workers in farm areas earned substantially less per hour than urban workers in the industrial sector and their employment was much less secure, their ability to save and borrow was limited, as was their willingness to use borrowed money—except to get a land title—for purposes within the government's development strategy.

Access to Credit—Urban

Although savings and credit societies were the chosen credit institutions of many workers, they were by no means the primary source. Permanent employees, especially supervisors, had access to advances on their monthly salaries, to commercial bank loans, and to hire purchase (installment credit) arrangements for cars, refrigerators, and television sets. Some companies provided cars as an incentive to taking employment, and government would lend its employees money for an auto through the National Bank of Kenya, requiring ten percent down on a used car and forty percent on a new car. The maximum loaned was Kshs 30,000 to be repaid in four years.

A civil servant could also get a salary advance once every two years of up to one month's salary with one year to repay, interest free. Companies often made arrangements for mid-month advances for their employees.

With a land title deed and/or insurance policies as security, Kenyans could get housing and other loans. Building societies and other finance companies asked for ten percent down payment on a new house and twenty-five percent on an old house, the loan to be repaid in fifteen years. Savings and credit society loans were often made to give members this access to other substantial credit.

Access to Credit—Rural

Various sources of agricultural credit were available to farmers, and it was estimated that between 500,000 and one million farmers were being reached by a wide array of public and private credit institutions in addition to personal sources.

Credit from informal sources—from trader to farmer, from farmer to laborer, and from a farming company to its tenants—was believed to be extensive. Formal sources of agricultural credit were provided by commercial banks, governmental parastatal institutions, the co-operative structure, and the Central Bank. Two specialized channels for agricultural credit were the Agricultural Finance Corporation and the co-operative movement, which included the Co-operative Bank of Kenya, the district co-operative unions and the primary co-operative societies.

Some of the money available for loans to the rural sector from the Co-operative Bank came from investments by urban workers' savings and credit societies that were members of the bank. By the same token, rural savings added to the bank's resources that were available to workers' savings and credit societies for loans.

The Central Bank of Kenya was pursuing a policy of promoting rural development by encouraging banks and other lending institutions to increase their lending to farmers. This policy was found necessary because the savings of the rural population were being used primarily to fund the concentration of lending in urban areas where earnings were higher.

Rural Savings and Credit Society Development

An estimated ninety percent of Kenya's 13.8 million inhabitants—over 12 million people—were living in and deriving their livelihood from the rural areas, so there was a vast potential for savings and credit society service, even after taking notice of the limitations imposed by the alternative services available. But this was not to say that the potential was unlimited—the actual numbers were hard to estimate. Less than half of the rural population was within the money economy, and of this number (the ILO/UNDP calls these people "working poor") only a fraction could conceivably operate savings and credit societies as they were structured.

The growth of commercial banks had been accompanied by branching and by some attempts to provide mobile banks, but while this may have stimulated savings, it had not given the average Kenyan effective access to credit. Although the POSB was relatively widespread, it offered no credit facilities.

There were, therefore, special opportunities for savings and credit societies to serve local government employees, artisans, farm laborers, and industrial workers in the rural towns and their environs. Some of the workplace societies we studied in rural towns were helping their members finance the purchase of small farms through co-operatives, and these activities tended to give the societies the recognition of being a community institution.

While there were few rural societies in Kenya (and only two were studied), these were among the most successful savings and credit societies in the country and had achieved international recognition. More emphasis on rural savings and credit society development was being urged by foreign donors. Meanwhile, the government continued to pursue its pragmatic policy of registering groups that had a reasonable likelihood of succeeding, while opening the door just a crack to the occasional rural community group that could prove its capability and persistence in order to qualify for registration.

Rural Co-operative Savings and Credit Schemes

Co-operative Production Credit Scheme

In 1966–67, Sven Lindquist, a Swedish credit expert, carried out a survey and feasibility study of credit and savings in the agricultural co-operative movement. He recommended reorganizing the marketing unions into multipurpose co-operatives with credit and savings facilities for members of the primary co-operative societies and making the Co-operative Bank the main bank for co-operatives. Marketing co-operatives would be encouraged to adopt this CPCS in which farmers would borrow for their crop inputs and repay these loans from the crop proceeds automatically credited to their individual savings accounts in the marketing co-operatives.

A substantial (£4 million) Nordic Project (Denmark, Sweden, Finland, Norway) aid program to implement this study was launched in 1969 which, in effect, reserved rural co-operative financing to the CPCS co-operatives. By the end of 1976 the CPCS had become the largest Kenyan farm loan scheme in terms of the number of farmers served—330,000—as compared with the Agricultural Finance Corporation dealing with 40,000 of the bigger farmers and larger loans.

The government policy on centralization of rural co-operative services, including banking, was expressed in the aforementioned *Sessional Paper No. 8:*

> From the time of independence, a structure has been evolved for the co-operative movement in which District Co-operative Unions are being developed as the focal point of Co-operative activity. In practically all areas of the country in which there is a co-operative enterprise, a District Co-operative Union has been registered, to which primary societies are

> affiliated and around which all co-operative development is being centered. In an effort to achieve a greater efficiency faster, some of the functions such as bookkeeping and accountancy, bulk purchasing of stationery, farm inputs and stores for resale, etc., have been centralized under the district unions with positive results. The policy is to continue to centralize more of the functions of primaries under the unions (including banking, etc.) as and when the latter prove their ability to render such services more efficiently.

The banking sections as of December, 1976, were operating in thirteen of the forty active co-operative unions. They were providing credit services to 298,200 members whose loan balances totaled Kshs 82.8 million and savings services to 238,000 members whose savings totaled Kshs 152.9 million. Another seven unions were serving 32,200 members with credit only; their loans totaled Kshs 3 million. No data were available regarding overall loan delinquencies.

Savings services provided real competition to the commercial banks as farmers transferred their commercial accounts to their co-operatives in order to finance the CPCS. Some unions promoted their savings services with mobile vans that enabled co-op members to make deposits and withdrawals conveniently.

The flow of excess co-operative union funds to the Co-operative Bank was one of the unfulfilled objectives of the original plan. Since the bank had no branches, some of the outlying unions found it too expensive to make frequent transfers of money to the bank's headquarters office in Nairobi. With very few exceptions, however, the farm co-operatives obtained all of their needed external funds from the bank. In the past several years the system experienced excess liquidity: savings of Kshs 152 million compared to loans outstanding of 86 million in 1976. Close collaboration between the Co-operative Bank and the banking sections of the co-operative unions had not been achieved, but progress in this direction was being made with the assistance of the World Bank and the Swedish International Development Agency (SIDA) through the Nordic Project.

Perhaps the most serious problem for the CPCS was the high proportion of non-Africans who have been needed since its inception in 1969. One-third of the government staff were foreigners (including ten Peace Corps volunteers) in 1977. Due to the scarcity of qualified Kenyan banking managers and their relatively high salaries, no easy solution was in sight. Another prevalent problem for the field staff was lack of funds for transport.

Integrated Agricultural Development Program, Smallholder Production Services and Credit Program, and Farm Input Supply Scheme

In addition to the CPCS program of the co-operatives, the Kenya agricultural credit system included numerous other financial institutions and credit schemes that supported the transfer of land from European to African ownership, provided services principally for large-scale agriculture and some help to smallholders. In the latter category was the IADP, which was financed by the World Bank and some Arab banks that provided a package of inputs for small-scale, mixed farming in selected areas in which multiple crops were raised.

The SPSCP (the Vihiga Project) that served indigent farmers in a western area not covered by CPCS was financed by USAID and assisted by the CDD, the Co-operative Bank, and the Agriculture Extension Service.

FISS, financed by the Danish International Development Agency (DANIDA), supplied below-subsistence farmers with materials to build storage units and with advice on their use. FISS worked in conjunction with the other assistance programs.

Loan Policy of Savings and Credit Societies

Ideally, Kenyan co-operative savings and credit societies were supposed to base their loans on a member's character, family situation, salary, savings, length of employment, use of payroll deduction, availability of his provident fund, and guarantors. However, nationwide societies have had to adopt more impersonal lending policies like the more rigid CPCS credit policies of the marketing co-operatives. This has led to a shift away from character loans to loans based on security and the use of lending formulas (multiplicands of savings) that minimize the need for personal judgment in the extension of credit to borrowers.

In November, 1975, a commissioner's circular tightened the rules on the granting of new loans to members. It also restricted the refinancing or granting of additional loans, especially to society officials. Disproportionately large loans made to office bearers, high officials, and supervisory personnel who later refused to repay them had become a major problem in some of the larger societies. Income-producing loans to big savers frequently were made at the expense of the small saver-borrower with equal or greater need. In nationwide societies where headquarters members tended to get the big loans, a campaign was under way to urge distribution of the available money among as many borrowers as possible, with special consideration to requests from the branch members in the outlying areas.

The average loan per society studied ranged from Kshs 1,000 to 15,000, depending on the size of the society; maximum individual loans ranged from Kshs 8,500 to 45,000. Limitations on loans varied from 1.75 times the amount of shares to 5 times shares, with an average share/loan ratio of 3 times the amount of shares. Loans were granted for periods of twelve months to five years, depending upon whether the loan was for school fees or for major projects such as building or buying a house or business. Most loans were expected to be repaid in thirty-six months.

Interest Tables

The figuring and collection of interest had proved to be a problem to some volunteer treasurers, so the government had prepared interest calculation tables. Co-operative officers were urging the use of these tables to reduce the local treasurer's work and help insure collection of interest.

Security for Loans

While guarantors were required, they were almost never called upon to make good on defaulted loans. Nevertheless, members were reluctant to become guarantors for their colleagues' loans; in many societies almost all members had loans themselves and had no surplus shares to guarantee any other loans. Only one society in the study reported collecting from a guarantor.

Several societies reported that they had rules prohibiting loans which, with the interest payment and compulsory savings requirement, would leave the recipient with less than one-third of his salary as take-home pay; others placed the bottom limit at fifty to seventy-five percent of monthly salary. Some societies did not give emergency loans (for deaths, funerals, illness) because these were taken care of by contributions from fellow workers, friends, or extended family members. However, most societies made arrangements for emergency loans of less than Kshs 500 to be issued immediately by the treasurer without the approval of a full credit committee meeting.

The money received on loan was not always used for the purposes stated on the loan application, and frequently the borrower asked for more (or less) money than he needed in order to be sure to get some money. In many societies, the misuse of loan money, if discovered, could be reason for refusal of more loans in the future.

In societies where loans were given almost exclusively on entitlement, the credit committee acted as a rubber stamp to the treasurer's recommendation, only deliberating on requests for exceptions to the two- or three-times shares rule. Oftentimes the credit committee granted the exceptions to keep on good terms with the borrower, hoping that the government officer who had to countersign the check would refuse to do so if the loan did not conform to the society's loan policy. All loans of over Kshs 30,000 had to be approved by the commissioner's office.

Loan Delinquency

With the use of payroll deduction, most loans were repaid on a regular basis, but serious defaults occured when workers lost their jobs and sometimes when they were transferred. However, it usually just took time to get a transferee reinstated on payroll deduction in his new assignment. When workers retired from the work force the situation was more serious. If they could be found and they refused to honor their obligations, the society could take its cases to a committee of lawyers set up by the commissioner of co-operatives to consider such cases. Upon the committee's recommendation, the society could resort to legal action. In one community society a field officer had been hired to call upon members and educate them as to their responsibilities in repaying their loans, in remaining a society member after the loan had been paid off, and in saving more money.

Management, Membership Participation, Bookkeeping

Society leaders and government officials were placing great emphasis on improving bookkeeping almost as an end in itself rather than as a tool of management. Their general feeling was that a society with a good and complete set of books was "under control," in spite of the fact that some embezzlements took a long time to come to light because of the "perfect" condition of the books. Thus, most training programs concentrated on bookkeeping, whether in KUSCCO seminars, ACOSCA study conferences, or Co-operative College courses. Only recently had training been focused, to any degree, on management skills.

The CDD was attempting to require all new societies to utilize KUSCCO's centralized record-keeping service for not less than three years before an application for exemption from the requirement could be submitted. Exemptions were to be based on the ability of the society to do the work currently and accurately at an acceptable cost to its members.

Of the eighteen societies studied, only three were using the KUSCCO bookkeeping service. Several of them reported plans to use the service in the near future; one planned to withdraw as soon as adequate staff was hired by the society. Apparently the policy of the government was awaiting implementation until KUSCCO could expand and upgrade its services. Aside from the problem of obtaining the source documents, KUSCCO's bookkeeping staff have had to spend much of their time "writing the books" and bringing them up to date for posting.

Two societies had a staff member provided by management; five societies hired a staff person, and one of these had KUSCCO bookkeeping service. This service was also used in two of five other societies that relied solely on volunteer management. One society had bought a posting machine similar to the machines used by KUSCCO bookkeeping services (actually it was tested in that society to see if it was adequate for KUSCCO). The machine proved so satisfactory that the society was considering renting out time on it.

Computerized bookkeeping, while a possible dream for the future, was generally believed to be no answer to Kenyan savings and credit society problems.

Strategy of Rationalization

With the concentration upon urban savings and credit societies has come a strategy of rationalization, seeking to apply scientific standards to chartering policies and modern methods of efficiency and mechanized solutions to society management problems. The insistence on payroll deductions as a prerequisite to registration, a loan security measure, and an aid to society record-keeping facilitated large-scale operations. It also contributed to a rationale for making salary and savings, rather than character and need, the basis for loans.

The shortage of available managers and bookkeepers was a

constant problem for both the societies and the government supervisory agency. Attempts to recruit experienced staff or even competent trainees met with limited success. A large foreign aid cadre was not being used in savings and credit societies as was the practice in the management of the marketing co-ops, which were assisted by SIDA and other Nordic staff.

Bookkeepers trained at the Co-operative College and in ACOSCA or KUSCCO seminars frequently moved to the private sector where demand for bookkeepers and managers was great and the pay better. However, a good number eventually returned to the less-pressured activities of the co-operatives.

In the staffing of managerial and supervisory jobs, people with general skills in management, bookkeeping, and auditing have had to suffice since few experienced managers or technicians were available. Recognizing these difficulties the CDD's recruitment program for co-operative officers to work with savings and credit societies was upgraded in 1975 to bring in as assistant co-operative officers more competent employees who could be trained to inspect societies' books and to understand their management problems. The government was also urging societies to hire trained bookkeepers as soon as they could afford to do so, rather than continuing to rely on volunteer assistance. Even with the bookkeeping service being provided by KUSCCO for smaller societies, the goal was for societies to become self-sufficient, with enough paid staff to manage them safely and efficiently.

Goal of Self-Direction

Despite the generally agreed upon goal of self-direction, there were those among government officials, international agency personnel, and some leaders of large societies who urged that a proportion of the members of the managing committees of large societies be appointed by the commissioner of co-operatives. It was also argued that having company officials assigned to societies would bring about a relatively faster development of the movement and would help improve management in such areas as the prevention of embezzlements and defaults and the proper investment of surplus funds.

There were equally strong voices—probably the majority—favoring the continuation and strengthening of the societies in their present form as grassroots, democratic, membership-governed institutions. The government seemed committed to this policy.

In the exercise of his supervisory powers, the commissioner for co-operatives had appointed management commissions to take over for a year the affairs of two mismanaged societies in our study. In one, a private management firm had been named to run the society; in the other, a co-operative officer, familiar with the society (having audited it and discovered the problems) and known to its members, headed the government-appointed commission and was the acting manager.

In addition to managing the society, the private firm in the first case was also drawing up management plans, systems, and manuals on the basis of this experience which could be used by other societies and was seeking government support in making these standard procedure.

Company Assistance

Where the parent company understood the benefits of society services for its workers, it often provided subsidies, which included office space, equipment (adding machines and typewriters), land for a building, time off for an accountant to do or supervise the bookkeeping, or even provision for a staff member to act as treasurer/manager. Although the twelve societies that were provided office space often considered it inadequate, few of these societies were planning to build their own office buildings; instead they planned to ask management for larger quarters.

One society owned its building but not the land it was on; one rented its space; one used the canteen building owned by the society; one rural society had offices in its own building and was, as the result of its own multipurpose activities, building another complex which would have substantial rental space as well as society office space; one operated in the treasurer's house; and one operated in the office of the paymaster who was also the voluntary treasurer of the society.

A major company contribution was commonly the provision of payroll deduction. This service, while originally not required by government, was strongly encouraged; newly organized societies were not being registered by the CDD without it. Sixteen of the societies had this check-off. In a number of them it had come only recently, after considerable government and worker pressure. One society had its payroll deduction privilege canceled when the company became suspicious and hostile because of trade union organizing efforts among the employees.

Multipurpose and Economic Development Activities

The rapid accumulation of assets in Kenya's dynamic and fast-growing savings and credit societies created investment opportunities for group development projects as well as for individual business and farm loans. This growth also created problems for the societies that had surplus funds to invest.

Government policy discouraged multipurpose activities, notwithstanding its diametrically opposite policy favoring multipurpose agricultural marketing co-operatives. Societies were being advised not to invest in related business activities but, instead, to grant individual loans to members who wanted to invest individually or in groups. This single-purpose co-operative discipline protected the societies, their management, and supervisors from spreading their abilities too thinly, but it did not always appeal to members who saw their societies as the natural center for other co-operative activities.

There have been a few cases of large societies that have become multipurpose, however. One, a well-managed rice farmers' society, was encouraged by government under special circumstances to buy into the ownership of a national rice mill and to finance a separate bran and transport co-operative; both of these additional activities were closely related to the farmers' livelihood, and the entire expanded development has been extremely successful. Another society had not been so fortunate in its management. Whether its major multipurpose venture—a two-million-shilling investment in a housing site—will eventually prove successful remains to be seen. One other large and well-managed society was apparently convinced that these housing plots were a good investment for its members, and it was making loans to enable them to build on the site. This third society also had another housing project under consideration which could test the multipurpose ruling.

Several societies with surplus funds seemed inclined to go along with the ruling, at least for the present. They were encouraging their members to borrow individually or to join into groups for building schools and rental properties and for opening retail shops and other businesses such as consumer shops, dairies, bakeries, poultry farms, or bars.

Women in Savings and Credit Societies

One or more women were serving on the managing committee of seven of the societies we visited; one was the chairperson of a very large society, one a secretary, and another a treasurer. Several women were serving on the credit and supervisory committees. Among the paid staff of these societies, three were women. There was one woman on the KUSCCO bookkeeping service team, and we met six female government co-operative officers. Where women were employed in the parent company society, officials reported increasing numbers of women applying for membership and loans as well as for paid jobs with the societies.

Government Supervision and Audits

The number of visits of co-operative officers to societies varied with the size of the area, the number of officers, and the availability of transportation. In Nairobi most societies were visited every two months. One society reported daily visits by the division co-operative officer and weekly visits by the district officer. Yet other societies reported they had never been visited by a co-operative officer.

Of the thirteen societies reporting on audits, four had not been audited after 1975, seven had last been audited in 1976, and two had books at the auditors for 1977. One reported books having been held for a full year for audit; another reported being without books for four months at the time of the study. Audit fees varied from Kshs 2,000 to 56,250. Some audits had been completed by government auditors; others by private auditors. There was some discontent with the private auditors since, according to society officials, they did not understand savings and credit society bookkeeping and were more expensive than government auditors.

We spent considerable time with one provincial auditor who discussed the problems in his province. He had had enough staff up to recently to provide all societies with annual audits, the scheduled dates of which were given to the societies in advance. Not all the societies had kept their books up to date, so the auditors had to spend a good deal of time updating before auditing them. This, of course, had increased the cost of the audits. Government charges, which were assessed according to the time taken, the grade of the auditor, and the income of the society, were running between Kshs 110 and 360 per auditor day.

In theory the audit section was supposed to be self-sufficient, but this had not worked. In many cases the section had to settle for less than the payment requested, and then only after lengthy negotiations.

Various new credit schemes being introduced in the rural

areas involving marketing co-operatives were making it impossible for the audit section to provide specialized savings and credit society auditors on a regular basis.

A Three-Way View of Savings and Credit Societies

Problems as Seen by Government Officials

The main problems, according to government supervisors, were inefficient management, ignorant and uninformed membership, lack of technical and financial resources, lack of long-range planning, lack of proper office accommodations, the inability of KUSCCO to perform adequately and efficiently, and political intervention.

Their recommendations included the societies' hiring of qualified and competent staff; increasing educational programs by the CDD, KUSCCO, and the societies themselves; emphasizing planning and a coordinated approach to growth; improving KUSCCO services so more societies could be encouraged to join; obtaining better society offices, primarily from employers; and increasing CDD vigilance, especially to prevent favoritism in granting loans.

Problems as Seen by Savings and Credit Society Officials

Poor record keeping was cited by society officials as their biggest problem—the cause of poor loan collection, embezzlement, and uncontrolled large loans. Books held for government audit for extended periods of time and delays in making audits created problems for some societies, and many societies reported the audit fees to be excessive. Hostile management was a problem for several groups. Inactive supervisory and education committees and the lack of promotional materials were areas of concern as was the need for trained staff. The loss of trained staff to better paying jobs elsewhere was also troublesome.

Other societies stressed their need for bigger office space and complained of problems with collecting "big fish" loans, of problems with corrupt leadership, with guarantors who refused to cooperate or who left the field of membership, and with having too little money to make good loans or having too much money but insufficient investment knowledge and guidance. Also mentioned was the need to educate borrowers on how to plan their loan needs, and, if necessary, how to ask for the bigger loans needed for more productive purposes. How to retain members after their loans had been repaid concerned other societies. Service-oriented society officers were concerned about this inability to lend money (because of the check-off requirement) to the hourly paid, casual and day laborers who had the greatest need, especially for small loans. There were also some complaints about computer errors on the payroll print-outs that made society bookkeeping difficult.

Branch operations presented additional problems: getting branch members a fair share of the total loans made, expediting the processing of loans, and helping borrowers to cash checks issued at headquarters.

Government Relations from Savings and Credit Society Point of View

Small and new societies found the strong government interest and involvement reassuring and helpful. The older and larger the society, the less management felt the need for government assistance, and, in fact, the more management was resentful of what had to them become "government interference."

A different viewpoint was expressed in one rural area where the secretary/manager told us that members who made loans thought they were borrowing from the government, which was keeping their money safe in a bank. Therefore they felt, "if I become a defaulter, the government will follow me up," and loan repayments were better because of this misunderstanding.

Most societies were in favor of the requirement for countersigning of checks by co-operative officers. In one society the officials felt strongly that countersigning helped catch mistakes even though that society had never had a check turned back by a government officer.

Strong government seemed to be respected in Kenya; government assistance, know-how, and support were acknowledged. However, conflicting government circulars sometimes created problems. There seemed to be great respect for the co-op officers; nowhere were they described to us as incompetent or disinterested. There were some cases, however, where inspectors had not come as regularly as the society would have liked.

To society leaders one of the more important functions of government was to provide some muscle to use on management—to get management to accept the societies, to provide check-off, office space, bookkeeping assistance. Hotel workers on the Malindi Coast felt that without the active support of the co-operative officers in their area, they would never have been able to get management to accept their society. Hours in the hotel industry were long, pay was low, the labor pool was large, and management feared for its profit margin should the experience in organizing a savings and credit society lead to organization of a trade union.

Education and Training

Much of the bookkeeping and management training continued to be done by the co-operative officers in their visits to societies and in the CDD offices when society personnel brought applications for loans with checks for approval and countersigning. More formal training was provided by KUSCCO seminars and meetings, sometimes in co-operation with ACOSCA. The highest level of training was provided through the Kenya Co-operative College.

Co-operative Department Manuals and Publications

In May, 1972, the CDD prepared a detailed *Handbook for Committeemen and Office Bearers of Co-operative Savings and Credit Societies.* Later, in August, the department released a *Staff Manual for the Urban Credit Section,* and in September produced a promotional booklet, *The Co-operative Savings and Credit Society: What It Is, What It Is For, How It Operates, How It May Benefit You,* which was revised from an earlier edition. At the same time, another promotional booklet, also revised from an earlier piece and titled *A Savings and Credit Society for Your Employees,* was circulated by the Kenya National Promotion Committee.

In November, 1975, a new series of manuals for societies was produced by the CDD: an accounting manual, a managing committee manual, and a credit manual. These were available to every society, and headquarters co-operative officers checked to see that these documents were on hand at the society when they made tours of inspection and supervision. However, we did not find these manuals being used in the societies we visited.

The education division of the Ministry of Co-operative Development, working with the KNFC and the Co-operative College, issued a revised *Guide to Member Information Pamphlet* in January, 1966, which was designed for use on Member Information Days by the co-operative training officer. The pamphlet had four lessons, each built around a series of pictures specially designed to stimulate discussion.

While three societies told us about holding Member Information Days, none of them discussed the above training package. In one society Member Day was described as an opportunity to exchange views, ask questions, and share food. At another society, the secretary/manager told us he "lectures" to his members. Other officials felt Member Days were a good idea to substitute for the annual meetings, which had to be postponed because of audit delays. Another society planned to hold a Member Day upon the payment of several outstanding insurance claims as a good advertisement of its services.

Co-operative College of Kenya

Co-operative education for members of the movement and for government officials supervising the movement had been recognized since 1952 when the East African School of Co-operation was established. After Uganda's withdrawal from the school in 1959 and Tanzania's in 1962, co-operative training became a branch of the Kenya Institute of Administration until the founding of the Co-operative College of Kenya in 1967. In 1970 the present site of the college at Langata, twelve miles from the city center of Nairobi, was made possible by collaboration between the Kenyan government and the Nordic Project, which provided eighty percent of the costs as well as administrative and teaching personnel. At the time of our visit, though, the college was manned almost entirely by Kenyans.

The Co-operative College is an agency of the government; it is not a product of the co-operative movement itself. Movement input comes through the representation of officials of the KNFC on the college committee and the coordination group for co-operative education. Although the college had been training co-operative officers who were expected to supervise savings and credit societies and although the college staff participated and held offices in CODEPT, there was no course on savings and credit societies as part of the regular curriculum until 1978 when one stream of thirty participants began studying the subject as part of their three-month course in administration, bookkeeping, and management.

The Co-operative College was hosting the ACOSCA Training Centre, which served students from all over East Africa. The first course was given in 1972 using ACOSCA and college staff. Through

1977, 135 East Africans had received training there, including 38 national association field officers, 7 volunteer organizers, 43 government co-operative officers, and 35 secretary/managers of societies. Because of ACOSCA's Tenth Anniversary Meeting in 1978 no course was held that year; from 1979 on, eight-week regional courses were to be held on a biennial basis.

Short seminars for savings and credit society personnel, sponsored by KUSCCO, were also being held at the college.

Kenya Union of Savings and Credit Co-operatives, Ltd.

KUSCCO, a nationwide service co-operative union registered under the Co-operative Societies Act, was organized in 1973 by a promotion committee created under government auspices (see pp. 82–84).

As stated in section 3 of its bylaws, the union's objectives are:

> i) To promote the organization and the development of sound Co-operative Savings and Credit Societies.
>
> ii) To develop and maintain the best possible public relations with the general public, the Government, the Private Business Sector, Trade Unions, Voluntary Organizations, National and International Co-operative Organizations.
>
> iii) To liaise with the Department of Co-operative Development and endeavour to secure constructive interpretation of the Co-operative Societies' Act, the Rules and these By-Laws.
>
> iv) To be alert and advise against any adverse legislation or restrictions.
>
> v) To establish and enforce among Societies and their officials, employees and members, a common code of ethics and practices based on co-operative principles.
>
> vi) To disseminate information concerning Savings and Credit Societies and co-ordinate their operating methods and practices; to maintain uniformity in bookkeeping and to foster education and training of members, officials and employees.
>
> vii) To help improve the internal management of Savings and Credit Societies and coordinate their operating methods and practices to maintain uniformity in bookkeeping and to foster education and training of members, officials and employees.
>
> viii) To arrange for a system to protect Savings and Credit Societies' funds against loss and to provide such other services as are of mutual advantage to Savings and Credit Societies, their members, and the Union.
>
> ix) To establish branches of the Union at Provincial level.

The policymaking body of KUSCCO is its annual general meeting in which each affiliated society has one voting delegate. KUSCCO operates in six geographical provinces through its provincial councils. The chairmen of the provincial councils make up the managing committee of KUSCCO.

Through its centralized accounting projects, KUSCCO was providing financial management advisory service to its affiliates in collaboration with the Ministry of Co-operative Development. This was primarily a centralized bookkeeping service that had been organized because of the low level of accounting knowledge of many of the volunteer treasurers, the inability of small societies to afford paid staff, and the inability to recruit professional staff in this field. KUSCCO was trying to develop ten bookkeeping centers with twenty-five bookkeepers, but only two of the centers were equipped with accounting machines. In 1978, 146 societies were participating in the bookkeeping service.

For the future, KUSCCO board members were discussing auditing services, an interlending fund, a stabilization fund, and the promotion of savings and credit societies in rural areas. Also for the future was a financial self-support plan that envisaged increased income from dues, bookkeeping and other service fees, stationery sales, and insurance commissions. KUSCCO's manager believed that income from the bookkeeping service could make the service self-sufficient, or even profitable, if only it could get more aid to purchase the necessary equipment. Meanwhile KUSCCO remained substantially dependent on grants from the KAF and the African-American Labor Center.

In 1977 twenty seminars planned and implemented jointly by KUSCCO and the Ministry of Co-operative Development were held with 820 participants. According to a KUSCCO report, there were in 1978 sufficient ministerial personnel exclusively involved with such educational activities to minimize KUSCCO's manpower problem in this field.

KUSCCO, through its fieldmen, was also reponsible for promoting new societies and recommending them for registration to the commissioner after conducting the preregistration meetings.

Through KUSCCO, societies were, at the time of the study, able to get the loan protection and life savings insurance of CUNA Mutual Insurance Society, but the future of the insurance program was in doubt due to management and bookkeeping difficulties.

In 1977 KUSCCO distributed to member societies 80,000 shillings worth of stationery.

KUSCCO as Seen by Its Members

All the societies visited were members of the union (a government requirement) but three large societies, registered before the formation of KUSCCO, were not paying their dues because they saw no need for its services. Two of them had their own insurance arrangements. Ten carried the KUSCCO insurance program (four reported that claims were paid promptly). Two others were considering joining the insurance program under government pressure; another had not paid any premiums for two years but planned to resume payments; and a third told us that, until very recently, they thought the insurance service came automatically with membership in KUSCCO.

A number of societies complained that KUSCCO bookkeeping stationery was so expensive that they had bought their own locally; others told of the stationery being unavailable for the two months previous to our visit. Government was urging the use of KUSCCO forms to improve system uniformity, facilitate data collection and centralized accounting, and prepare for a computerized system when that should come about.

The training given by KUSCCO staff was considered good, but seminars were too short. Most of the societies that sent delegates to the annual meeting felt they had learned a great deal. However, the treasurer of one large society felt it was a waste of time. The officials attending the Co-operative College courses, either those sponsored by KUSCCO or by ACOSCA, were pleased with them and felt they provided substantial learning experiences.

Societies quite distant from any KUSCCO branch office reported that they were never visited by fieldmen nor did they get much in the way of service. One of the societies in Nairobi also said it had never received a visit from a fieldman. Apparently the government co-operative officers performed most of the society visits and gave direct help to individual societies while KUSCCO provided services that could be offered at the KUSCCO headquarters and branches.

Problems as Seen by KUSCCO Leadership

1. Accounting services, which KUSCCO was being pressured by government to expand, were not only running at a loss but also had little hope of becoming self-supporting because small, financially limited societies could not affort to pay the costs.

2. Foreign aid had gotten such favorable publicity that the government and union members did not feel as much pressure for KUSCCO to become self-supporting as they would if that cushion were not available.

3. There were differences of opinion with the CDD in spite of the close relationship between the government and KUSCCO. They disagreed on whether or not there should be a special savings and credit society law and whether KUSCCO should have a central fund or should be required to use the Co-operative Bank for its centralized financial services.

4. Large societies, especially those registered before KUSCCO's time, did not see any need for the type of services offered by KUSCCO. KUSCCO's expertise in financial management was limited, and the KUSCCO staff did not have the experience necessary to advise the large societies. Nor did these societies feel any evangelical responsibility for expanding the movement.

5. Transportation for field staff was lacking and/or limited to public transportation, which was slow and unreliable.

6. Promotion in rural areas was difficult and expensive.

7. Relationships with ACOSCA were still being sorted out. The proximity of the international agency presented both problems and bonuses.

8. The insurance program was in trouble both because participating societies didn't have current and correct bookkeeping records on which to base the coverage and premiums and because of KUSCCO's chronic management problems.

KUSCCO Branch Office (Mombasa)

In our visits to Coast Province societies we were hosted by the KUSCCO Mombasa branch manager, a retired senior co-operative officer, who accompanied us on all our visits. He was generous with his time in describing the operations of his office as well as the activities of the provincial managing committee, which he served as secretary.

The provincial managing committee of nine members was elected by the provincial council, which was made up of all KUSCCO member societies in the province. The province was represented on the national managing committee by two representatives; the chairman of the Coast committee was a member of the executive committee of KUSCCO.

Seventy of the ninety-five societies registered in the Coast

Province were affiliated with KUSCCO. Of these, forty societies (5,686 accounts) were using the bookkeeping service, and more were in the process of joining. The bookkeeping service which started in 1969 under the former Mombasa Chapter Union required the societies to carry standing bank orders to cover KUSCCO dues, insurance premiums, and bookkeeping costs. Each participating society submitted monthly a bank statement, a check-off list of monthly member activity, and subsidiary papers, including checks and vouchers. As part of the bookkeeping service, copies of the monthly bank reconcilements and trial balances were sent to the society, its branch office, the district co-operative officer, and KUSCCO/Nairobi.

The service prepared budgets for each society, figured dividends, and readied the books for audit. A bookkeeping machine had recently been introduced, but of the six bookkeepers only two knew how to use it. At the time of our visit, all books were three months behind. The main problem, according to the manager and bookkeeping staff, was getting the societies to deliver correct source documents on time.

Another problem to the manager was how to evaluate the productivity of the growing bookkeeping staff. The full staff included, in addition to the bookkeepers, two typists and two office messengers. An additional bookkeeper was to be placed in Malindi, about 125 kilometers north, where eight societies were located.

While we were at the office, the branch representative of a Nairobi-based society came to complain about the problem members of the branch were having in getting their checks cashed in local Mombasa banks. Members in great need had been traveling all the way to Nairobi in order to get cash. A local bank manager told us later that the problem was one of identifying authorized signatures on the checks; he felt the society should open a Mombasa bank account.

This was just another of many problems to the busy KUSCCO branch manager. In addition to checking all the trial balances and overseeing the work of the bookkeepers, he also attended all the general meetings and managing committee meetings of KUSCCO's member societies. (The local co-operative officer was also supposed to attend such meetings.) In addition, he was responsible for soliciting KUSCCO membership among nonmembers, for servicing the thirty-three societies that carried KUSCCO insurance, and for conferring with six societies that were considering it. He felt frustrated in being tied to his office with so much field work to be done. He described the KUSCCO seminars that he helped to arrange as being very well attended. In fact, some societies joined KUSCCO in order to get training for their officials and staff. These seminars were given at no charge to the societies, nor did the societies pay the participants a "sitting fee" for attending. According to the manager, participants would even have paid for the privilege of attending had they been asked. The government was planning to help meet this demand for education with a monthly program in Mombasa, to which most society members could come by bus.

The Co-operative Bank of Kenya, Ltd.

The Co-operative Bank of Kenya is the principal financing institution of the entire co-operative movement and one of the main links between the savings and credit societies and the rural marketing co-operatives.

The bank was registered as a co-operative society on June 19, 1965, but did not start operations until January, 1968, when it was also registered as a commercial bank under the Banking Act. Its objectives have been to mobilize the financial resources of the co-operative movement and use the funds for relending to the movement. It does business only with its member-shareholders, the registered co-operative societies (including savings and credit societies). Membership has grown from 161 members at the beginning to over 951 members. It had almost Kshs 17 million in shares on June 30, 1977, when the bank's total assets were Kshs 553 million. The bank can only lend eighty percent of its deposits; a twenty percent liquidity reserve is maintained. All of the co-operative financing and foreign aid for co-operatives is channeled through the bank.

The ten-person bank board of directors has six directors representing the co-operative movement and four directors representing the Kenya government. Savings and credit societies were apparently on the way to becoming a majority of the bank's members. Even though societies outside Nairobi were unable to use it as their depository because the bank had no branches, their deposits in the first quarter of 1978 were flowing in at the rate of Kshs 15 million a month.

The bank has granted loans to savings and credit societies to meet their members' recurrent peak loan demands such as for seasonal school fees and has also helped them finance major investments, including the two-million-shilling Harambee Co-operative Savings and Credit Society maisonette housing project. Loan maturities were usually five years, but the increasing buildup of share capital was expected to permit longer-term loans in the range of eight to ten years. The bank had been paying a patronage refund of interest, credited to members' shares; dividends paid on shares moved up from seven and a half percent in 1972 to a proposed ten percent for 1977. One of the bank's major investments as of June 30, 1977, was a fifty-one percent holding in the shares of a new Nairobi skyscraper, Co-operative House, which was being built to house the bank, KNFC, KUSCCO, the Co-operative Insurance Society of Kenya, and the CDD.

The savings and credit societies studied uniformly reported being shareholders in the bank, their investments ranging from Kshs 400 to 366,666, and they were making concentrated efforts to increase their shareholdings in order to get more substantial loans from the bank for housing and other productive projects. Originally it was planned that their savings mobilized in the urban areas would be channeled through the bank to the rural areas to increase agricultural productivity and bring about a more equitable distribution of income within the country. This strategy had worked out to the extent that monthly savings and credit society deposits were stabilizing the bank's liquidity position. On the other hand, farmers tended to be savers rather than borrowers, and their savings from high coffee prices in the past years had been channeled through the banking departments of their marketing co-operatives into investments in urban rental property or businesses with a higher return than was anticipated from rural financial activities. Similarly, a successful rural savings and credit society invested its surplus funds in a Nairobi building and loan association. Lacking any inducement to divert their surpluses into projects that would otherwise encourage more equitable income distribution, neither the savings and credit societies nor the rural co-operatives nor the Co-operative Bank were making any effort in that direction.

Although savings and credit society development had been concentrated in urban areas where there were few other co-operatives, the societies in Kenya have always considered themselves a part of the total co-operative movement. Participation of the societies in the work of the KNFC, the Co-operative College of Kenya, and the Co-operative Bank of Kenya was growing. KUSCCO wanted to get direct representation on the boards of KNFC and the Co-operative Bank, thus insuring that savings and credit societies would "speak with one voice" at the KNFC and Co-operative Bank general meetings. KUSCCO also wanted to effect a reallocation of bank delegate seats on the basis of one delegate for every ten member societies—to allow the proliferating societies to exercise their very considerable voting strength and to assert their growing importance in the financial affairs of Kenya's co-operative movement.

16. Conclusions

In Kenya, membership in savings and credit societies is viewed mostly as a way of "getting ahead." The societies have taken a long stride toward their transition from an altruistic financial co-operative to a specialized developmental loan agency. As an industry, they seem poised for explosive growth, awaiting the influx of professional managers, who, once secure in their jobs, may be answerable mostly to, and directed mostly by, the government,

Once a rebellious colony of the British Empire, Kenya today is America's key ally in the Horn of Africa and is wooed by Great Britain and other Western countries whose economic and strategic interests in Africa and the Indian Ocean add to the inflow of hard currency, resources, and long-range support.

Kenya's "White Highlands" are no longer a white enclave—white faces predominate only in the luxury tourist hotels and the exclusive country clubs. Most of the good farmland belongs to black Kenyans, and most of the country's businesses, factories, and hotels are either nominally owned by or answerable to Kenyan directors. Luxury automobiles, clothing, and jewelry bespeak the fact that some Kenyans are getting ahead, especially the few who have managed to consolidate and build their personal fortunes in "kenyanized" business ventures backed by foreign investors and Asian silent partners. Racial conflict continues to smolder in the Africans' animosities toward the visible Asian population concentrated in the retail trades.

The Kenyan elite with their commitment to a trickle-down economic system may be buying time for their tenuous control of the nation's destiny by giving hope and stability to a rising middle class—the wage earners of government, commerce, and industry—who themselves have a vision of someday entering the magic circle of wealth, privilege, and prestige. It is this "secondary elite" who hold the key to the future of Kenya's savings and credit societies. Barring a political upheaval or a catastrophic reversal in Kenya's fortunes, her salaried workers should enjoy increasing prosperity as jobs, salaries, and benefits increase. The availability of savings and credit societies will play no small part in their upward mobility.

Obviously, savings and credit societies in and of themselves cannot eradicate the inequalities so deeply embedded in Kenya's lopsided economy. But they can contribute to the growth of the middle class. They already show promise of becoming the financial development centers of a more socially motivated generation who see comforts, opportunity, and security for themselves in housing, farms, businesses, and other investments that create jobs for the *wananchi* (ordinary people).

Although they have been totally ignored in the prestigious studies of the World Bank, American University, ILO, and Rand McNally, savings and credit societies are becoming a household term in Kenya, especially among workers who once had only the well-publicized POSB for savings and no place to borrow. The societies' assets exceed the POSB deposits, and they are growing at a faster rate than those of the POSB. Savings and credit societies have the potential for mobilizing even larger sums of money that can be plowed back into loans and investments in the nation's interests.

In the absence of government policies that would more adequately address the transfer of incomes from the top income groups to the working poor, as recommended by the ILO, the productive loans made by these societies for small business and other entrepreneurial activities are a way of spreading the incomes of those who are employed among the unemployed—often members of their own extended families.

Leaders of Kenya's societies and government officials are conscious of the trust, prestige, and power that attaches to a movement with such an enormous potential, and thus far they have worked together in harmony. But they will be hard-pressed to cope with the problems of growth unless there is a better division of responsibilities between the overly protective government supervisors and the elected officers of the societies whose management performance leaves much to be desired.

Savings and credit societies' assets more than doubled in the period between 1975 and 1977, and billion-shilling totals are foreseeable by the late 1980s, excluding a major setback. There is, however, the ever present threat of an adverse government policy or head-on competition from the banks. Indeed, critics inside government have already started asking questions about the amounts of money going into these co-operatives.

Particularly vulnerable to criticism are some of the largest nationwide societies whose business would be most lucrative to the banks. Yet few of these societies' leaders have sensed the threat of banking competition or the need for an organization to defend their interests. Ironically, they look instead to government, which by its omnipresence is becoming a major obstacle to overall savings and credit development.

Singularly responsive to the government's view that "growth is progress," these big societies are growing at a pace that makes it difficult to maintain a democratic, member-controlled organization.

Money is coming into savings acounts faster than it can be invested in loans. Needed are new and more flexible lending policies, more flexible lending procedures, more character lending, and additional investment outlets. Working together, the savings and credit societies and the Co-operative Bank might provide Kenya's workers with the kind of "workers' bank" envisaged by Mboya who unfortunately did not live to see the realization of his concept. Member Day celebrations are becoming popular as an antidote to membership apathy; yet to be explored is their potential for maximizing membership use of idle funds.

The original government strategy of channeling surplus funds from urban savings and credit societies and other financial institutions into rural development by corporate transfers has not worked as planned. But, in effect, urban societies have become rural development agencies. Their members are buying farms, hiring labor, and buying seed and fertilizer with individual loans. Moreover, the branch offices of the nationwide societies, which are already active in some rural towns, have a potential for becoming rural development centers. They could offer technical assistance and encouragement to savings and credit societies newly organized among farmers and village residents. Alternately, the branches might be permitted by government to include these persons in their field of membership.

KUSCCO

If planning and study could guarantee success, KUSCCO should by now be on its way to becoming a star performer in the Kenya co-operative system. But after nine years of deliberations prior to organizing their league in 1973 and some eight years of trying to make it work, Kenyan savings and credit society leaders, their government, and their well-wishing donor agencies must face the fact that KUSCCO is neither a replica of the United States and Canadian leagues on which it was modeled nor a uniquely Kenyan answer to the needs of Kenya's co-operative savings and credit societies.

KUSCCO has had to make vital concessions in fitting itself into the operations of the two other, more senior, co-operative institutions—the Co-operative Bank and the Co-operative College—that are in the business of providing several very important services to Kenya's savings and credit societies such as corporate interlending and management development. Without these services to offer, KUSCCO will have a hard time becoming a self-supporting organization.

Insofar as financing is concerned, the league is alive today because several donor agencies have been willing to provide essential funding for services designated as KUSCCO's responsibilities by the government while overlooking the serious weaknesses of KUSCCO's management. The government's use of KUSCCO as an extension of its own staff has detracted from KUSCCO's "independent" role and has weakened any claim KUSCCO might have to savings and credit society financing by giving it the appearance of being a parastatal agency.

Even if it is to become a parastatal operating on subsidies, KUSCCO must nevertheless make difficult choices as to what services to offer and what subsidies to accept. The insurance program, for example, is a potential income-producer, but it is a questionable KUSCCO service because it focuses attention and concentrates resources on symptomatic bookeeping problems almost to the exclusion of the more fundamental management deficiencies in both the league and the societies. Similarly, societies that are required to use KUSCCO's subsidized, centralized bookkeeping service are in danger of becoming as dependent as KUSCCO itself on outside assistance.

Kenya has made no excuses about its intention to use foreign aid to achieve economic growth. The entire agricultural co-operative marketing system has long been dependent on a corps of non-African managers who were originally supposed to be on temporary assignment. In this milieu, KUSCCO's dependency seems to be normal, at least until there is some resistance on the part of donors. Given Kenya's strategic importance to the United States and the Western bloc and the unique advantages of a Nairobi headquarters for any non-African organization seeking to maintain a presence on the African continent, it is unlikely that Kenya's savings and credit movement will want for either government aid or nongovernmental organization donors.

Predictably, this generosity will lead to the introduction of expensive, sophisticated, electronic machines and computer programs which will have considerable appeal to the large nationwide societies. The question is whether KUSCCO will be bypassed, leaving it with the unprofitable responsibility of catering for the small societies, and thereby making it even more dependent.

Some rethinking of KUSCCO's structure, services, and financing seems inevitable, possibly by calling for a return to a decentralized system of provincial councils that eventually would become the foundation for a more representative national association. Or KUSCCO might, through an accommodation with the Co-operative Bank, become more of a second-tier financing organization like the U.S. and Canadian central credit unions. KUSCCO might also be integrated with and/or function as a satellite of the KNFC, becoming even more closely identified with the Kenya co-operative movement. The government of Kenya will unquestionably have a strong voice in the ultimate solution.

17. Selected Profiles

A Sampling of Savings and Credit Societies

The sampling of savings and credit societies in Kenya is not being done on a regional basis as was Tanzania because many of the Kenyan societies are national in membership and are headquartered in Nairobi or Mombasa. Nairobi and its environs have been described in some detail in previous chapters. Where a unique feature of a profile responds to the geographic location of a society, some extra descriptive background is given. We have chosen to review societies in Kenya that reflect differing membership bonds and management styles.

National Employee Co-operative Savings and Credit Societies

CODEPT Staff Co-operative Savings and Credit Society Ltd., the first society organized in Kenya to serve a national ministry, was registered April 24, 1969, to provide services to employees of the Ministry of Co-operative Development. Actually, CODEPT provided an opportunity to see if savings and credit societies could work. The staff of the CDD had many doubts about their own abilities to run such a society even though many of them were directly involved in supervising marketing co-operatives and even some of the early savings and credit societies. Some assistant commissioners hesitated to join because they were afraid they would lose their money. Some senior staff members felt it would be bad to mix senior and subordinate staff in a single organization. Some of the senior staff, when they did join, put in very small amounts of money so they would have little to lose should the society succumb to the management and other problems they were seeing in the marketing societies.

Since the staff recognized the importance of *trust* as an ingredient for successful savings and credit society development, the society was run by the CDD in its first year, with a senior co-operative officer as treasurer and charged by the commissioner of co-operatives to keep the books. Full participation was encouraged by the commissioner, Nyanjom, and the society is said to "have taken off" with the election of Diane Opondo, the commissioner's secretary, as chairman.

After the treasurer retired in 1972, the managing committee was left to run the society on its own and was faced with continuing problems in trying to use exclusively department personnel. In 1973 the committee hired a full-time secretary from within the department and provided training for him at the African Business Management Institute and at the ACOSCA course at the Co-operative College. While the secretary was in training there, the society office was moved to the college to allow him to work on the society books with the chairman, a member of the college faculty. The secretary/treasurer was further trained at a full-term co-operative management course at the college and then went on to study at Coady International Institute in Nova Scotia, Canada. Upon completion of all this training, he left the society and accepted a job with KUSCCO.

In 1976 a new secretary/manager (a nonvoting member of the management committee) was employed. He came from the banking industry and had succeeded in bringing the books up to date with the help of a clerk paid by the society and another provided by the assistant commissioner for co-operative development. The department in 1978 was also providing a fully furnished office in the building that housed the Nairobi Co-operative Development Office. Even though all society members were on check-off, some did call in person at the society office with general inquiries, to check on their accounts, to pay off their loans in cash, and to take out other loans.

In the year 1977 a very strict loan policy was initiated. Previous to that time (especially during 1972–75) "big seniors" (senior officials of the department) were getting loans of Kshs 20,000 on the security of Kshs 1,500 in shares (and the standard two guarantors), even though the generally accepted practice was to give no more than three times a member's savings. Some of these big takers were also defaulting.

At the time of the study the society did not have enough money to meet its total loan demands so each request was being scrutinized carefully, and the three-times shares formula was not considered automatic. The committee found that the member usually did not need as large a loan as he asked for. Therefore the committee was instituting an educational program to get the member to say honestly what his needs were; the committee would then try to honor the total request. With each loan, two guarantors from within the society were required, but guarantors had never been called upon for repayment. Loans were usually for school fees, income tax, home improvements, and house building. The society's standing overdraft of Kshs 100,000 at the Co-operative Bank of Kenya was used most frequently in December, the time of the holidays and the time when school fees were due.

The supervisory committee of the society, elected by the members, checked the books regularly. The managing committee of nine members plus the manager were meeting once a month; the manager always had a current end-of-month trial balance to present. The society continued to grow with approximately thirty new people joining each month, while only four or five were leaving.

We met with the board chairman, a member of the staff of the Co-operative College who was also vice-chairman of KUSCCO; the vice-president, also a staff member at the college; and the honorary secretary, a woman who was a supervisor of consumer co-operatives in the Nairobi area. In a written report prepared by the manager of CODEPT, the following points were given to us:

The total membership of 1,400 out of 1,260 eligible members reflects that a number of members transferred to work in other agencies have chosen to remain with this society. The monthly deductions through check-off have been Kshs 310,000. Accounts had been audited up to December 31, 1976. Accounts for 1977 had been submitted to the CDD's audit division, and the audit was to have been completed in May, 1978. The total share capital through 1977 was Kshs 3,220,393, while the total loans were Kshs 3,321,289.

The maximum individual loan was Kshs 37,000, and the maximum period of repayment was thirty-six months. The highest individual monthly share contribution was Kshs 1,600. There were seventy loan defaulters owing a total Kshs 240,000. The Office of the Commissioner had appointed an arbitrator to help with collection. Dividends had been paid as follows:

Year	*Total Amount Paid*	*Rate*
1973	Kshs 44,178	5%
1974	Kshs 78,033	6%
1975	Kshs 106,332	6½%

The last general meeting was held in 1976, and arrangements were under way to hold one in August, 1978.

Tembo Co-operative Savings and Credit Society, Ltd., a company-based national society, served the 5,000 employees of Kenya Breweries in all of its locations: Nairobi, Mombasa, and Kisumu. It was registered on January 24, 1972, with 72 members. As of December 31, 1977, there were 2,467 members with total assets of Kshs 8.5 million.

Kenya Breweries has been a "family set-up" with one hundred percent Kenyan holdings, and the employees have shared in the profits of the company. In addition to granting payroll deductions, the employers have played a very paternal role in the running of the society. When the managing director of the company became concerned that the people who were running the society were not competent because they came from the junior level of company administration or from the less skilled workers—it was alleged that votes for leaders had been bought with beer—he gave the managing committee six hours to resign. A meeting was then called by the government at the manager's request. It was attended by over 1,000 people. Four members of the new committee were proposed by company management, and an open election was held for the remaining eight places. The company sales manager became chairman; in fact, all four table officers were brewery managers, with the company auditor serving as volunteer treasurer/manager.

The managing committee, which met monthly, was paid "sitting fees": Kshs 80 per sitting for members and Kshs 100 for officers. The treasurer/manager stated that the society really needed a full-time paid manager and paid officers. He was keeping the general ledger himself, while the individual ledgers were being maintained by the society staff of three, one of whom was paid by the company. The other two employees were paid by the society. The company management has felt that democracy has had to be sacrificed to get efficiency.

As of December 31, 1977, Tembo had shares of Kshs 7.7 million, loans outstanding of Kshs 5.8 million, bank deposits of Kshs 3.1 million, statutory reserves of Kshs 333,000, and a surplus of Kshs 446,860. The treasurer/manager expected the society to have assets of Kshs 10 million by August, 1978. At its rate of growth, the society, he estimated, could have Kshs 28 million in assets by 1984.

The treasurer/manager was not happy with the expense of league membership (the society paid maximum dues of Kshs 12,000 annually), since he felt the society received no service from KUSCCO. The society was self-insured, putting an additional one percent of net earnings into the statutory reserve. Up to March, 1978, they had written off only two debts. The last KUSCCO annual meeting that he attended as a delegate was a waste of time in his opinion—the meeting had "too free a set up." Those with practical experience were not being heard. He would like to see twenty percent of KUSCCO's officers seconded by the government.

Loans in this society were primarily for projects which would earn money. The entire managing committee was meeting monthly to consider loan applications. Eighty-five to ninety-five percent of all loans were going toward buying farms, most of them on lease-hold and not within the land title system. (Kshs 20,000 would finance ten acres.) Investments in sugar plantations were considered good productive loans. Home improvement loans had to be repaid in thirty-six months, and all expense invoices were checked by the manager within the first three months after the loan was made.

Loans for school fees had to be repaid within twelve months; no loans were made for income tax payments nor for funerals and other emergencies that were taken care of by contributions.

The largest single loan made was for Kshs 40,000. The borrower's monthly savings and monthly loan payment could not be more than one-third of his take-home pay. This society did not follow the usual two- or three-times the amount of savings formula but used its own formula, which encouraged large savings. Guarantors were required only as a formality.

There have been some auditing problems. According to the treasurer/manager, the government assigned an incompetent auditor to reconstruct the 1976–77 books before the present management took over. The new management did its own reconstruction of the books, which did not agree with the findings of the government-selected auditor. The government refused to accept the accounts of the society auditor and refused to release payment of a 7.5 percent dividend for the combined years of 1976 and 1977. There had been a big *shauri* (argument) over getting the signature of a qualified chartered accountant on the management's audit report, but the commissioner of co-operatives was expected to approve the balance sheet.

The society was considering using its Kshs 2.5 million surplus for a residential housing development for Tembo members on lease-hold land given by the company. A possible thirty-million-shilling investment was being considered since financing of up to ninety percent was available for such projects. The plan centered around chartering a new co-operative mortgage company in which the society would have a ten percent share, the brewery company a ten percent holding, and individual members' investments would comprise eighty percent of the capital. Meanwhile Tembo had made loans secured by land titles to members to purchase housing plots in the housing development financed by Harambee Co-operative Savings and Credit Society.

Rural Community Co-operative Savings and Credit Societies

The hillside farmlands north of Nairobi leading to Mt. Kenya were beautiful to see. The landscape of small farms looked like a fisherman's knit design done in red (the earth) and green (the vegetation). Twelve years after our first visit to Mwea Tabere Co-operative Savings and Credit Society, Ltd., the visible changes included many more people working the land, walking along the roads, shopping in the small villages that seem to be prospering as good roads brought people and trading goods in from the surrounding countryside.

In our first visit in 1966, we met with the society's management committee in a small warehouse surrounded by rice fields squared off with red earth bulwarks glistening in the Kenyan sun. We were told that although beautiful, this area and its people were poor. The members were all part of a rice scheme, and getting a good harvest was essential for only productive farmers could remain with the scheme. The farmers did not own the land they farmed; it belonged to the government. The rice scheme was operated by the National Irrigation Board, which also managed the rice mill jointly owned with the savings and credit society. All of this was detailed in our notes taken at the meeting:

> Operating since November, 1963, Mwea Tabere was first registered as a co-operative thrift society February 2, 1964, and registered as credit society July 22, 1965. Eight hundred and two members started saving to buy a rice mill. Their first rice crop brough Kshs 215,000 in April, 1964. All of this was loaned out to members, at Kshs 200 per member, to buy rice sprouts to raise the next crop. The interest rate charged on 1964 loans was twenty percent per annum. This was later reduced to six percent on 1975 loans, and five percent on 1966 loans. Total savings to date, including undistributed earnings, are Kshs 705,000 for 1,192 members. There are Kshs 220,000 in crop loans.
>
> The members are tenants on a government settlement scheme, 130 kilometers north of Nairobi. Most had no experience in farming; they may have once rented an acre to raise food for families, or squatted. Ninety-nine percent Kikuyu, they came from central provinces. Half of them are now between fifty and sixty years old. They endure the hard work of day-long exposure in the water, picking weeds, etc., because they know that their only security is in their savings. They have no

demand for luxury goods, but are forming a consumer co-operative for necessities.

Many of the settlers have families living elsewhere since the houses on the scheme are not big enough for an ordinary family. They are planning and saving to buy farms which they can own; groups of forty to sixty people have already started to buy co-operative farms. Similarly, other groups have formed companies with as much as Kshs 140,000 capital and have bought farms and hired laborers to raise wheat on them.

The average farm on the scheme is four acres with 32 bags of rice as the average yield, although 160 bags are possible depending on the quality of land and skill of the farmer. Children who live with parents have some schooling available but are also expected to transplant and weed the rice seedlings, work in which they excel because of their light touch.

Kenya gets ninety percent of its rice from this scheme; by 1970 Kenya expects to be self-sufficient in rice production. The scheme is self-supporting, the biggest of its kind in Africa, and expects to have 10,000 acres in production by 1970. It now has 6,000 cultivated acres.

The estimated total cost for the rice mill, including feeder roads, etc., is Kshs 4 million. The National Irrigation Board, which operates the scheme, will form a company to build and operate the mill; it will own sixty percent of the stock and the society members will own forty percent. By reducing the farmer's costs of transportation and processing, the mill will give him a bigger net return for his crop. Government will continue to market the rice for the farmers and will receive a commission for this service.

Sixteen hundred tenants now live on the scheme. The average income is Kshs 2,400 per year, and the average savings is from Kshs 250 to 400 per year. Members of the society are confident of their ability to raise Kshs 80,000 for their projected consumer shop; they have already paid for a primary school and are building a secondary school.

Volunteer officials are assisted by two paid employees: a secretary who gets Kshs 250 per month (since July, 1966) and a clerk who gets 150 per month (since May, 1966).

At our visit twelve years later, we found the society and its Mwea Farmers' Co-operative in their own offices adjacent to each other in a commercial center that looked much like an Old West frontier town in the United States—wooden buildings, wooden market stalls, wooden walkways, bars and restaurants, muddy and potholed roads. But just across the main highway from the offices was rising a modern three-million-shilling, three-story building, scheduled for completion in 1978 and paid for entirely with society funds. The ground floor was to be rented to commercial banks, commercial enterprises, and shops. The next floor was to house a restaurant, hotel accommodations of single and double rooms, and some apartments. The top floor would house the offices of the society and would also accommodate some government offices.

It was on the advice of the co-operative officer in the area that the society did not buy a building in Nairobi as an investment but instead chose to put the building where the members could see where their money was invested, in a building that would advance economic development in the local area.

This society was described by its officers as "moving from strength to strength." The members numbered 2,843 out of a possible 3,000. It had just been granted permission to invest another five percent interest in the rice mill, bringing the society's share to forty-five percent of the total capital of this business. There was a paid professional staff of four serving both the savings and credit society and the trading co-operative. The co-operative also hired fifteen drivers for its fleet of five lorries and provided the sole transportation service for delivering white rice to the Sagina Maize and Produce Board. The co-operative also marketed bran, a by-product of the mill.

The paid manager had been with the society since 1966, when he was understudy to the manager, and in 1969 was named full-time manager. The total assets of the society as of December 31, 1977, were Kshs 6,205,974; the Mwea Farmers' Co-operative had approximately Kshs 1.5 million in assets.

The society had been using its own bookkeeping forms but in the future was going to purchase stationary through KUSCCO. The officers of the society thought KUSCCO had a great potential for service, especially in the field of education and in providing insurance services. The management welcomed the daily visits of the division co-operative inspector who was stationed in Kerugoya and the weekly visits of the district co-operative officer. These inspectors were competent to go over the books and discuss society activities. "They check what they wish to check," said the manager. The officers felt that the private auditor appointed by the government charged too much for his audit, especially since the society employed a bookkeeper who kept all records current.

The major purposes of loans at this time were for employing labor (from inside and outside the settlement) to level rice fields, transplant, and weed the rice, for school fees and uniforms, for food, and for family needs such as for marriages, burials and hospital care. The society made direct payment to doctors and hospitals upon presentation of the invoice by the member. These loans were to be repaid in one year. The maximum loan had been Kshs 20,000, which fell within the formula of not being more than three times the member's share contribution and within the member's ability to repay. The society used guarantors to sign for any amounts loaned above shares but had not yet asked any guarantor to pay off a bad debt.

Members were still being encouraged to buy lands around the irrigation area. The deals were negotiated by the society with the commercial banks to help the member buy land with freeholding title, which most members had done. Land costs were over Kshs 4,000 per acre. The society was authorized by the member to pay the seller direct after checking all the papers with the Land Control Board.

The society has been holding an annual meeting regularly, and almost all members turned up to vote on the declaration of a dividend. In 1977, 2,700 members met in a small field at the division administration headquarters when a dividend of two percent was declared. The rice mill returned to the society a ten percent dividend—the maximum allowed—on its investment. Last year the society earned Kshs 600,000, only one-half of which it used as a return to members and, as of our interview, was undecided about use of the remaining Kshs 300,000. The society was not able to purchase more shares in the mill because the government was unwilling to give up more of its investment in such a money-maker.

Since 1971 the settlement scheme management has kept individual record of all credits earned by the farmers and all deductions made for their farm inputs and has turned over a single check to the society along with a list of each individual's account activity. This simplified society bookkeeping and permitted management time to be used for other activities.

Not only was the society thriving, but members were no longer described as "really poor people." The community around the scheme provided a village polytechnic school, a family life education center, a ginnery, an airport, and a police headquarters. However, the hope of this irrigation scheme providing enough rice to make Kenya self-sufficient had not materialized, and several similar schemes were in operation in other parts of the country.

Quite a different community savings and credit society from Mwea Tabere was Ahero Co-operative Savings and Credit Society, Ltd. Ahero, registered in mid-1971, was organized through the efforts of a native Kenyan, Brother Luke, who was stimulated and supported by his priest and the local Catholic church mission.

In 1969–71 Brother Luke attended credit union courses given by a UNDP credit union specialist at Maseno Government Training Institute and studied the printed papers that were passed out, as well as books on the subject borrowed from the mission library. He had also received three months of ACOSCA training at the Kenya Co-operative College and, when we spoke to him, was applying to the Coady International Institute for a year's study.

Brother Luke began organizing societies by talking about them among the catechists of Ahero parish, and they, in turn, began recruiting members among people living and working within the twenty-one-square-kilometer Kano area which spreads inland from the eastern shores of Lake Victoria. About two hundred thousand small farmers, teachers, small businessmen, farm laborers, and traders reside in the area.

Brother Luke was not present at our meeting with the secretary, the treasurer, and employees of the society. The officers spoke with pride of the society's accomplishments. They commented on other groups taking notice of Ahero's successful service record and coming for advice on organizing themselves into a similar society. But the government was holding the others off until Ahero had grown stronger.

The society had about 1,900 active members and 100 dormant members; most of them were Catholics although church affiliation was not required for membership.

The society rented an office at a local community center. Since check-off service was not available and all transactions were on an individual basis (except for a few group depositors described later), the officials felt that the office was too small for the amount of traffic. Most transactions were in cash; checks were issued only for loans of over Kshs 1,000. Small deposits were encouraged by the society—two to three shillings—which were held until Kshs 20 had been saved, at which time the member was issued a receipt for one share. Many traders and farmers had accumulated twenty to twenty-five shares by bringing their few shillings either at the end of each day or once a week. Members also came in person to pay on their loans and to request emergency assistance.

Every morning some cash was available for emergency loans, which were usually authorized by Brother Luke or the parish priest but could also be approved by the society's secretary or treasurer, both of whom were headmasters of local schools. Tuesday was the local market day, and the office was especially busy in the afternoon when the market people brought in their day's income to be deposited in savings or used for loan repayment.

The credit committee met in the office each Saturday to accept loan applications and on the following Tuesday informed the members of the disposition of their requests. Approved loans were disbursed within the same week. The society lent up to four times members' shares at one percent per month interest on unpaid loan balances. All loans were secured; among the types of security were savings in the society, land title deeds, and salary assignments. Two guarantors from among the society's members were required for each loan. The largest single loan ever made was for Kshs 15,000 to be repaid over a three-year period.

Most loan purposes were for building houses, paying school fees, and buying farm inputs. Even the poorest farmer had a piece of land and could use money to develop it. The society had been using loan applications written in the vernacular (Luo) but was severely criticized for this by government inspectors who ordered the society to use loan application forms written in English. Loan application forms in the vernacular were allowed to be drafted only for the benefit of those who did not understand English, but the required signatures had to appear on official English-version loan applications.

The 1977 books were being audited at the time of our visit. We were told that the 1976 audit took six months, and the total assets were given as Kshs 500,000. A later unaudited government report showed that at July 31, 1977, 1,500 members held Kshs 243,368 in shares and Kshs 155,237 in deposits; their loans outstanding amounted to Kshs 319,279. While the officers felt dividends would be appreciated, it would be three to five years before a dividend would be declared because the society had chosen to put its surplus into investments such as Kshs 364,000 in a Nairobi building association and Kshs 10,000 in the Co-operative Bank.

The society accepted group memberships, and the officers cited as an illustration the membership of a school that collected money in small amounts from parents at various school meetings and deposited the total collected in a single savings account. This allowed the school to borrow money to build a new school building. The loan would be paid off by the parents' continued small donations to the school.

Brother Luke had helped manage the society and for five years did the bookkeeping (including the general ledger, trial balance, and the balance sheet), but he had relinquished his responsibilities to the elected officials and the two paid staff members, a bookkeeper and a fieldman. The field officer was employed specifically to make home visits to educate the people about the value of society services, to collect loans, and to help borrowers understand the value of staying with the society even after a loan had been repaid. Members were encouraged to borrow individually to finance productive group projects as well as to take larger loans, if they could be used profitably.

The society, with the help of the KUSCCO branch manager from Kisumu, held Member Days for education purposes twice a year; one was the annual general meeting at which time a financial statement and balance sheet were read by the government officer. As the figures were read, they were placed on the blackboard since most of the members could read and thus follow the officer's discussion. As many as nine hundred have attended these meetings in a large community hall. Last year four hundred participated in a three-hour meeting at which the treasurer, educational committee, supervisory committee, and loan committee each gave full reports.

The next Member Day was to be held when pending insurance claims would be paid. The members were very interested in the insurance coverage and felt it was a good service of KUSCCO. There were three women on the managing committee: one on the loan committee and two on the education committee.

Most of the help of the society came through the church. The government officer visited about three times a month. Since the society did not have its members on check-off, it was not eligible to be served by the KUSCCO bookkeeping center in nearby Kisumu. KUSCCO's branch manager served such a large area that he was not able to be in very close contact with Ahero.

The society's first paid bookkeeper disappeared, with Kshs 12,926 of members' funds, when he learned a meeting was to be held to which all members were to bring their passbooks for comparison with their personal ledgers. But this had not discouraged savings; instead, it had made the committee members even more faithful in the performance of their duties. The secretary of the society visited the office weekly to check on society affairs. The supervisory committee met regularly and periodically audited the passbooks of members coming to the office.

Brother Luke told us in a separate interview about eleven other similar savings societies he had organized which were awaiting savings and credit society registration after one year in which they were limited to, and registered only for, savings activities. It was important to them to be registered as savings and credit societies in order to become eligible for KUSCCO insurance. Prior to registration they were to have the choice of remaining together or becoming separate, individual societies. Among their plans were group investments in land, rental property, and where the soil was weak, in fish ponds.

The parish priest who had a car collected the savings from these societies and took the money to the bank. The diocese headquarters in Kisumu served the eleven societies. Since no loans could be made, whatever emergency loans were needed were made by the diocese, whose office of development also covered Brother Luke's travel expenses to work with the managing committee. Each month the treasurers of these societies met with him to discuss how the money comes in and how to increase savings. Two workshops were being organized to discuss what to do with money and how to beat inflation. Brother Luke considered his teaching of committee members as "training the trainers" who would spread the savings and credit society word. Brother Luke also organized workshops in the missions where he tried to reach some of the 3,000 to 4,000 potential members: peasants, farm laborers, and a small number of teachers.

Since government auditors kept their books for as long as two months, necessitating the opening of new records, the societies cut expenses by stenciling their own stationery.

Local Employee Co-operative Savings and Credit Societies

Kericho District in the Rift Valley Province is the center of Kenya's outstanding tea estates. The amount of rainfall, the climate and soil provide a special growing condition for tea. Traveling on an excellent two-lane highway, we saw bright green tea plants stretching like a never-ending carpet across the rolling countryside. Upon closer inspection, we became aware of people in dark aprons with large baskets on their backs moving noiselessly between the rows of tea plants, picking tea leaves.

The Tea Hotel, managed by African Tours and Hotels, a Kenyan parastatal company, had been a landmark hostelry since colonial times when the settlers came to the cool, beautiful highlands for a weekend of relaxation or a longer vacation with their fellow estate and plantation owners and managers. Time seemed to have stood still. The hotel and grounds were elegant and well-kept and service and food excellent.

According to the district co-operative officer, there had been some savings societies in the area designed to encourage savings by paying interest, but no loans were given. All had failed. The three active savings and credit societies in the district had been registered only recently: two on tea estates, one in town. Three national civil servant societies had branches in Kericho: Post Office, Kilima (Ministry of Agriculture), and CODEPT.

The town of Kericho had 11,000 residents, the majority of whom were Kikuyu, Luo, and Baluyah. The tribes did not mix socially.

Since tea was being planted throughout the year and there was a regular work force on each tea estate, the co-operative ministry planned to push savings and credit societies for about 30,000 estate workers in the area. The average pay of a regular worker was about Kshs 600 per month plus a house. Casual tea pickers earned only about Kshs 275 per month. Some regular workers had their own garden plots on the tea estate on which they raised food or products to sell at the Sunday market. The father, mother, and children of fifteen years or older who were not in school picked the tea. Typically, the family often opened a business in town that the wife ran while the husband and children continued to pick, since anything sold could become the basis of a small business.

Research Tea Co-operative Savings and Credit Society had as its field of membership the employees of the Tea Research Institute of East Africa, an institution run by representatives of the international tea companies doing business in Kenya. Itinerant tea pickers were not served by the society. The managing committee was made up of educated young men who served in the institute's four main departments: chemistry, botany, agronomy, and crop environment. These leaders were very frustrated by the company's June, 1977, elimination of payroll deduction for the members. The society had been organized in July, 1975, after discussing the credit union idea with a KUSCCO representative; thirty-five members out of a field of membership of seventy were charter members.

By 1977 sixty employees were members. However, fifteen members resigned out of fear of losing their jobs when the management withdrew the check-off service. They felt this action was a rejection of the society and its members. Also, this action came just at the time some workers were also trying to organize a trade union. With the loss of these members, business activity had decreased by one-half.

When government officers had come to talk with company management, they had been told there was no law requiring management to give check-off or other supports to the savings and credit society. However, the district co-operative officer who came to the last membership meeting said he was confident check-off would be reestablished.

Both savings and loan repayments were very slow because of the great self-discipline needed to bring the society cash "off the top of the paycheck." The society had also found that if the officers kept after a member to repay his loan, he resigned altogether. Even members who were repaying loans were not putting in any savings.

As of June 30, 1977, shares were Kshs 54,691, loans Kshs 30,575, cash Kshs 25,766. Loans were for home building materials, school fees, and emergencies. The member himself decided the time he would need to repay the loan within the limit of two years. The average loan was Kshs 1,000. Loan policy set limits on loans to no more than twice the member's monthly salary and required the signature of one guarantor. In his loan application, the borrower not only pledged his shares but also authorized the company to cover any loan balance at the termination of his employment out of his final pay and/or provident fund benefit.

In the beginning the company postman took the society checks to the co-operative office in town to get the co-operative officer's signature, and then the checks were cashed through the company. However, the society was taking in just about as much money from loan repayments as was being requested in new loans, so no banking was necessary. The loan committee continued to meet monthly.

While the supervisory committee had started out good, it had become slack. The volunteer treasurer said he prepared a special report for the monthly managing committee meeting. Since there was no office, he kept the books with him in his home.

The society carried life savings and loan protection insurance with KUSCCO, and the treasurer had attended one KUSCCO-sponsored training seminar in Kericho and four in Nakuru. He has had to take his annual leave to attend these seminars as the management refused to allow any paid time-out for society business. Even trips to the bank or the CDD were charged against his annual leave. However, the officers reported they continued the struggle to provide services because there was no alternative lending facility, and individual members could not afford time to go to the town to bank. The district co-operative officer has been giving the society encouragement to continue.

Miwani Co-operative Savings and Credit Society, Ltd., located in Kenya's sugar belt, was serving the employees of the Miwani Sugar Mills, an Indian-owned company. Complete reports, prepared by the society's paid staff—a bookkeeper (who posts by hand) and a typist—were ready for us upon arrival. The officers and committee members of the society who met with us were knowledgeable and enthusiastic about their operation. Their report included the following general information:

- Objects of Society: Promotion of thrift by affording opportunity for accumulating savings from which loans can be made for provident and productive purposes at fair and reasonable rates and interests.
- Formation: The society was formed in 1971 with 89 members holding shares of Kshs 2,220.
- Progress: Of the potential membership of 1,760, there were 1,512 members as of February 28, 1978, with shares of Kshs 1,609,319; 1,076 of these members had outstanding loans totaling Kshs 1,486,264.

  Loans granted from 1973 to February, 1978, amounted to Kshs 3,703,840; total income was Kshs 286,468.

  Investments included Kshs 10,000 in the Co-operative Bank of Kenya and Kshs 50 in KUSCCO.
- Meetings: The managing committee meets once a month. The loan committee also meets monthly. The supervisory committee meets at least three times a year.
- Relationships:

  Ministry—Helps in auditing, countersigning checks, and supervision of books.

  KUSCCO—Helps in providing seminars, stationery, and insurance.

  Parent company—Assists the society by providing a free rental office, but the society proposes to build its own office with full facilities.
- Plans for future: To grant large loans to help members buy farms, build houses, etc.

  To invest more money in the Co-operative Bank of Kenya in order to borrow the money needed to make these loans.

The society, as mentioned in the report, was planning to build a facility to house society offices and to provide space for businesses on land donated by the company near the town market. It had previously considered and rejected building on a plot in the government reserve, which was out of town where there was no security. The businesses would be financed by groups of ten members who would receive individual loans totaling approximately Kshs 200,000 for such activities as a bakery, corn mill, and dairy with grade cattle for milk. The society had an appropriation account (undivided earnings) of close to Kshs 100,000, but the members were not interested in multipurpose co-operative activities for the society itself.

The government co-operative field officer introduced the savings and credit society idea, and the society has had full support of management, including check-off (Kshs 120,000 is received monthly). The society owns the office equipment and furniture. Among its other assets an amount of Kshs 130,353 was receivable from Miwani Sugar Mills on February 28, 1978.

Most of the individual loans were for land purchase, business purchase, family needs, and school fees. Except for emergency loans of up to Kshs 500, all loans had to be fully secured by the shares of the borrower and his two guarantors and could not exceed three times the borrower's shares or thirty-six-months maturity. The interest rate was one percent per month.

Members were required to make share deposits of not less than Kshs 20 per month.

A dividend of seven percent was earned in 1973, nine percent in 1974, and nine percent in 1975; the entire amount was paid as one dividend. The government was auditing the 1976 books during our visit, and payment of a dividend was anticipated. Because there would be a substantial surplus even after paying the dividend, a budget for production of promotional and educational materials was to be proposed to the next general meeting.

At least a quorum (one-third of the membership) attended general meetings. Last year two meetings were held to discuss allegations that the office bearers were operating as moneylenders within the society, which allegations were disproved. The officers felt that member grievances must be aired even though criticism such as this could endanger their jobs with the company.

The society had first used KUSCCO stationery but had been able to get it reproduced locally at a much reduced cost. The officials were enthusiastic about KUSCCO loan protection insurance because loans were so large, and society members tending to travel in groups along the highways posed the possibility of a severe loss to the society due to an accident. They have had five insurance claims honored. The earlier claims took two to three months to process, but the last took only one month.

The KUSCCO Kisumu branch, with its high turnover of staff and problems of transport, had not provided much assistance to the society. There was one woman on the managing committee, and the board felt this was notable representation since there were only twenty women members because the mill hired few women.

The leadership for development of co-operative savings and credit societies was in place in Mombasa in 1965 and 1966. Mwea, co-operative officer of the province, had returned from a U.S. training visit (October, 1964, to September, 1965), and Sister Rose (now Antoinette-Rose Potvin) of Star of the Sea Convent had come back to Mombasa after a year's study at Coady International Institute, followed by an intensive course in group dynamics in Belgium.

Potvin, a Canadian and the first Kenya nongovernment promoter, contacted civil servants, railway workers, police, tailors, and textile workers. She would make her first call to the firm's industrial relations officer, tell him briefly about credit unions, and, having gotten his support, ask for the names of leaders among the work force. She would then call a meeting of the group recommended and ask them to select a few persons as potential officers with whom she would decide on a series of meeting dates.

In these meetings she encouraged the participants to discuss their economic problems and in that sharing of ideas helped them build a group spirit. The credit union idea was then introduced as a possible solution to some of the problems expressed by the group and only then was the organization of a savings and credit society discussed and the group encouraged to concentrate on government rules, management responsibilities, and bookkeeping.

Torch Co-operative Savings and Credit Society, Ltd., was organized in 1965 and became the first society in the Mombasa area; it was registered in February, 1966, to serve workers in the Mombasa oil refinery. The credit union idea had already come to their attention from a fellow worker from Trinidad, and they were ready to listen to Potvin. Within nine months of its registration the society had 101 members out of a potential membership of 220, Kshs 27,000 in shares, and Kshs 16,000 out in loans.

Loans at that time were for school fees, medical expenses, new roofs for homes, buying farms, part payments on cars. Ten years later, Torch had 239 members, shares of Kshs 1,099,320, and outstanding loans of Kshs 1,050,600. Loans were being requested for buying farms, cars, and household items, and for down payments on purchases of houses, school fees, and business investments.

We attended a regular monthly managing committee meeting of seven committee members, two government officers, and two other guests at the society's office on refinery property. The society was considering investing in a plot of land with housing for members; the selection committee reported that the property recently visited was highly overpriced in view of the poor quality of the houses built so far and recommended that the search continue for more suitable home development properties.

It was reported that the balance sheet sent for audit had still not been returned from the co-operative commissioner's office, and the managing committee was seeking ways to hasten its return under pressure from society members. The society expected to declare a 6.7 percent dividend and would call the annual membership meeting as soon as the audited books were returned. The managing committee was certain of a good turnout.

Insurance information was still being awaited from KUSCCO at Nairobi, as the committee was considering purchasing KUSCCO insurances. The committee also planned to hire a bookkeeper as soon as possible and drop the KUSCCO bookkeeping service.

The remainder of the meeting time was spent trying to reconcile two conflicting government circulars in order to provide a necessary service for a member. One directive prohibited loan refinancing and one recommended against loan balancing (paying off loans with transfers from shares). Each directive had been issued after bad experiences. Loans were being refinanced to larger amounts for a few members of a society, often at the expense of loans to the rest of the members. Loan balancing was frowned on after there had been runs on several societies whose income and assets suffered sharp declines when members withdrew their shares to pay off their loans.

In this particular case, the managing committee, which had sufficient funds to lend, was faced with a dilemma when an officer of the society, a trusted company employee, wanted to take advantage of an offer of a company car (which the employee needed for his twenty-four-hour-on-call job) at a bargain price.

He had sufficient funds in his share account to pay off his present loan with enough money remaining in shares to allow him to take out a new loan within the bylaw limitation of Kshs 25,000. He had enough money in shares plus his provident fund to provide the security for refinancing his present loan to the total amount of the old loan plus the auto loan, but the loan committee felt the applicant would be overextended—his monthly payments would be too high for him to handle within his salary. So the committee agreed to the member's original plan to balance his old loan with a shares transfer and take out a new loan for the auto. He further pledged Kshs 100 to his monthly savings, in addition to his loan payment, in order to rebuild his share account. The member was not present during the discussion.

Torch provided leadership for the original Mombasa chapter formed in 1969 to provide central bookkeeping and a central fund for area societies; the society was still providing leadership for the provincial council activities under KUSCCO, and the secretary of the society served as vice-president of the council.

Co-operative Savings and Credit Societies Intervened by Government

Mombasa Port Co-operative Savings and Credit Society, Ltd., was the second largest savings and credit society in Kenya and, at the time of our visit, had been "intervened" by the CDD and was being managed by a government-appointed commission.

We met with the chairman and manager of this society, both of whom were members of the commission appointed to serve for one year. The commission was charged with resolving the problems resulting from the mismanagement of the society by its elected officers, bringing the bookkeeping up to date, and restoring the confidence of the society membership. While the members were not happy with commission management, they had accepted this particular commission because they knew these men. The manager was the government co-operative officer (an accountant/auditor who had made the audit that uncovered the various mismanagement problems).

The savings and credit society office had been closed from April, 1977, until the commission took over management on July 14, 1977, at which time they found a difference of Kshs 1,900,000 in the loan accounts and Kshs 2,000,000 in the share accounts. The only annual balance sheet on record showed share holdings of Kshs 14 million and loans of the same amount.

The society's troubles began when the original pioneer group of officers were replaced in an annual election in 1975. The new managing committee began to take large loans for themselves which they didn't repay, gave excessive and illegal loans to their friends whether or not they were society members, falsified checks, and failed to charge or collect interest on loans. The whole mess came to light when the members complained to the co-operative officers in the area.

In the first seven years that the government had supervised the society, no audits had been made. The 1974 audit was completed, and a five percent dividend was paid in early 1977. The 1975 audit was completed in 1977 and a five percent dividend was paid in January, 1978. The 1976 audit was being made by a private auditor; the balance sheet was in Nairobi so we could not see it. There were seven accounts clerks employed by the society who were bringing the books up to date and keeping the current records. They had received special training at the Kenya Co-operative College.

Another problem faced by the society occurred with the break-up of the EAC when the East Africa Cargo Handling Company became the Kenya Cargo Handling Company and all Ugandan and

Tanzanian nationals left the area. Outstanding loans of the Ugandan nationals had been collected, and an agreement had been reached with the Tanzania government to try and recover the outstanding loans of its nationals who had returned to Tanzania to work.

Mombasa Port was registered in 1966 to serve mainly dock workers who were often illiterate and the sole support of their urban families. Since then, the company had been providing classes so that workers not only learned to read more than the "cargo handling marks" but also to write. Before the society was formed the company reserved Kshs 40,000 to provide loans to its 9,000 employees. Since not all of them could get the loans they needed, the co-operative officer in the area introduced the idea of credit unions, reinforced by Potvin.

The society was started with 200 members and Kshs 3,600 in savings and for the first six years accepted only savings. No loans were made until 1972 when it started to give Kshs 2,000 to 3,000 loans. By 1974 there were 5,000 members. The membership peaked in 1975 with 6,000 members, but when the mismanagement became apparent several thousand members resigned. In 1977, with the appointment of the commission, old members returned, and membership once more began to grow, especially after dividends were paid in 1977 and 1978. As of December 31, 1975, the latest audited figures available, there were 6,150 members with shares of Kshs 10,137,003 and an equal amount outstanding in loans. According to the manager, the society was approaching Kshs 17 million in shares.

The society had not been paying dues to KUSCCO since the managing committee members felt they were mature enough to have their own paid management staff, having been in business long before KUSCCO. At one time KUSCCO had put in two bookkeepers to help the society, but they had not done a good job. KUSCCO's bookkeeping stationery had never been used—the society designed and printed its own forms. However, the society had recently bought KUSCCO shares and, under government pressure, was resigned to paying KUSCCO dues.

Loans were being made for no more than three times shares with a maximum of Kshs 30,000 to be repaid in thirty-six months. Most of the members felt they had the right to borrow three times their share account, not the privilege of borrowing just what they needed. Loan purposes included purchasing houses to rent, buying farms and businesses, paying school fees. The credit committee was thinking about extending the time for repayment and granting larger loans since some members had over Kshs 18,000 in shares in their individual accounts and there was a surplus of money.

Employees of the Kenya Cargo Handling Company actually had three loan sources:

1. The savings and credit society where the financial position of the member was considered for each loan.
2. LASCO Club (Landing and Shipping Company of East Africa) where members could get goods on hire purchase.
3. The parent company, which would lend Kshs 10,000 for development loans, especially to nonmembers of the society. More money could be negotiated through the managing director of the company; the money was loaned to top staff at five percent interest.

Some savings and credit society members also belonged to LASCO.

The society had insisted on the signatures of guarantors but had never collected from a guarantor. Recently, however, a member with a loan was fired and had disappeared, so the managing committee was considering calling for payment from the guarantors.

The office at the port was provided by the company, which also provided check-off. Each employee's pay slip showed his share balance and his loan balance. To correct the problem of nonpayment of interest, the loan officer was now taking the time when presenting the loan check to explain that interest must be paid on the loan and to work out with the member a monthly level payment installment to cover the principal and interest due. To remain a member in the society, the worker must save at least Kshs 20 monthly.

The society was now in the process of opening an account at the Co-operative Bank. It was also looking for a plot for a tenant-purchase housing development, which it hoped to fund using surplus savings and borrowed money.

Harambee Co-operative Savings and Credit Society, Ltd., the largest society in Kenya, was reported to have 16,000 members with shares of Kshs 24 million in March, 1978, and was expected by year end 1978 to have 20,000 members and over Kshs 30 million in assets. At the time of our visit Harambee was being managed by a government-appointed commission, which in turn had hired a private management services firm to run the society. This firm was training a manager-designate.

The society was organized in February, 1970, among civil servants on the payroll administered by the Office of the President and included five ministries plus the police. While they knew of CODEPT, they were not helped by other civil servants. The Harambee group thought of Potvin of the Kenya National Promotion Committee as being their organizer.

Although the idea was slow to take off, once the potential

members understood that saving a little would enable them to get a lot, they began to pour in savings, which were accompanied by demands for loans. With this growth came problems, including inadequate bookkeeping, favoritism in giving loans, the lack of service to up-country (outside of Nairobi) members, and the misdirection of finance because of the lack of proper controls. A high rate of loan delinquency and losses resulted from the raiding of the society by "big fish" who instructed clerks, fearful of losing their jobs, to withhold reporting loan check-off information to the payroll office or had them reduce the amount of repayment agreed to on the loan application. Also, over an extended period of time, there was outright embezzlement by officers and managers of the society.

In late 1976 the commissioner of co-operatives appointed a management commission to put the affairs of the society in order, and on May 12, 1977, this commission, upon government recommendation, selected a management team to run the society from among a panel of management consultants available in Nairobi. Technoserve, Inc. management team (partially funded by U.S. and German donors) was brought in for one year to provide managerial services and to supervise reconstruction of the society's books. The management commission was scheduled to return the active management of Harambee to its own duly elected managing committee in November, 1978.

In its report to members on January 10, 1978, the Technoserve team stated that "apart from a cash flow problem, which has caused some delay between loan approval and payment, the society is now very sound financially and members may confidently expect dividends on their shares after the 1977 audit has been completed around mid-1978. . . . Of the loan defaults of 3.54 million shillings as of May, 1977, about 2.5 million has now been recovered or reinstated." However, in March, 1978, the bookkeeping was not yet current or in balance.

The credit committee of four members held one paid meeting a month to consider loan applications and met after that as many times as necessary (without pay) to consider loan requests that represented exceptions to the loan policy of the society. At least two members had to be present to do business. Loans that the manager recommended after verification of the validity of the two required guarantors and that fell within the general rules of entitlement were routinely approved by the credit committee. A member could have as many as two loans, but they could not add up to more than three times his shares. Loans of over Kshs 30,000 had to be approved by the commissioner of co-operatives. Loans for Kshs 1,000 or less for emergencies were handled by the team manager.

Analysis of Harambee Loans Approved, 5/12/77 to 12/31/77, by Category

Category/Description	*No.*	*%*	*Amt. in Kshs*	*%*	*Avg. size in Kshs*
Land purchase	877	26.09	3,786,675/30	26.53	4,317/75
Land improvement	310	9.22	1,392,940/00	9.76	4,493/35
Bldg. or house purchase	1,314	39.10	6,040,535/45	42.32	4,597/05
Bldg. or house improvement	160	4.76	667,315/00	4.68	4,170/70
Business purchase	85	2.53	493,800/00	3.46	5,809/40
Business asset purchase	88	2.62	386,970/00	2.71	4,397/40
Personal asset purchase	73	2.17	290,746/40	2.04	3,982/85
School fees	188	5.59	317,630/00	2.22	1,689/50
Medical expenses	48	1.43	96,219/15	0.67	2,004/55
Debt financing	46	1.37	212,241/80	1.49	4,613/95
Investments	80	2.38	361,124/35	2.53	4,514/05
Wedding expenses	42	1.25	124,260/00	0.87	2,958/55
Other	50	1.49	102,905/00	0.72	2,058/10
Total	3,361	100.00	14,273,362/45	100.00	4,246/76

The table above, prepared for the January 10, 1978, report, analyzes the loans approved for the period from May 12, 1977, to December 31, 1977, by category and value.

The society planned to maintain a tight lending policy for five more years in order to extend loans to more members and to give the "little people" a chance to borrow to participate in the country's development. This policy would, however, allow for the investment of surplus funds in productive projects such as the society's more than two-million-shilling investment in housing and its investment of Kshs 310,860 in shares of the Co-operative Bank. The management team was conscious of the importance of returning earnings to the members who were trying to build a retirement nest egg.

The society was giving time off with pay to employees to participate in education and training programs. Eight were studying to become CPAs, two were taking secretarial studies, and one was away for a co-operative course in Moscow. The society also paid for staff training at the Kenya Institute of Management.

KUSCCO dues were not being paid because the society felt that the dues schedule was too high and that KUSCCO provided no services needed by Harambee. The society itself had obtained the agency for all types of insurance and received agency commissions, which helped pay dividends to the members. In this insurance effort, the society was co-operating with Jubilee Insurance Company, Ltd., Pan African Assurance Company, Ltd., and Pioneer Assurance Company, Ltd. Payments for the premiums on these policies were being remitted through Harambee.

PART V

Foreign Aid

18. A Twenty-Year Perspective

During the past twenty years leagues and other associations of credit unions in North America and abroad have become a part of the development sector, engaged in the business of foreign assistance. Imperceptibly, donors and recipients who benefited from pure altruism, in the tradition of the visionary philanthropist Edward Albert Filene, have been moving toward a calculated give-and-take relationship more commonly associated with government-to-government foreign aid. This is essentially the story of the Tanzania-Kenya programs, with their considerable initial successes and subsequent problems.

The altruism of the 1960s among Saskatchewan and Michigan credit unions, which funded the Tanganyika Project, combined with a number of other factors to favor grassroots help from North America: local African leaders were already engaged in credit union development; a relatively small amount of money was required; personal relationships had been established with high level officials of the East African governments; the goals were limited; a base of operations was available away from the capital; great flexibility and freedom were given to a qualified technician with an adventuresome family.

The problems with this type of assistance began to surface when initiatives for creating a league in Tanzania indicated that relatively sizable amounts of money would be needed for an extended period of time. Instead of a very limited education, training, and consultation program utilizing a single technician who had to rely on the existing institutions and staff, an entirely new institution was to be created which would require its own staff, vehicles, and offices.

Local leaders and government officials pressed for the creation of this league. It was a logical next step in strengthening the existing societies, organizing new societies, and providing a wide range of services based on the examples they had personally witnessed, or at least read about, in the United States and Canada. They were encouraged in this by the willingness of a number of donors to provide assistance and funding. Later on, when some of these donors began to vie with each other for the privilege of providing help in their own self-interest (as governments do), it became clear to the Tanzanians, as it did to the Kenyans later, that they had mastered a basic technique in attracting foreign aid.

None of them seemingly recognized the inherent problems of creating a nationwide institution in a large country still struggling with inadequate roads, communications, schools, and a relatively uneducated population just entering the money economy. Nor were they prepared for the tremendous differences between the leagues of the North American credit unions and the unions of co-operatives in East African countries.

When the East African governments exercised their authority over the leagues, the direction of their activities, and the use of their donor-funded resources, they diverted attention from the goal of self-support. With every successful negotiation for more outside assistance, the gap widened between the original ideal of a self-supported league and the reality of a donor-funded organization. Moreover, foreign aid from various sources invariably brought in as many competing goals, strategies, and management concepts as donors, their contractors, and their technicians. The conflicts confused and discouraged the societies' leaders; consequently they impaired the abilities of the leagues to make any consistent plans for their own support.

Thus, from their very inception the Tanzania and Kenya leagues were placed in an untenable position. They could satisfy neither the government, nor the donors whose funding made their existence possible, nor their member societies. As their foreign funding increased and credit union successes were publicized, league leaders found themselves surrounded by newcomers with a more worldly outlook on the uses of gifts from wealthy Europeans and Americans. At the same time they felt frustrated in answering to foreign technicians assigned by the donors to police their respective grants: a far cry from the early days when no guarantee was needed to assure that every donated shilling was used for its assigned purpose.

Unable to support themselves, these leagues were in no worse position than ACOSCA, which they had helped to found. ACOSCA was even more important to the development community because it stood alone as a Pan-African, co-operative-based, Western-oriented association that was steadily gaining acceptance in anglophone, francophone, and Arabic-speaking countries. But no sooner had it taken off with its multi-donor cargo of well-intentioned, if overly ambitious, service programs than it began to lose power. Nongovernmental organization funding uncertainties, brought on by the darkly clouded threats of a worldwide depression, were compounded by growing antagonisms among and between the rich countries and the poor countries. Foreign aid programs were being justified more candidly as a commitment to the long-range political, economic, and security interests of the individual donor nations. With their humanitarian facade stripped away, private donor-government partnerships in support of ACOSCA were in danger of losing their altruistic constituencies.

By 1982 even WOCCU, the apex organization which needed ACOSCA to round out its worldwide operations, was having to tighten its belt and was becoming more concerned about ACOSCA's deficiencies. Having taken over CUNA's global contracts with AID, the World Council was feeling the weight of its responsibilities to the United States movement—a principal contributor to its budget and a concerned supporter of the Africans. If ACOSCA should fail, the repercussions would not take long to reach American leaders in the CUNA Mutual/CUNA World Credit Union Center where WOCCU has its headquarters.

One strong tie that binds U.S. credit unions to the World Council is a genuine concern for the thousands of credit unions they have helped to establish in other countries. Those credit unions are now represented through their own leagues and confederations in WOCCU. Many of them still need help, and that very fact from a U.S. viewpoint is one of the justifications for WOCCU's existence.

At this time, self-support for individual country leagues and for ACOSCA must be viewed as a long-range goal and like the African nations' independence, more rhetorical than real. Given more time and more experimentation with different types of income-generating activity, the leagues might possibly achieve solvency. More likely they will have to wait, just as the countries themselves will have to wait, for something like the N.I.E.O. or the Brandt Commission's proposed World Development Fund to provide the resources for a self-sufficient movement.

As an ongoing exercise, Tanzania-Kenya credit unionism demonstrates how many facets there are to foreign assistance. Fortunately for the Africans, people-to-people help preceded and laid a foundation for the government and nongovernmental organization support that followed.

PART VI

Credit Union Legislation

19. *Major Features of Tanzania and Kenya Legislation, Bylaws, and Government Regulations*

The legislative climate in Tanzania and Kenya has been hospitable to savings and credit societies, although the laws are much more attuned to the principles of governmental promotion, supervision, and management of marketing co-operatives.

The co-operative societies ordinances of the former colonial administrations have given way to the co-operative societies acts of the new nations. Non-African government registrars and their co-operative officers have been replaced by Tanzanians and Kenyans, but that has not changed the co-operative-government relationship. In fact, both governments have consistently tightened their grasp on the co-operatives in their countries. This makes it all the more remarkable that there has continued to be the kind of legislative-supervisory setting in which savings and credit societies could take root and prosper.

Among the most important decisions made by the government authorities of Tanzania and Kenya after consulting with North American credit union advisers were those authorizing the registration of savings and credit societies as co-operative societies under the provisions of their respective co-operative societies acts. While North American experience clearly supported the view that specialized savings and credit society laws were essential to the proper functioning and protection of savings and credit societies and their members, it was agreed that the legislative process might considerably delay the introduction of such societies and that better legislation might be obtained if specialized laws were to be enacted by the two countries on the basis of their own experiences. The existing statutory framework may have been stretched and twisted by government administrators to accommodate savings and credit societies, but it remains basically unchanged.

As recently as 1973, savings and credit society specialists in

Tanzania and Kenya decided, with legal advice, that special legislation was not at that time a pressing need in either country. However, this does not mean that the special legislation question is settled. Currently in Kenya the introduction of a savings and credit society statute is one of the top priorities of KUSCCO.

Only the Tanzania Co-operative Societies Act of 1968 has specific references to savings and credit societies as such. Part I defines a savings and credit society to mean "a registered society whose principal objects [are] to encourage thrift among its members and to create a source of credit for its members at a fair and reasonable rate of interest"; Part III(2) (a) (ii) names it a co-operative registered with limited liability. Part XIII, 105(2) limits the use of the words "savings and credit society" or their equivalent to bona fide savings and credit societies registered under the act.[1] Aside from these specific references, the Kenya Co-operative Societies Act (Chapter 490, Laws of Kenya Revised Edition 1972 [1967]) is similar to the Tanzania act in its provisions relating to the registration, operation, dissolution, supervision, and auditing of co-operatives, including savings and credit societies.

Experience has thus far demonstrated that reasonably effective rules and regulations can be promulgated, and, even more important, that workable bylaws unmistakably North American in origin can be written within the provisions of the co-operative societies acts. (In regard to their credit union bylaws, Tanzania, Kenya, Canada, and the United States all speak the same language.)

As seen below, the basic provisions of the Tanzania and Kenya bylaws are much the same.

Basic Provisions of Tanzanian and Kenyan Co-operative Savings and Credit Societies Bylaws and/or Relevant Acts, Rules, and Regulations

Item	*Tanzania* *Bylaw No.	*Tanzania* Provision	*Kenya* *Bylaw No.	*Kenya* Provision
Minimum age of voting member	3(b)	eighteen	7(b)	eighteen
Minimum age of director/committee member	3(b)	eighteen	Rules 33(b)	twenty-one
Liability of member	20	limited to amt. of paid up shares	28(a)	limited to nominal amt. of shares held
Nationwide society voting procedures	—	no provision	40	managing committee may establish special procedure for elections in outlying locations; no proxies
General meeting quorum	24(3)	1/5 of membership or 100 members, whichever is less	37	25 or 1/4 of total no. of members, whichever is less
Officials	27–28	board of directors (5) elected by and from membership	44	managing committee (minimum 7) elected by and from membership;
	33	credit committee (3) elected as above; supervisory committee members and society employees excluded	55 47(o)	managing committee elects chairman, vice-chairman, treasurer, and secretary from its number; may employ and fix compensation of manager
	41	supervisory committee (3) elected as above	60	managing committee appoints from its no. credit committee members, none of whom shall be executive officers
	37	credit committee may appoint loan officers	64	supervisory committee members, none of whom may be members of other committees, elected by general membership
	25(5) 75	honoraria may be paid to honorary treasurer and assistant treasurer(s) if society has no salaried employees, as approved by general meeting	41(i)	honoraria may be paid to retiring officer or committee member as approved by general membership and commissioner
Borrowing by society:				
from members	31(5)	deposit accounts authorized by board of directors	29–30	loans from members and deposits and loans from

Item	Tanzania *Bylaw No.	*Provision*	Kenya *Bylaw No.	*Provision*
from nonmembers	25(6) 20	maximum amt. fixed by general meeting up to 50% of total paid up shares		nonmembers subject to maximum approved by general meeting, subject to approval by commissioner as to amt. and terms; interest not to exceed market rates except with written permission of commissioner
Par value of shares	14	Tshs 5	22	Kshs 20
Maximum individual shares	15	20% of total shares	22	1/5 of total shares
Dividends on shares	59 80(a)	annual or semiannual, authorized by board of directors up to rate of 5% per annum	77(b) (1)	as decided by general meeting subject to approval of commissioner up to rate of 10% per annum
Limitations on loans to members				
Amount	51	maximum amt. not to exceed Tshs 500 or 10% of society's total assets, whichever is more	86	maximum amt. not to exceed 5% of society's total share capital and reserves
Maturity	—	no provision	86	two years, provided that loans for capital expenditures may not exceed 3 years
Purposes	46	provident and productive purposes only	81	worthy purposes that will benefit the borrower; credit committee required to insure that loan is used for purpose for which given

Security	46	terms and security approved by board of directors	88–89	as deemed necessary by credit committee; shares and deposits may be used, but credit committee may rely on known character, honesty, and industry of borrower, together with his income prospects
Loans to officials	55	loans in excess of their shareholdings must be approved jointly by board, credit committee, and supervisory committee	87	loans to executive officers, committee members, and employees of society must be on terms not more favorable than those to other borrowers, conform to bylaws, and be approved by credit committee and thereafter by managing committee
Interest on loans to members	47	1% per month on unpaid loan balance	79	1% per month on declining balances
Interest refund	31(3) 60 80(b)	authorized by board of directors	77(b) (2)	as decided by general meeting at close of financial year, subject to approval of commissioner
Investments	31(9) 62	board of directors may authorize investment of surplus funds in: capital shares and certain other issues of organizations restricted to societies and organizations of societies designed to serve or assist society operations; obligations of Tanzania government	47(k) Act 43	managing committee may authorize investments only in: deposits in POSB; investments and securities authorized for trust funds; shares of any other

Item	*Tanzania* **Bylaw No.*	*Provision*	*Kenya* **Bylaw No.*	*Provision*
		or securities fully guaranteed as to principal and interest thereby; shares of registered co-op organizations not to exceed 10% of shares, deposits, and surplus of societies; any investment legal for savings banks or trust funds in this jurisdiction; obligations of this jurisdiction or any subdivision thereof; loans to or shares of other societies not to exceed 25% of investing society's assets		registered society; deposits of any bank registered under Banking Act; stock of any statutory body established in Kenya and approved by the commissioner; any limited liability company approved by commissioner which is registered in Kenya and whose business is analogous to that of society; any other manner approved in writing by commissioner either generally or in any particular case
	Act 45	registrar may direct society to invest all or part of its funds in: deposits in POSB; interest bearing deposits in NBC; shares of any other registered society; such other investments as minister may, by order published in the *Gazette*, declare to be authorized investments		

Cash reserve	—	no provision	97	minimum of 10% of total share capital shall be maintained in cash in hand, society's current bank account, savings account, and/or fixed deposits
Reserve fund	56	minimum of 25% of net earnings transferred annually until registrar otherwise directs	32	minimum of 25% of net earnings transferred annually. More can be authorized by general meeting and approved by commissioner. Also, entrance fees except amount used for initial organizing expenses of first 2 calendar years, recoveries of loans, and other losses charged to reserve previously
	56	all entrance fees, late charges, fines, and transfer fees (after payment of organization expenses) added to fund		
	57	more can be recommended by board of directors and approved by general meeting		
Miscellaneous				
Affiliation with league/union and/or apex organization	31(14)	may be authorized by board of directors	47(t)	may be authorized by managing committee subject to approval by general meeting
	25(8)	general meeting elects delegates to league or other meetings		
Financial year	79	January 1–December 31	68	January 1–December 31
Language	—	no provision	85	loan repayment form, if not written in borrower's language, shall contain clause stating that borrower has had meaning explained to him and he understands it

Item	*Tanzania*		*Kenya*	
	**Bylaw No.*	*Provision*	**Bylaw No.*	*Provision*
Checks	64	all disbursements must be made by checks signed by treasurer or assistant treasurer and two members of board of directors jointly	76	all documents, including checks, shall be signed by chairman or vice-chairman, treasurer, and secretary unless otherwise decided by general meeting
Check-off system	—	no provision	11(b)	statement of account may be used in place of passbook
Required reports	66	monthly financial and statistical report sent to registrar, SCULT, and regional co-operative officer. Annually, audited balance sheet and accounts of preceding year sent to registrar all bookkeeping and other forms used must be approved by registrar	58	monthly financial statement to be posted for information of members; financial reports to be prepared for commissioner as he may require

Note: The citations of the Tanzania legislation are from The United Republic of Tanzania No. 27 of 1968, Co-operative Societies Act, 1968; Rules and Regulations, Part XII of Co-operative Societies Act, 1968; and Masharti Ya Shirika La Akiba (Savings and Credit Society, Ltd., Bylaws), Revised, December, 1968. The Kenya citations are from Laws of Kenya, Co-operative Societies Act, Chapter 490, Revised, 1972; Co-operative Societies Rules, Section 84, Chapter 490; and Model By-Laws of Co-operative Savings and Credit Society, Ltd., Revised, September, 1972.

*Unless otherwise noted, references are to bylaw numbers.

PART VII

Reflections

20. *The Credit Union Movements of Australia, the United States, and Canada*

With the help of a number of credit union leaders we look now to the credit union movements of Australia, the United States, and Canada to describe some experiences, developments, or trends that may have meaning for Tanzania and Kenya (see Appendix for statistical data).[1]

Australia

Australia's movement, which started slightly ahead of the two African movements, developed in three phases: the 1950s marked the introduction of the credit union idea brought from abroad; the 1960s were a period of rapid expansion; and the 1970s were a time of growing up and accepting the responsibilities of a maturing movement that was fast becoming an industry.

Australia's physical isolation and the fierce independence of its people created a receptive environment for the pragmatic idealism of credit unions, and they became the focal point for a new, exciting, and satisfying activity in which working people could achieve personal recognition and fulfillment while solving economic problems for themselves and their communities. The volunteer leaders had minimal outside help and few guidelines to stifle their individual ideas and initiatives.

About half of the early credit unions were parish/community credit unions encouraged by the Catholic church as socioeconomic institutions inspired by the Canadian Antigonish Movement and were centered in the state of Victoria. The others were industrial credit unions at first organized mainly among government employees and then among other workers. (All employee credit unions in Australia are referred to as industrial credit unions.) Today, New

South Wales has over half of all credit unions and credit union resources.

Credit unions originally were tax exempt. The little government supervision they received allowed them great freedom, and at the same time, employers were not only friendly but generous in providing office space, payroll deduction, and in some cases, paid staff.

As Australia developed its heavy industry, national policy encouraged immigration, and employers went all out to subsidize the credit unions whose services they were publicizing as a job benefit. Later on, some of these credit unions formed their own association, setting themselves apart from those who joined the state leagues.

A wave of prosperity swept over Australia in the 1960s. Credit unions—and their volunteer directors—were borne along on the crest of full employment and high expectations. And then came roadblocks that caused them to detour from one of their basic policies. Their tax exemptions were reversed in a series of government and court rulings in one state after another. To avoid paying taxes, the credit unions shifted from being heavily taxed mutual shareholders' organizations to being deposit institutions that could avoid paying taxes by paying out their earnings and retaining minimal reserves. Handsome rates of interest on deposits and interest refunds to borrowers effectively reduced the taxable credit union income, but as a consequence reserves for bad loans and other contingencies dropped to dangerously low levels. The financial effect went unnoticed at the time since credit unions were prospering.

Also unnoticed but perhaps even more significant was the subtle weakening of the members' feelings of responsibility. In effect they were becoming customers rather than co-owners of their credit unions, whose solidarity was also disintegrating.

It had taken about ten years in each state for the credit unions to form their leagues out of an altruistic interest in spreading the credit union gospel. Leagues gained support and recognition as representatives of credit unions during the struggle over the taxation issue, but they found themselves working at cross purposes with each other since what was good political strategy in one state sometimes worked to the disadvantage of credit unions in another state. Once the leagues got a foothold they took only a few years to conclude that a national association was needed to spearhead credit union legislative activity. In 1966 AFCUL, the Australian Federation of Credit Union Leagues, was organized by two state leagues and became fully active in 1967 to represent the organized movement in Australia and internationally as a member of CUNA International.

As credit unions stepped up their political lobbying activities, AFCUL succeeded in making an important incursion into national politics by convincing the Opposition Party (Labour) to write into its platform policy two of the most important credit union legislative objectives: tax exemption and recognition as an approved savings institution in the Commonwealth Housing Assistance Scheme. Specialized credit union laws were not obtained, except in New South Wales whose Credit Union Act (1969) became the first (and up to the date of this study the only) such legislation for credit unions. Australia does not have a federal credit union act.

Individual leagues had already been sending delegates to CUNA meetings, and with AFCUL's membership in CUNA International came the opportunity for Australian leaders to learn more from their U.S./Canadian counterparts about a number of lessons that the North Americans had picked up in forty years of experience: the need to recognize that credit union movements as they mature attract different kinds of leaders; that the effective "lifetime" of a volunteer is limited, and many of them have a limited capacity to grow into managerial material; the need to prepare for bad debt losses and operating failures with stabilization programs. It all seemed so simple. Armed with this knowledge, the Australians thought they could prepare for all these contingencies and accomplish in a few years what had taken the others so many years to do.

They soon decided, however, that they wanted no part of the Americans' schooling in movement politics, and most emphatically they did not wish to be used by the contending factions of CUNA International and CUNA Mutual Insurance Society that, in trying to lure the newcomers into their respective camps, were inciting controversies in Australia. Neither did they wish to become embroiled in making decisions solely affecting North Americans and the United States in particular. When support began to build for the creation of WOCCU as a more internationalized apex organization helping credit unions worldwide, the Australians were among the strongest advocates of the proposal.

But international altruism had to take a second place to Australian credit union survival problems in the 1970s. When the Labour government came to power in 1973 it made good on its promises to give credit unions tax relief and a competitive savings role among all the financial institutions. Within three years, however, the government administration changed again, and as the recession of the early 1970s worsened into a depression in the mid- to late 1970s, the entire banking industry came under more intensive supervision. Problems multiplied for the credit unions, the leagues, and the government.

Well-managed credit unions proved that they could survive with or without league affiliation, but there were enough casualties to shake up the entire movement and cause a loss of mutual confidence. Suggestions made by the leagues often triggered resentment—and withdrawal—by troubled credit unions. League membership dropped while league responsibilities and demands on staff were multiplied by the credit unions that were willing to accept help. Many of the volunteer credit union officials' deficiencies had been obscured by the years of prosperity; pressured by their unpleasant and demanding responsibilities, they surrendered their positions to league staff and government officers.

Nevertheless, credit union members have suffered few losses. Mergers and amalgamations, backed by stabilization funds in some states, have compressed and reshaped a loosely knit movement into an industry. The 1980s will test the ability of the Australians to forge a new unity that is crucial to the success of that industry. Organizational and political leadership may come not from the idealists but from the same managerial cadre increasingly being entrusted with the responsibility for maximizing financial returns on members' money.

Strategic opportunities await the credit unions that are prepared to provide checking (which is on the horizon), automated teller machines, credit cards, and other new financial services. But not everyone is enthusiastic about the prospect of more pooling of credit union resources and decision making through centralized institutions. And there can be little satisfaction, even among the most ardent advocates of growth, in the trend to depersonalize members' relationships with their credit unions or in the widening gulf between the interests of savers versus borrowers.

However, among the idealistic and troubled volunteers and managers there are still those who are determined to corral the supremely self-reliant Australian individualists into groups in which they can argue, if not always agree on, the possibilities of economic co-operation. As befits a country so proud of its democracy, the Australians continue to search for the best ways to sustain democratic membership involvement while meeting increasing business competition.

United States of America

United State credit unions are the multibillion-dollar product of an affluent society that is now in the process of adjusting to changes so fundamental as to invite comparisons with the Industrial Revolution. Just as credit unions have secured their place in the business of consumer credit, America is said to be moving from an industrial society to an information society in which the entire concept of "consumerism" has yet to be defined. Some of the most successful occupational-type credit unions, representing a large part of credit union membership and money, face wrenching contraction if steel, automobile, railroad equipment, machinery, shoe, and textile industries continue to be relocated outside the United States.

Notwithstanding, the credit union movement remains committed to the encouragement of thrift, the wise use of credit, and prudent management of personal and family resources. It professes an unshaken belief in democracy, co-operation, and worldwide advancement of the credit union idea, while adjusting to technological change in the maturing global economy.

U.S. credit unions have weathered the Great Depression and subsequent recessions. Whether they will survive this century in their present form is not as important as whether their concepts of self-help, co-operation, and democracy will endure in the restructuring of America. Their history says much about their ability to adjust to changing times, and perhaps foretells their response to the future.

The historical origins of U.S. credit unions go back to the beginning of the twentieth century when money was scarce and credit was unavailable to the low income worker except on usurious terms. Americans today feel at home in banks; they are knowledgeable about interest rates; they know how to use credit (and abuse it). In the early 1900s banking was a total mystery to most people and certainly to office and factory workers afraid to risk their few dollars of savings in any kind of loan scheme. Some workers had the experience of mutual self-help with close friends or relatives, but it took well-to-do, public-spirited leaders and credit union ideas imported from Canada and other countries to convince American wage earners of the notion that "the little man" could manage his own money.

Up until the 1950s credit unions were not taken seriously by their competitors, but at least they were spared the hysterical opposition encountered by the trade unions. An eminent and generous patron, Filene, had given them entrée to the strongholds of American power, and his emissary Roy Bergengren had described the idealistic "brother's keeper" role for them within the American capitalistic system. Although credit unions did little to change U.S. societal patterns or politics between the 1950s and the 1980s, they succeeded in demolishing the myth that only professional bankers can manage money.

The idealism of getting people to save together so some of

them can get small loans has proved to be good credit union business (banks have capitalized on it as well), but conservatism and inflation have taken their toll of character lending. When borrowers had nothing to offer except their good name and reputation as security for a loan, credit unions were responsive to their needs, although they had no collateral. Credit unions provided low cost loans with no hidden charges, and as leagues became active in the 1950s they began to speak out for the credit unions against overpriced credit life insurance, unfair finance company practices, and other abuses in the consumer loan industry. Simultaneously, overextended, credit-happy consumers were able to go to their credit unions for counseling services in some states, adding to the reputation of credit unions as consumer-oriented lenders. In the 1960s and through the 1970s, flourishing credit unions were setting yardstick standards for other lenders—but even as they were raising their unsecured loan limits, they were also feeling the effects of consumer protection and bankruptcy legislation that made character lending more difficult and more risky. The booming economy, until it stalled in the mid-1970s, poured out an avalanche of consumer goods that credit unions were eager to accept as security for their members' loans. Borrowers were more than willing to mortgage their new possessions—a mere formality—since with inflation rising they expected to repay their loans with cheaper dollars. As recession turned to depression in the early 1980s, this philosophy faded. Concurrently, credit unions felt themselves being homogenized along with other lenders.

Today the ringing credit union motto "not for profit—not for charity—but for service" has been muted as credit unions try to balance their membership rhetoric with a marketing ideology. It is difficult now to distinguish the large credit unions from their competitors in the banking industry. Many of the spokesmen for the movement-turned-industry are the managers and technicians recruited from government, small loan companies, and banks who are recreating the banking mythology.

And yet the volunteers are also heard. Their enthusiasm and tenacity, like that of the once-ridiculed amateur bankers, still keeps the "movement" philosophy alive in America's materialistic society.

Looking back in a legislative perspective, both state and federal laws have helped to create and nurture U.S. credit unions, but 1934, 1970, and 1978 were the watershed years because they gave credit unions—both federal and state chartered—the unmistakable imprint of U.S. government control. In 1934 Congress enacted the law that provided for the first steps (excluding a central bank) toward establishing a federal credit union system for "people of small means." In 1970 federal share insurance was added—a measure that accelerated the transformation of the credit union movement into a credit union industry under a new government agency, the National Credit Union Administration (NCUA). And in 1978 the Central Liquidity Fund (CLF) was created to provide NCUA with a liquidity facility that has some but not all of the powers needed by a central bank to complete the system envisaged in 1934.

The central bank concept goes back to the draft legislation that became the Federal Credit Union Act of 1934. Title II of the draft, which was never approved, made provision for state central credit unions with access to the Federal Reserve System. Unable to agree among themselves and faced with implacable opposition, credit unions have been unable to restore the centralizing element that would have made them a system and have had to accept the CLF and a piecemeal assortment of corporate central credit unions that serve as interlenders. The most powerful of these is the U.S. Central Credit Union, which operates in conjunction with CUNA and the corporate centrals. However, neither the U.S. Central Credit Union nor CLF, which has been relegated to stabilization functions in NCUA, has the authority to act as the unifying central bank.

The most important unifying activity continues to be the well established network of voluntary associations typified by the local chapters, state leagues, and CUNA. Unlike the closely regulated credit unions they function without government supervision and finance themselves by collecting dues and fees. Along with a variety of credit union special interest associations they enjoy great freedom to lobby and to provide technical, training, and public relations services. Moreover, their commercial affiliates such as CUNA Mutual Insurance Society (which is now absorbing the Michigan league's insurance companies) give them additional services, bargaining power, and financial resources.

These different constituencies create a healthy diversity of business options and political opinions—the lifeblood of democracy. Witness the contest over federal share insurance, a major objective of the government since the 1950s. Despite CUNA's longstanding resistance (which collapsed only at the last moment) and the unwavering opposition of the leagues' International Association of Managing Directors, now known as the Association of Credit Union League Executives, federal share insurance became law largely due to the efforts of the National Association of Federal Credit Unions (NAFCU), a comparatively new, small, and financially limited organization.

The National Share Insurance Act of 1970 effectively put all credit unions, state and federal, under the control of the NCUA. A number of factors combined to convince Congress of the wisdom of such a far-reaching measure.

- Foremost was the rationale for all deposit insurance to use government guarantees to protect the money and banking system of the United States against any loss of confidence that could be caused by a failing financial institution.
- Many credit unions (not only those represented by NAFCU) and especially the large institutions felt they needed and deserved the prestige of government insurance to compete with insured banks and savings and loan associations. They also wanted to be able to guarantee their members against loss.
- Credit union competitors did not oppose the legislation because it was strategically more advantageous to impose additional regulation on credit unions than to be concerned with their competition.
- Some credit union members had lost their savings, and though there were few disastrous cases, congressional attention was focused on the weaknesses of the self-policing protection afforded by league stabilization programs.

Share insurance thus far has worked out much as predicted by both its proponents and its opponents. A growth spurt in the 1970s accompanied widespread insurance publicity. The move to this compulsory insurance by federal credit unions was joined by state credit unions that became eligible for NCUA or similar coverage. Several thousand of the largest credit unions have benefited tremendously; their assets have doubled and redoubled with the input of large accounts seeking guaranteed safety—and high yields. Their new buildings are replete with state-of-the-art computers and smartly attired staff. The federal and state regulatory bureaucracies have grown, and jobs for careerists have multiplied in the credit unions and their lobbying associations.

Share insurance has also spawned a mass of regulations that, along with consumer protection requirements, has become so burdensome, especially to the small credit unions, as to raise doubts about the viability of volunteer management. It has also accelerated other countercooperative trends. Membership responsibility in some credit unions has become so meaningless that proxy voting is already predictable. Co-operative saving for mutual self-help is all but gone. Even the largest credit unions have become vulnerable to the competition of the unregulated money market funds, which add to the extreme volatility of the large accounts. They must look as much to the money market as to their members for funds, in competition with the government itself. It will be government more than ever that determines how the competitive game is played. And although credit unions now have access to the Federal Reserve System, the game will be played on the turf of the banking industry, whose leaders are entitled by law to direct the "Fed's" policies.

The years of ambivalence about credit union goals—social or economic—may be coming to an end. What might be called their split personality is forcing credit unions apart. At least two different types of credit unions function with little more in common than a shared name. The lines have been drawn, although no overt steps have been taken to separate them.

One group believes credit unions must grow to survive. They conceive of a totally integrated credit union industry that can compensate its officials and/or pay taxes if necessary, cope with complex regulation, and still meet and beat the competition in the deregulated financial system envisaged by 1986. Employing Electronic Funds Transfer technology, they would give credit union members instantaneous access to their accounts and a wide spectrum of financial services at minimal cost and maximum return. Mergers and amalgamations of the smaller credit unions would be required to take advantage of the economies of scale, and membership involvement would have to be adapted to large-scale credit unions. All credit unions would have to surrender some of their autonomy to credit union central authorities that would have almost the identical powers of government to direct and discipline participants in the system.

Traditionalists, conversely, see their credit unions as independent, tax-exempt co-operatives, minimally regulated, directed by volunteers, and totally responsive to the immediate needs of their members for basic savings and loan services that can be provided without expensive staff, buildings, or equipment. They are content to remain small, but they are open to opportunities for upgrading their operations, possibly through service centers, in order to survive.

The blurred image is as troublesome to political friends of credit unions as it is to credit union leaders themselves. Congressional warnings have already gone out to NCUA that recently extended powers of credit unions were intended not to encourage growth as an end in itself but to improve credit unions' performance as distinct deliverers of basic financial services. And NCUA's former chairman has admonished credit unions against head-to-head competition with the banks.

The problem, of course, is that what is basic financial service at the end of the twentieth century is quite different from what it was at the beginning of the century. And to complicate matters, there are also quality-of-life considerations. One might think that the new generation of credit union members—affluent, educated, and young—would lean toward growth and competition, but a Harris poll in late September, 1977, showed that Americans are basically far more concerned with the quality of life than with the unlimited acquisition of more physical goods. They want to participate in community decisions affecting their lives; they prefer to co-operate rather than compete; they want to experience life directly rather than watch it on television; and they welcome challenges to their creative abilities.

The opportunity for a new crusade might seem at hand were it not that U.S. credit unions generally have never defined an explicit social role for themselves. There have always been so few community credit unions that community responsibility never became a major concern of the movement as a whole. However, the problems facing the nation today call for citizen action to implement the government's programs in such areas as neighborhood renewal, energy, and environmental protection. And citizen action, to be effective, will have to start with organizations such as credit unions that have had good experience mobilizing resources and activities at the local level.

In an era when community decisions may call for group financing of projects as an alternative to individual borrowing, there should be opportunities for credit unions to join forces with local businessmen, if not with other co-operatives, to help revitalize the American economy. Co-operative financing, one of the oft-voiced goals of past and present credit union leaders, has been pigeonholed in recent legislative maneuvering that created two separate institutions where one might have served both credit unions and co-operatives. The National Consumer Co-operative Bank (NCCB) was chartered by Congress in 1978 along with the CLF to promote, assist, and finance other co-operatives. If they succeed as planned, these co-operatives will someday own and control NCCB. With their own bank, the consumer co-operatives may soon be sharing the limelight with credit unions—or upstaging them.

Except for the services it offers to low-income credit unions, the bank has no credit union function, but it has started business under the shadow of a friendly NCUA (whose former chairman also chaired the first bank board). In 1981 the bank managed to escape dissolution as recommended by the Reagan administration, but it was forced into a premature independence that redoubles its need for credit union organizational and financial support. Strong consumer co-operatives could provide allies or alternatives to credit unions. Working together the two systems might strengthen the consumer movement and do something neither movement has been able to do on its own—help low-income Americans break out of the economic-racial poverty circle. Consumer co-operatives might also become independently strong enough to extend their services into consumer financing, with savings and credit departments that could challenge credit unions with new service concepts tied to merchandising.

Apart from their business activities, U.S. credit unions are also faced with more appeals to reinforce their international commitments. They have the resources to give generously, and they have given, but they have never explored the boundaries of their own potential—it has been much easier to rely on AID money. It will be the task of the new CUNA Foundation to revitalize the movement with more recognition of its idealistic members such as those in the National Credit Union Youth Involvement Board who are already asking to help.

Canada

Canada's credit union movement, the first on the North American continent, has developed out of a healthy diversity that reflects the absence of a national credit union law, the differences between Canada's French and English cultures, the contesting demands of its agricultural, maritime, and industrial economies, and the geographic rivalries of its far-flung provinces. Canada's long-standing credit union relationship with the United States has made for bonds of friendship between the two countries, not the least of which is an exchange of ideas and assistance and a pooling of efforts in support of Third World co-operative development.

Each Canadian region has a distinct credit union history.

Caisses Populaires

For many years the Catholic church played a major role in extending caisses populaires among French Canadians in the province of Quebec. These were the first credit unions to get started in North America at the turn of the twentieth century. Ideas for co-operative people's banks, borrowed mainly from Germany, proved to be the answer to usury and exploitation in French Canada. As a racial and religious minority in Canada, the French Catholics' community activities revolved around their parish life, and so it was with their caisses populaires, which became the trusted financial institutions of their communities by serving workers, businessmen, and professional people in close and knowing proximity to each other. As their leaders predicted, these banks have had a beneficial effect on their communities. Today the caisses populaires of Quebec (some also operate in Ontario and New Brunswick) are a self-contained system with their own insurance company, educational institutions, and overseas development institute.

Antigonish Movement

The maritime region is best known for its Antigonish Movement. It was in Antigonish, Nova Scotia, in 1928 that the extension department of Saint Francis Xavier University began to specialize in a new concept of adult education—helping the poor people of the Canadian maritimes find the answers to their economic and social problems through adult study groups, which lead to local economic group action. Credit unions, simple and viable, served as the initial demonstration activity, encouraging study groups to take the next steps into other co-operatives, labor unions, and community organizations to create a better life. Credit unions and leagues in this region are relatively small and concerned with basic services. They are still very localized, involving their members in decision making at every level of group activity.

The Antigonish study group method has spread not only over Canada but also into the United States and the developing countries of the world through the work of Coady International Institute, as the extension department is now known. The farmers and fishermen of the Atlantic provinces who were inspired by the Antigonish Movement have become the inspiration for widely scattered Coady alumni who believe that they too can become masters of their own destiny.

Ontario

Canadian credit unionists who live and work in Canada's "golden horseshoe," the industrialized and densely populated region that spans the area between Windsor and Montreal, have been strongly influenced by the success of the caisse populaire movement in neighboring Quebec and even more by the active assistance of CUNA and their fellow credit union enthusiasts across the border in the United States. Credit unionism failed twice to establish itself before it caught on in Ontario—once its beginnings were snuffed out by World War I, and again it was demolished by the Great Depression.

With the entry of CUNA Mutual Insurance Society into Canada in 1937 to provide much needed insurance services, development revived, and by the late 1930s credit unions were multiplying rapidly. Momentum picked up with the idealism of World War II, when Canadians wanted to create a better world for their returning soldiers. Ontario's credit unions, their Ontario Credit Unions Act (1940), and their Ontario Credit Union League (1941) were a part of their plans.

CUNA's emissaries were welcomed in Ontario during the formative years because of their experience in organizing credit unions. (Within just a few years Ontario and other provinces would send managers, teachers, technicians, and table officers to CUNA, CUNA Mutual, and some of the most important U.S. leagues and credit unions.) Although the Canadian leagues formed their own national association, NACCU, in 1958, the Ontario league declined to join up until 1970, possibly because it had more in common with CUNA and the U.S. movement than with other Canadian leagues.

In 1951–52 credit unions were growing faster in Ontario than anywhere else in Canada or in the United States. At the end of 1957 Toronto had the world's largest chapter. The Ontario movement continued to burgeon in the mid-1950s, a period of feverish volunteer organizing activity that accompanied general Canadian growth and prosperity.

When it became evident that Ontario credit unions needed more supervision, government and credit unions turned to the Ontario Credit Union League in order to keep government intervention in credit union affairs to a minimum. In 1957 the league was given additional responsibilities to supervise and examine individual credit unions.

Meanwhile, in this rapid growth period a bitter rivalry broke out between two factions fighting for leadership of the movement. The immediate conflict was provoked by competition between the Ontario Co-operative Credit Society (OCCS), formed in 1954, and the League Central Credit Department for control over the increasingly important credit union interlending business. Differences were not resolved until 1972 when League Central bought out OCCS. This dispute and the refusal of some credit unions to pay dues they considered too high cost the league some of its largest members.

The 1960s opened a new decade for Ontario credit unions with government-approved, full-time, paid staffs, a league stabilization fund, and a move toward fewer and bigger credit unions to meet the increasing competition of banks, which could offer full-service convenience through their branches. Government restrictions on community credit unions were eased, which led to a proliferation of community credit unions accompanied by mergers and liquidations of small credit unions. By the end of the 1970s credit union offices were everywhere, models of modern, computerized management techniques.

The Ontario movement in the 1980s is a major force in Canadian credit union and co-operative development, committed to maintaining credit unions' competitive position while retaining their individuality.

British Columbia

During the depression, various community groups in British Columbia became convinced that, independent as they each had to be to survive, their best hope for improving their total economic situation was to act collectively. Thus, in 1936 the first credit union in British Columbia was organized. An adult education program of the extension department of the University of British Columbia, with teaching assistance from Saint Francis Xavier University staff, introduced the credit union idea to members of fishermen's co-operatives, trade unions, and communities in which the fishermen lived.

The British Columbia credit union movement remains community and co-operative centered. In the economic field this movement has closely allied itself with other credit unions and co-operatives throughout Canada to pool surplus funds and to undertake major loans and investments in other related corporations. In the social field the movement has been in the forefront of efforts for improved housing, truth in lending, help for the disadvantaged, and youth-related programs, particularly in education. Politically, it has been active in updating credit union legislation provincially and nationally and in initiating other legislation that would help credit unions and/or their members (such as farmers and fisheries loan legislation). The new British Columbia Credit Union Centre, owned by the British Columbia Central Credit Union (BCCCU) and other co-operatives, is a major addition to Vancouver's False Creek waterfront redevelopment area.

With growth and increased competition with the chartered

banks have come new concepts of community charters with an "open" common bond and an extreme diversification of financial services. A new type of competition now challenges credit unions as they vie with each other for the same potential members. Some credit unions have grown very large while some of the smaller credit unions have disappeared through merger and dissolution. And yet there are also credit unions which have not changed appreciably since the late 1940s.

As a result, the British Columbians are rethinking their strategies and their services during a period of economic adversity when credit unions are also very visible to government and to their competitors. Growth objectives of the past no longer suffice for the development of a movement in which population differences, social differences, shifting economic foundations, and the contending convictions of leaders have all become unpredictable factors in the credit union equation.

The Prairie Provinces

> The settlement and development of Western Canada was promoted as a means to defend the western plains from annexation to the United States and to develop eastern commerce and industry. . . . The building of the transcontinental railway, the tariff policy as well as the inducements to settle the plains region all were intended to serve these purposes. In the process, the Canadian agricultural industry always was subservient to the needs of other industrial and commercial development.[2]

Canada's agricultural prairie provinces (Saskatchewan, Alberta, and Manitoba), isolated by thousands of miles from the eastern centers of power and dependent on a single crop—wheat, became the birthplace of some of the nation's strongest co-operatives. These early co-operatives were organized by farmers to process and market their farm products, and they laid the foundation for a system of specialized co-operative organizations in which credit unions play a major role.

During the Great Depression credit almost disappeared in the prairies as the banks consolidated their branches, and as a result, a money co-operative had to be created. Loans of even the smallest amount made the difference between the end or the survival of the family farm. Step by step, credit unions moved from small, short-term lending based on small savings to becoming the communities' banks. As economic conditions improved, the chartered bank branches returned; intense competition demanded that credit unions take the next steps to centralize their finances and technical support. Credit union leaders have had to rationalize the advantages of efficiency compared to the disadvantages of large, impersonal organizations.

Co-operation is big business on the prairies today. Wheat pools with their thousands of elevators handle some eighty percent of Canada's cash grain crop. Insurance, retirement funds, and estate administration are also handled co-operatively. The Co-operative College of Canada in Saskatoon has become a center for the advanced training of managers and technicians for Canada and the developing countries Canada assists.

The Canadian movement's growth has been marked by conflicts and crises. Even now divisive forces and financial problems threaten to rip some of the leagues apart. However, leaders of impressive foresight and creativity have always emerged to achieve the harmony necessary for democratic progress. A. Rod Glen, one giant of the Canadian movement who died recently, left this farewell message:

> For 30 years credit unions have had everything going for them—a vacuum in the market-place which they were quick to fill with consumer loans, and mortgage loans and loans to small businesses—an early recognition that ordinary people with their small savings could be mobilized into a powerful financial and social institution—and an expanding economy which made it easy to obtain laws and experiment with new services. In the process, I think, some people, some leaders, came to the conclusion that individual accomplishment was superior to group attainment. That is the paradox of our times. The more independently we have been able to operate, the more interdependent we have become. What we have built, in effect, is a system which has allowed many options. But nonetheless, it is a system upon which we must all rely and which must continue to be improved as events indicate it should.[3]

Glen's successors are striving to bring their organizations together in support of a nationwide co-operative development program. With a projected 54.5 percent of the population expected to be credit union members by 1985, they foresee not only a tremendous potential market for a wide range of co-operative services but also a membership clientele that is already predisposed to participate. Credit union is now a household word throughout Canada. Membership and resources have increased even as amalgamations and mergers have reduced the number of individual societies. The Canadian credit union experience points to the validity of new and different concepts of credit union organization in which the traditional common bonds are reinterpreted in terms of need, understanding, and commitment on the part of the organizing group to permit open charters.

French Canadians with their strong independent Desjardins movement are beginning to pool the technical resources of their La Societe de Development International Desjardins with those of the Co-operative Development Foundation of their English-speaking neighbors in helping with overseas credit union development programs cosponsored by CIDA.

At the national level the provincial centrals are now linked together with other Canadian national co-operatives in the CCCS. As the financial arm of the Canadian co-operative movement, the CCS could—through such pivotal enterprises as CO-ENERCO (Co-operative Energy Corporation)—give Canadians a measure of control over their own industries and perhaps even permit them to buy back some of their resources from U.S. and other foreign investors.

Appendix
Worldwide Credit Union Statistics

	Number of Credit Unions	Number of Members	Shares/ Deposits	Loans Outstanding	Reserves	Assets
Total Credit Unions Affiliated with WOCCU	39,481	52,308,628	$74,420,280,591	$55,678,707,588	$150,125,704	$81,894,703,582
Total Nonaffiliated Credit Unions	121,204	79,485,014	$27,748,720,257	$23,677,753,990	$703,222,902	$33,928,333,969
Total Credit Unions and Co-ops	160,685	131,793,642	$102,169,000,848	$79,356,461,578	$853,348,606	$115,823,037,551
Total Related Societies	17,241	21,321,027	$179,202,690,998	$155,712,077,489	$8,832,259,613	$254,211,275,153
WORLD TOTAL	177,926	153,114,669	$281,371,691,846	$235,068,539,067	$9,685,608,219	$370,034,312,704
Africa (ACOSCA) Totals:	10,638	1,510,613	$136,482,239	$93,723,539	$39,831,279	$184,254,973
Benin[7]	16	767	24,772	3,227	660	25,432
Cameroon	204	44,778	9,755,945	6,783,864	399,020	10,154,965
Ethiopia	163	19,630	2,210,760	1,603,726	121,630	3,028,125
Ghana	410	57,000	16,500,000	10,500,000	181,800	16,681,800
Ivory Coast	61	6,359	780,563	391,833	17,003	936,571
Kenya[8]	630	300,000	38,000,000	36,000,000	30,000,000	68,000,000
Lesotho	56	24,194	1,283,220	876,105	43,157	1,547,490
Liberia[4]	17	7,292	762,455	744,624	21,320	993,967
Malawi	26	8,667	443,531	441,723	12,497	519,033
Mauritius	47	8,600	550,000	420,000	50,000	600,000
Nigeria[7]	7,732	717,268	48,732,000	26,492,304	8,525,300	60,074,222
Senegal[9]	20	1,917	22,349	7,173	200	23,000
Seychelles	1	1,327	191,334	183,034	12,000	206,253
Sierra Leone	212	10,892	979,923	1,548,717	196,075	1,175,998
Swaziland[10]	25	1,222	40,626	14,266	6,108	46,734
Tanzania	375	67,567	6,716,754	5,057,560	140,864	9,201,032

Togo	97	4,974	486,820	301,102	1,852 (E)	544,907 (E)
Uganda	353	158,850	196,765	103,675	3,071	205,411
Upper Volta[4]	33	1,200	102,777	48,342	22,604	144,251
Zaire[4]	70	44,417	3,362,244	512,017	N/A	4,000,000
Zambia	90	23,692	5,339,401	1,690,247	76,118	6,145,782
Asia (ACCU) Totals:	3,923	1,432,628	$470,294,334	$432,903,946	$12,045,673	$532,520,514
Hong Kong	52	14,361	2,652,162	2,425,349	125,402	3,060,393
Indonesia	749	73,468	3,477,819	3,589,359	107,237	4,074,769
Japan	57	8,236	1,438,872	926,416	89,635	1,528,507
Korea	996	701,551	379,841,023	344,662,140	7,851,456	427,610,609
Malaysia	37	1,820	110,000	70,500	5,000	120,000
Papua-New Guinea[1]	33	84,064	35,424,116	32,224,950	1,692,730	41,602,471
Philippines	1,511	485,702	25,402,340	26,342,670	905,902	28,718,450
Taiwan, Republic of China	291	45,597	20,728,839	21,382,279	1,183,023	24,152,548
Thailand	234	19,649	1,329,163	1,350,783	90,288	1,772,767
Australia (AFCUL) Totals:	406	1,111,648	$1,698,000,000	$1,471,000,000	$37,356,000	$1,811,200,000
Canada (CCCS) Totals:	1,780	4,446,711	$12,629,640,000	$10,331,180,000	N/A	$13,539,020,000
Caribbean (CCCU) Totals:	429	429,648	$216,383,763	$215,117,621	$9,337,025	$240,681,576
Antigua	6	563	75,000	77,771	29,434	90,000
Barbados	24	5,500	2,944,123	2,662,918	130,659	3,228,031
Belize	22	12,382	1,879,991	1,775,776	85,900	2,093,620
Dominica	22	29,088	4,473,810	4,491,273	110,438	4,584,248

	Number of Credit Unions	Number of Members	Shares/ Deposits	Loans Outstanding	Reserves	Assets
Grenada	22	5,493	1,386,840	1,494,295	91,309	2,235,504
Guyana	57	31,766	2,400,898	1,714,628	175,341	2,831,616
Jamaica	96	220,166	96,740,945	98,443,494	3,842,380	114,720,680
Montserrat[10]	1	402	40,703	24,560	1,437	42,140
Nevis	1	602	86,297	84,045	2,711	104,897
St. Lucia[7]	12	3,721	650,809	571,346	29,415	773,662
St. Vincent	7	3,365	233,056	245,513	22,487	437,347
Surinam	39	6,000	2,334,839	2,239,562	254,514	2,461,828
Trinidad and Tobago	120	110,600	103,136,452	101,292,440	4,561,000	107,078,003

Latin America (COLAC) Totals:	2,123	2,154,193	$417,580,278	$470,006,993	$28,698,761	$573,497,780
Bolivia	190	209,089	30,029,097	26,997,046	2,595,107	37,072,959
Brazil[7]	232	235,000	16,000,000	18,500,000	1,115,200	17,090,365
Chile	100[11]	60,000[11]	6,637,000[12]	8,141,000[12]	331,850	7,374,444
Colombia[10]	217	124,568	13,050,563	44,219,882	1,139,314	50,000,000
Costa Rica	32	18,086	4,325,413	6,559,397	648,811	7,288,219
Dominican Republic[10]	118	70,500	12,600,000	11,900,000	1,034,460	12,945,648
Ecuador[4]	118	235,312	93,819,511	93,800,762	994,486	124,909,480
El Salvador	44	17,000	4,320,000 (E)	4,348,628	209,572	5,239,310
Guatemala[10]	90	90,400	9,884,136	8,994,600	278,732	13,980,390
Honduras[10]	112	34,981	11,150,000	13,650,000	759,315	15,000,000
Mexico[3]	176	129,973	30,338,775	37,149,840	4,134,960	42,001,852
N. Antilles	75[13]	11,290[8]	3,407,500[13]	3,406,500[13]	117,218	3,622,687
Nicaragua[7]	43	12,577	1,917,050	2,103,993	85,692	2,691,351
Panama	91	32,761	18,977,993	25,354,777	727,682	29,143,421
Paraguay	48	20,332	6,032,579	10,574,675	441,158	18,772,723
Peru[7]	290	775,000	144,419,900	144,437,300	13,936,520	174,631,076
Uruguay[7]	52	32,870	1,375,000	1,600,000	57,775	1,807,291
Venezuela[8]	95	44,454	8,935,761	8,268,593	90,909	9,926,564

United States (CUNA) Totals:	18,983	40,552,191	$58,565,866,000	$42,393,340,000	N/A	$64,704,680,000
Free Standing Totals:	1,162	669,176	$285,923,977	$271,364,989	$22,851,966	$308,728,739
Fiji	378	38,697	6,996,381	6,632,613	229,222	7,907,389
Great Britain	68	14,200	2,646,000	2,419,000	60,480	2,895,480
Ireland	459	512,157	241,037,246	228,768,024	21,571,171	261,690,427
New Zealand	257	104,122	35,244,350	33,545,352	991,093	36,235,443
Nonaffiliated Totals:	121,204	79,485,014	$27,748,720,257	$23,677,753,990	$703,222,902	$33,938,333,969
Australia	144	210,620	282,752,028	263,372,478	N/A	301,658,668
Argentina[3]	92	276,000	438,500,000	390,225,000	38,423,000	512,600,000
Australian Capital	1	6,585	7,388,678	5,917,014	N/A	8,134,770
Cameroon	45	9,415	257,618	2,000,000	N/A	2,526,927
Kiribati and Tuvalu[4]	2	220	11,332	24,981	7,204	32,026
India—Non-Agricultural[6]	21,797	13,183,000	723,460,659	817,760,415	93,591,751	1,350,258,898
India—Agricultural[5]	95,187	54,140,000	639,339,226	1,919,902,589	129,475,427	2,832,370,218
Ireland	4	5,376	4,194,479	4,285,730	457,971	4,031,096
Korea	460	106,203	33,889,506	28,387,227	161,948	35,752,757
Canada	1,627	5,312,179	17,157,055,000	13,399,522,000	438,678,000	18,336,430,000
Mariana Islands	1	2,588	790,350	907,658	76,193	936,900
Marshall Islands	4	2,333	2,801,427	3,200,308	N/A	3,246,877
Vanuan	5	745	72,218	24,357	4,666	65,815
Palau	20	994	1,245,892	1,153,546	100,408	1,480,747
Ponape, Yap, Truk, Kosrae	7	3,699	3,536,557	4,165,552	240,059	4,190,734
Tonga	67	4,248	291,287	245,135	6,275	297,536
United States	1,681	6,220,809	8,443,134,000	6,836,660,000	N/A	10,533,320,000

	Number of Credit Unions	Number of Members	Shares/ Deposits	Loans Outstanding	Reserves	Assets
Related Societies Totals:	17,241	21,321,027	$179,202,690,998	$155,712,077,489	$8,832,259,613	$254,211,275,153
Austria	1,030	1,500,000	9,430,850,551	9,478,667,107	418,779,420	24,348,803,526
Belgium	407	170,267	3,939,024,762	2,255,378,977	157,281,155	4,366,346,399
Cyprus	753	240,000	152,359,000	176,672,000	3,100,000	210,972,000
Finland	371	388,375	4,619,986,200	4,662,626,495	137,695,492	5,928,058,878
France	3,069	3,403,233	12,926,426,554	7,543,452,232	520,841,014	18,188,790,216
Germany	3,935	9,300,000	104,117,000,000	85,816,000,000	4,812,000,000	129,180,000,000
Hungary	261	1,515,712	618,965,822	104,914,969	27,006,073	642,279,750
Japan	47	297,237	15,409,776,700	9,387,109,200	521,055,900	18,084,660,100
Luxembourg	69	13,621	185,184,758	138,036,749	18,477,989	314,129,728
Malaysian Federation	327	505,000	140,000,000	99,500,262	35,000,000	205,000,000
Netherlands	970	950,000	21,067,691,000	31,204,666,000	1,896,228,000	44,747,039,000
Portugal	176	88,000	103,772,615	145,297,984	11,166,923	231,451,830
Zimbabwe[4]	480	18,000	250,500	195,390	12,525	278,833
Singapore	39	29,904	15,041,585	10,371,024	2,927,532	18,998,859
Republic of Sri Lanka	1,158	193,249	4,784,889	5,180,557	636,810	7,503,416
Sweden	409	407,299	4,051,924	2,769,048	202,720	4,382,777
Switzerland	1,207	260,000	6,213,000,000	4,436,000,000	255,000,000	7,511,000,000
Thailand[4]	280	535,647	126,507,716	219,246,997	6,344,134	169,627,635
Tunisia[7]	17	30,483	9,954,840	5,856,044	1,117,720	15,123,241
Turkey	2,236	1,475,000	18,061,582	20,136,454	7,386,206	46,828,965

Source: The World Council of Credit Unions Statistical Report and Directory, 1981–82. Courtesy of World Council of Credit Unions, Inc.
(E) Estimated; N/A Not Available; all monetary amounts are in U.S. dollars.

[1]June 30, 1981.
[2]September 30, 1981. [Note 2 not cited in published source.]
[3]November 30, 1981.
[4]December 31, 1980.
[5]June 30, 1980.
[6]June 30, 1979.
[7][illegible]
[8]December 31, 1978.
[9]December 31, 1975.
[10]December 31, 1977.
[11]November 30, 1979.
[12]October 31, 1979.
[13]June 30, 1977.

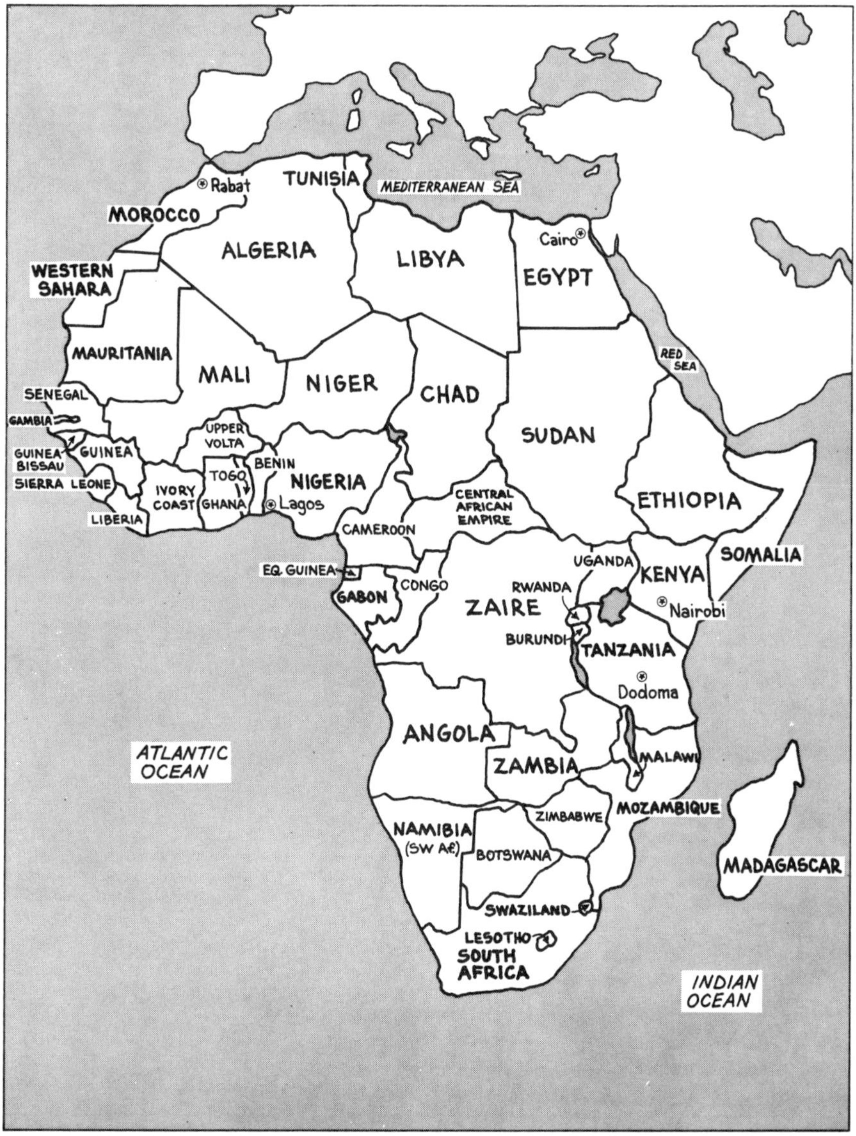
MEDITERRANEAN SEA
TUNISIA
Rabat
MOROCCO
ALGERIA
LIBYA
Cairo
EGYPT
WESTERN SAHARA
MAURITANIA
MALI
NIGER
CHAD
RED SEA
SENEGAL
GAMBIA
GUINEA-BISSAU
GUINEA
UPPER VOLTA
SUDAN
SIERRA LEONE
IVORY COAST
TOGO
GHANA
BENIN
NIGERIA
Lagos
LIBERIA
CENTRAL AFRICAN EMPIRE
ETHIOPIA
CAMEROON
UGANDA
KENYA
SOMALIA
EQ. GUINEA
GABON
CONGO
RWANDA
ZAIRE
Nairobi
BURUNDI
TANZANIA
Dodoma
ANGOLA
ATLANTIC OCEAN
ZAMBIA
MALAWI
ZIMBABWE
MOZAMBIQUE
NAMIBIA (SW Af.)
BOTSWANA
MADAGASCAR
SWAZILAND
LESOTHO
SOUTH AFRICA
INDIAN OCEAN

Africa.

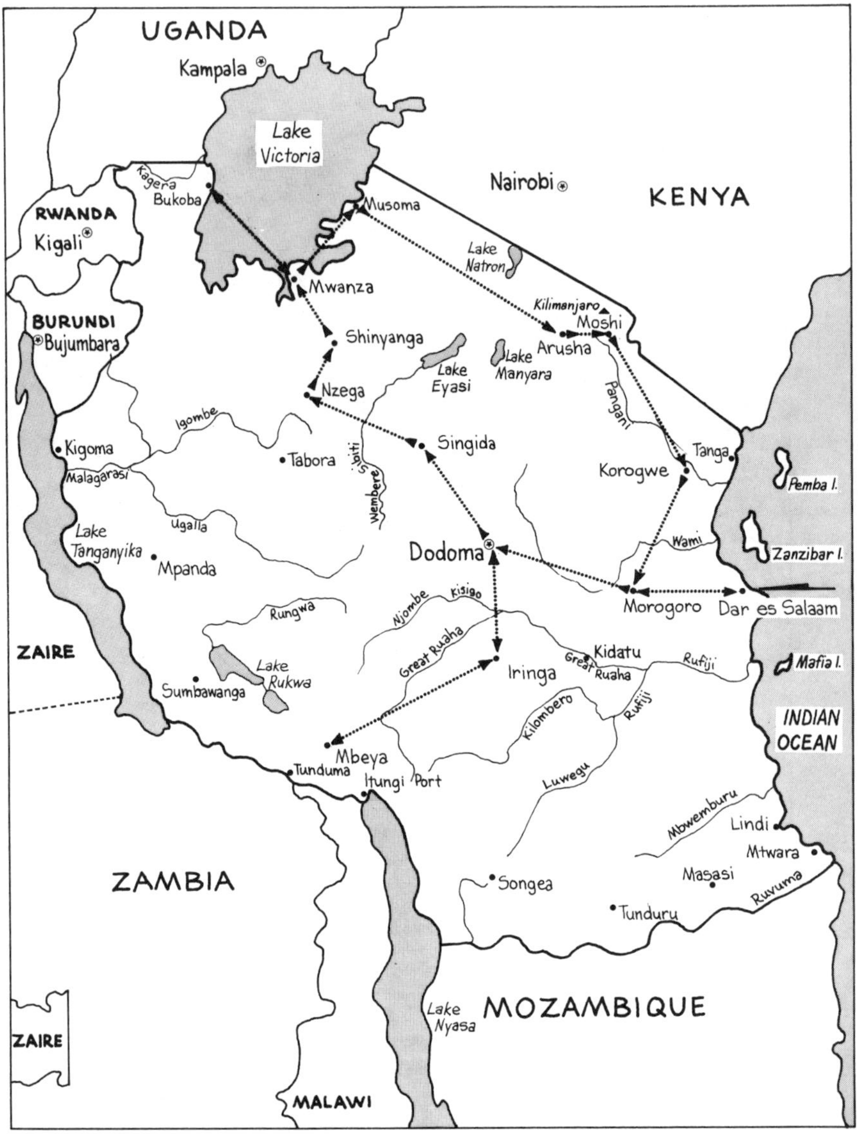

Tanzania. The dotted line with arrows indicates the route of the Dublin trip.

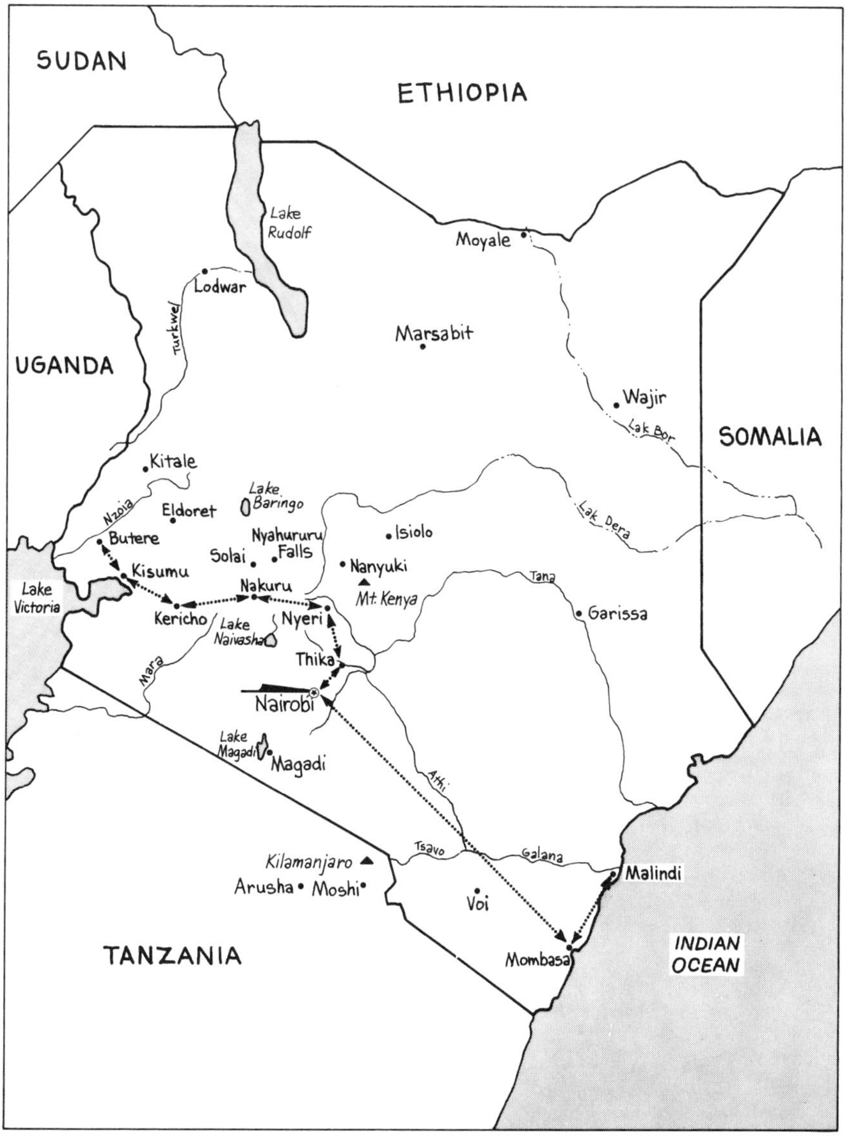

Kenya. The dotted line with arrows indicates the route of the Dublin trip.

Notes

Notes to Chapter 1

1. Koff, p. 1.
2. Lapham, p. 47.
3. Vance, "America and the Developing World," p. 4.
4. This chapter draws on a variety of published materials, the most important of which are Aggarwala; Arnold; Barnet; Barnet and Müller; "Communism in Africa"; de Blij; Kaplan, *Tanzania; Kenya: Into the Second Decade;* Moorehead; Nyerere, *Freedom and Unity;* Nyerere, Remarks on "Issues and Answers"; Resnick; Rodney; and Slater.

Notes to Chapter 2

1. See Jack's recount of his interview with President Nyerere in Chapter 5.
2. Malecela, p. 2.
3. "Kibaki's Plan to Make 'All' Kenyans Rich," p. 9.
4. *Kenya: Into the Second Decade,* p. 5.

Notes to Chapter 3

1. Principal sources for this chapter are *Central Banking;* Donald; Kirsch; Kirsch and Göricke; Loxley; Miracle, Miracle, and Cohen; and Münkner, *Credit Union Development in Africa.*

Notes to Chapter 4

1. Moody and Fite, p. 318. See also *Abridged Minutes, Joint Meeting, Credit Union National Association, CUNA Mutual Insurance Society, CUNA Supply Co-operative,* report of managing director, p. 3, and report of president, pp. 3–4.

Notes to Chapter 5

1. The first credit union in Dar es Salaam was Kianga Credit Union, Ltd., organized on Oct. 7, 1961, among members of a group from the Pare District, who had formed the Wapare Union of Dar es Salaam in 1935.

2. Dublin, J., letter to Betty Smith.
3. "Four Hundred Credit Unions Is the Target," p. 2.

Notes to Chapter 6

1. Nyerere, *Freedom and Unity*, p. 90.
2. Madery and Mwasha, *Travel Report*.
3. "Progress Report Covering First Six Months of Operation."

Notes to Chapter 7

1. *Report of the Presidential Special Committee of Enquiry*, p. 36.
2. *Co-operative Senior Officers Conference and Seminar*, pp. 114–15.
3. Binhammer, p. 82.
4. Howarth, p. 7.
5. Kirsch and Göricke (p. 73) estimate that sixty percent of SCULT's member societies with savings of some US $540,000 were thereby divorced from the movement. SCULT's 1978 report to ACOSCA shows that between July, 1973, and December, 1974, the number of society members dropped from 62,662 to 41,872 and their shares from Tshs 13,969,427 to Tshs 7,906,310. By April, 1978, members had increased again to 48,491 and shares to Tshs 23,669,569. Presumably the reported gains of 1974–78 were made in the worker-type savings and credit societies.

Notes to Chapter 8

1. *Report of the Working Committee*, p. 12.

Notes to Chapter 9

1. Bailey, A. A., "Report on Field Trip to Africa."
2. *Ten Years toward Self-Reliance*.

Notes to Chapter 10

1. We found Jack's book *Credit Unions: Theory and Practice* in a number of the libraries and noted that the copies had been checked out repeatedly.

Notes to Chapter 11

1. *SCULT Country Report on Savings and Credit Societies*.

Notes to Chapter 12

1. In January, 1980, the government dissolved SCULT and transferred its assets, its functions, and its personnel to a new savings and credit department within UCS. In 1982, a new co-operative societies act specifically designated savings and credit societies as one of the nation's major co-operative enterprises. This action and the recent decision to permit regions or districts to reestablish co-operative unions might have favorable implications for the revival of SCULT as a second-tier organization for savings and credit societies.

Notes to Chapter 15

1. "Kibaki's Plan to Make 'All' Kenyans Rich," p. 10.

Notes to Chapter 19

1. Additional references to savings and credit societies appear in the Tanzania Co-operative Societies Act, 1982, which was adopted following a governmental change of policy in 1981 to permit the revival of the co-operative marketing system. Although by-laws, rules, and regulations pursuant to the new law were not available at the time of this writing, some of the sections are of prima facie importance. Among these are section 16 which permits the primary societies to form secondary societies or unions and secondary societies to form an apex organization, and section 18—(2)(e) which specifically mentions the operation of a secondary society "to establish and operate a co-operative savings and credit service for member societies."

   Other sections specifically relating to savings and credit societies are quoted below:

   > 41. A co-operative savings and credit society, in this Part referred to as a credit society may be registered for the promotion of thrift among its members and the creation of a source of credit for its members at controlled rates of interest, exclusively for provident or productive purposes.
   >
   > 42. One or more of the words "savings" and "credit" shall form part of the name of every society registered exclusively for the purposes mentioned in section 41.
   >
   > 43. Subject to the provisions of section 44 the membership of a credit society shall be drawn from groups of persons having a common bond of occupation or association or from a group living within a well defined neighbourhood or community, or within a rural or urban district.
   >
   > 44.—(1) A credit society may, with the approval of the Registrar, admit as members another credit society or other society and any of the following organisations—
   >
   > (a) a local authority or other public body performing a function of government or providing a public service;
   > (b) a religious organisation;
   > (c) a labour organisation, an agricultural organisation or benevolent or fraternal organisation;
   > (d) an organisation operated exclusively for charitable, educational or community welfare purposes, no part of the income of which is payable to or otherwise available for the personal benefit of any proprietor, member or shareholder thereof.

(2) A society, local authority or other organisation mentioned in subsection (1) which is a member of a credit society, may vote in accordance with the by-laws.

(3) The terms and conditions under which a member society or organisation may obtain loans from a credit society shall be set forth in the by-laws, and shall not be inconsistent with the provisions of this Act, and the total amount of all loans made by the credit society to member societies or organisation shall not at any time exceed an amount equivalent to one quarter of the combined paid up capital and deposits of the credit society.

(4) Except with the approval of the Registrar no credit society shall admit to membership another credit society or other organisation unless their membership is drawn from the same general group as that composing the membership of the credit society.

45. For the purposes of carrying out its objects, every credit society may, subject to the provisions of this act and the rules—

(a) receive the savings of its members as payments on shares and as deposits either in individual or in joint accounts, and receive deposits from the societies, the Government of the United Republic or any department, board, bureau or agency thereof, any local authority performing a function of government or providing a public service, and any company the majority of the shareholders of which are members of the credit society;

(b) make loans to its members for provident or productive purposes:

(c) deposit money in the Tanzania Rural Development Bank established under the Tanzania Rural Development Bank Act, 1971 or any other financial institution as may be approved by the Registrar;

(d) invest in any stock, bonds or securities of the Government of the United Republic: Provided that the total amount of investments made by a credit society under this paragraph other than in stocks, bonds and securities of the Government of the United Republic shall not exceed one half of its capital;

(e) borrow money as provided by section 46.

46.—(1) Subject to the approval of the Registrar a credit society may borrow—

(a) upon a vote of at least three fourths of the members of the committee—

(i) moneys not exceeding in the aggregate one quarter of its combined capital surplus and deposits; or

(ii) money not exceeding in the aggregate an amount equal to the total of the market value of stocks, bonds and securities of the Government of the United Republic held by the credit society;

(b) upon a special resolution passed by the members of the credit society approving a recommendation of at least three fourths of the members of the committee additional moneys from time to time so long as the balance owing by the credit union in respect of all money borrowed at no time exceeds one half of its combined capital surplus and deposits.

(2) The Registrar shall review annually the borrowing powers of a credit society under subsection (1) and may at any time withdraw his approval of further borrowings under that subsection.

(3) A credit society may with the approval of the Registrar charge, hypothecate, mortgage or pledge its immovable or movable property, rights and powers, undertaking, franchises, book debts and unpaid calls of the credit society, to secure any liability for the repayment of moneys borrowed under subsection (1).

47. No credit society shall commence lending operations until it has furnished satisfactory evidence to the Registrar that such number as he may specify have subscribed for the minimum number of shares prescribed in the by-laws for each member, and have made the payments initially required thereon.

48.—(1) Every loan made by a credit society shall be for a provident or productive purpose.

(2) Every application for a loan shall be on a form provided by the credit committee, and shall set forth the purpose for which the loan is desired, the security, if any, offered and such other information as may be required by the committee.

(3) The credit committee shall inquire carefully into the character and the financial conditions of each applicant for a loan and his sureties or guarantors, if any in order to determine his ability to repay the loan and shall determine whether the loan applied for is for a provident or productive purpose and will be of probable benefit to the borrower.

(4) Except for loans of such small amount as may be prescribed in the rules, the credit committee shall require security to be given on all loans and shall determine the particular security to be taken in each case.

(5) An assignment of shares or of deposits or a negotiable instrument endorsed by a guarantor may be accepted as security for a loan.

(6) The security for a loan shall be in the possession or within the control of the society before the loan is made and where security covering immovable or movable property is required for the purpose of securing the repayment of a loan, the proceeds of the loan shall not be made available to the applicant until all documents necessary to establish the claim of the credit society or the security in case of default have been duly executed and if so required, registered.

(7) Notwithstanding the provision of subsection (6) the lending of money on mortgage of any description of immovable property shall be subject to the approval of the Registrar.

(8) Where more loan applications are pending than can be granted by the credit society from the funds available preference shall be given by the credit committee to the applicants for the smaller loans in the order received if the need for the loan and the security offered compare favourably with the need and the security offered with respect to application for larger loans.

49.—(1) No loan shall be made by the credit society if it would cause the borrower to become indebted to the credit society for an amount in the aggregate of all loans made by the credit society to the borrower, in excess of eight percentum of its paid up capital, surplus and deposits, or in excess of such lesser percentage as may be provided in the by-laws.

(2) Notwithstanding the provisions of subsection (1) the by-laws of a credit society may authorize the making of loans for amounts in excess of eight percentum of its paid up capital, surplus and deposits, to a local authority, or to a statutory body performing a function of government or providing a public service or to a society:

Provided that the total of all loans made to all such borrowers shall not at any time exceed an amount equivalent to one quarter of its paid up capital surplus and deposits.

50. A credit society shall not, without the approval of the Registrar make any, or any further loans if the aggregate of its reserves consisting cash on hand and on deposit with a bank or other organisation authorized to accept money on deposit, is less than ten per centum of its combined paid up capital and deposits.

51. No officer of a credit society shall be allowed to borrow in excess of the value of his shares and deposits, assigned as security to the credit society and the market value of any stock bonds or securities of the Government of United Republic held by him and so assigned unless the application is approved by a majority vote taken in the absence of the applicant, of the majority of the members of the credit committee;

52. Subject to the provisions of section 44 no credit society shall lend money to or accept deposits from a person who is not a member of the credit society.

53.—(1) No officer or employee of a credit society shall lend money from the funds of the credit society to an applicant for a loan unless the application and the loan have been approved as required by this Act.

(2) An officer or employee who contravenes this section shall be guilty of an offence.

54. The interest rates on loans made by a credit society shall not exceed one per centum per month on unpaid balances.

169.—(2) No person other than a *bona fide* savings and credit society shall trade or carry on business under any name or title of which the words "savings and credit society" or their equivalent in any other language is part without the sanction of the Registrar.

Notes to Chapter 20

1. For recommended readings for this chapter see Arneil, *Forming and Running a Credit Union;* Bergengren; Boyle; Bromberger, *Conflict and Co-operation;* Clements; Dublin, *Credit Unions;* Ellsworth; Hill; Kenyon; Moody and Fite; "The Restructuring of America in the Decade Ahead"; Runcie, *Credit Unions in the South Pacific;* and Schroeder.
2. Bromberger, *Conflict and Co-operation,* p. 5.
3. "A. Rod Glen," p. 21.

Bibliography

Abdallah, A. *The Central Bank of Kenya and National Development.* Nairobi: Central Bank of Kenya, Research Department, February 23, 1978.

Abridged Minutes, Joint Meeting, Credit Union National Association, CUNA Mutual Insurance Society, CUNA Supply Co-operative. Madison, Wis., February 12, 1953, p. 3. Report of managing director.

Abridged Minutes, Joint Meeting, Credit Union National Association, CUNA Mutual Insurance Society, CUNA Supply Co-operative. Madison, Wis., February 12, 1953, pp. 3–4. Report of president.

Accounting Manual for Co-operative Savings and Credit Societies. Nairobi: Ministry of Co-operative Development, November 1975.

Adam, M. Mlamali. "Nyerere under Fire." *New African,* September 1979, pp. 11–15.

Adams, Dale W.; Chen, H. Y.; and Hsu, C. Y. *Rural Capital Markets and Small Farmers in Taiwan 1952–1972.* Columbus: Ohio State University and Joint Commission on Rural Reconstruction, December 1972.

Adelman, Ken. "Seminar in African Diplomacy." *Harper's,* September 1978, pp. 22–27.

Africa, January 1978.

"Africa . . . Continent of the Future." *Ebony,* August 1976.

"African Socialism and Its Application to Planning in Kenya." *Sessional Paper No. 10.* Nairobi: Government Printer, 1965.

Africa South of the Sahara. London: Europa, 1974, 1977–78.

Aggarwala, Narinder K. "Media, News, and People: A Third World View." *Media Asia* 5, no. 2 (1978): 78–81.

Agricultural Credit Tables through 1977. Nairobi: Central Bank of Kenya, 1978.

Ahsan, A. S. M. Fakhrul. "On the Nature and Significance of Banking without Interest." *Bangladesh Bank Bulletin* 56 (February 1978): 1–7.

Allen, Hayward F. "WOCCU: The World Council of Credit Unions." *Review of International Co-operation* 71, no. 1 (1978).

Annual Report and Statement of Accounts 1976–1977. Nairobi: Co-operative Bank of Kenya, October, 1977.

Annual Report 1959. Nairobi: Department of Co-operative Development, 1960, p. 67.

Annual Report 1976. Nairobi: Co-operative College of Kenya, 1977.

Arneil, Stan F. "The Antipodean Question: To Be or Not To Be." Unpublished paper of November 29, 1979, prepared for the authors.

———. *Forming and Running a Credit Union.* 2nd rev. ed. Sydney: Alternative Publishing Co-operative, 1979.

Arnold, Guy. *Kenyatta and the Politics of Kenya.* London: Dent, 1974.

"A. Rod Glen." *Enterprise* (Vancouver, B.C.), July–August, 1979, pp. 20–21, 25. Publication of the British Columbia Central Credit Union.

Arusha Declaration: Answers to Questions. Dar es Salaam: Information Services Division, Government Printer, 1977.

Bailey, A. A. Letter to Father J. Van den Dries, Nairobi, February 22, 1967. Copy supplied to Jack Dublin.

———. "Report on Field Trip to Africa March 6 through May 4, 1962." Undated internal memorandum to O. H. Spetland, Chief, World Extension Division, CUNA.

Bailey, Martin. *Freedom Railway*. London: Collings, 1976.

"Banks Nationalised." *Standard* (Dar es Salaam), February 8, 1967, p. 1.

Barnet, Richard J. "A Reporter at Large (The World's Resources)." *New Yorker*, March 17, pp. 45–81, March 31, pp. 40–91, April 7, 1980, pp. 46–115.

———, and Müller, Ronald E. *Global Reach*. New York: Simon & Schuster, 1974.

Barnicle, E. Anthony, Jefferson City, Mo. Letter to Jack Dublin, August 11, 1977, enclosing copy of his paper "Casa Credit Union."

Beling, Willard A. *Modernization and African Labor: A Tunisian Case Study*. New York: Praeger, 1965.

Beltran, Luis Ramiro S. "Communication and Cultural Domination: U.S.A.–Latin American Case." *Media Asia* 5, no. 4 (1978).

Bergengren, Roy F. *CUNA Emerges*. Madison, Wis.: CUNA, 1935.

Bienefeld, M. A. *A General Theory of Trade Union Development: Some Lessons from Tanzania*. Economic Research Bureau Paper No. 72.3. Dar es Salaam: University of Dar es Salaam, July 1972.

Binhammer, H. H. *The Development of a Financial Infrastructure in Tanzania*. Dar es Salaam: East African Literature Bureau, 1975.

Black, Maggie. "Africa's Co-operative Talent." *Africa*, September 1977.

Blue, Richard N., and Weaver, James H. "The Tanzania Model of Development." Draft prepared for the Consultation on Self-Reliance and Solidarity in the Quest for International Justice, Ecumenical Institute of World Council of Churches, Geneva, April 3–9, 1976.

Bomani, Paul. *Co-operatives Must Care for the Farmer*. Dar es Salaam: Co-operative Union of Tanganyika, April 1967.

Borowiec, Andrew. "Nyerere Plan Perils Nation." *Evening Star* (Washington, D.C.), June 16, 1967, p. A–11.

———. "Rocky Road for Tanzania." *Evening Star* (Washington, D.C.), June 17, 1967. p. A–14.

Boyle, George. *The Poor Man's Prayer*. New York: Harper & Bros., 1951.

Brett, E. A. *Colonialism and Underdevelopment in East Africa*. Nairobi: Heinemann Educational Books Ltd., 1973.

A Brief History of CUNA's Involvement in Worldwide Credit Union Movement. Washington, D.C.: Global Projects Office, CUNA International, Inc., December 3, 1976.

Bromberger, Norman. *Conflict and Co-operation*. Regina: Saskatchewan Co-op Credit Society, March 30, 1973.

———. "Saskatchewan Credit Unions." Tape recording prepared for authors, Regina, November 1979.

Brown, Lester R. *Seeds of Change*. New York: Praeger, 1970.

Bye-Laws: Co-operative Thrift and Loan Society Ltd. Kampala: Co-operative Development Department, Government of Uganda, n.d.

Bye-Laws: Savings and Credit Society Ltd. rev. ed. Masharti Ya Shirika La Akiba, United Republic of Tanzania, December 1968.

By-Laws: Kenya Union of Savings and Credit Co-operatives Ltd. Nairobi: Kenya Union of Savings and Credit Co-operatives, n.d.

Central Banking in Socialist Transformation of Tanzania 1966–1976. Dar es Salaam: Bank of Tanzania, 1976. Special publication to commemorate tenth anniversary of founding of Bank of Tanzania.

CEPO Seminar. Nairobi: Kenya National Federation of Co-operatives and Coady International Institute, February 1977.

Charbonneau, G. A., Toronto. Letter to Jack Dublin, November 14, 1979.

Clark, W. Edmund. *Socialist Development and Public Investment in Tanzania, 1964–1973*. Toronto: University of Toronto Press, 1978.

Clements, Muriel. *By Their Bootstraps.* Toronto: Clarke, Irwin, 1965.

Cliffe, Lionel, and Saul, John S., eds. *Socialism in Tanzania: An Interdisciplinary Reader.* Vol. 1, *Politics,* Vol. 2, *Policies.* Nairobi: East African Publishing House, 1972, 1973. Reprinted Nairobi: East African Publishing House, 1975.

Coady International Institute. *Review 1978.* Antigonish, Nova Scotia: Saint Francis Xavier University, 1978.

Cole, C. M. *Investigation into an East African Savings Scheme.* Dar es Salaam: Government Printer, 1955.

Colman, David, and Nixson, Frederick. *Economics of Change in Less Developed Countries.* New York: Wiley, 1978.

"Communism in Africa." *Current Policy No. 99.* Washington, D.C.: Bureau of Public Affairs, U.S. Department of State, October 18, 1979.

Connell, Lawrence, Jr. "Credit Unions: A Base of Economic Development in Third World Countries." Address to tenth anniversary educational conference and fifth biennial meeting, ACOSCA, Nairobi, Kenya, August 16, 1978.

Co-op Development Division Report. Dar es Salaam: Ministry of Agriculture, Food, and Co-ops, September 1969.

"Co-operation of the Socialist Countries in the Year 2000." Joint document prepared by Central Co-operative Unions and Societies of Bulgaria, Hungary, GDR, Poland, Czechoslovakia and the Soviet Union for XXVII Congress, International Co-operative Alliance, Moscow, October 1980.

"Co-operative Development Policy of Kenya." *Sessional Paper No. 8.* Nairobi: Government Printer, 1970.

"Co-operative Education and Co-operative Development: A Study of Problems in Organization Building." Dar es Salaam: Tanzania/Nordic Study Team, September 1972.

"The Co-operative Education System in Tanzania: Some General Observations and Recommendations." Dar es Salaam: Tanzania/Nordic Study Team, July 1972.

Co-operative Future Directions Project. *Patterns and Trends of Canadian Co-operative Development.* Saskatoon, Sask.: Co-operative College of Canada, 1982.

Co-operative Movement in the Countries of Socialism. Moscow: Centrosoyu, 1980.

The Co-operative Production Credit Scheme. Nairobi: Ministry of Co-operative Development, August 1971. Staff manual.

Co-operative Savings and Credit Societies and Tanzania Rural Savings and Credit Scheme. Dodoma: Prime Minister's Office, March 1977. A village management training program.

The Co-operative Savings and Credit Society. rev. ed. Nairobi: Ministry of Co-operative Development, September 1972.

"Co-operative Savings and Credit Society Development in Kenya." Paper delivered at Ninth African Conference on the Mobilization of Local Savings, Addis Ababa, Ethiopia, August 23–27, 1971.

Cooperative Senior Officers Conference, Mwanza, September 30–October 5, 1969. Dar es Salaam: Ministry of Agriculture, Food and Co-operatives, n.d.

Co-operative Senior Officers Conference and Seminar, Moshi, November 3–12, 1970. Vol. 2. Dodoma: Co-operative Development Department, n.d.

The Co-operative Societies Act, 1967, Chapter 490. rev. ed. Nairobi: Government Printer, 1972.

The Co-operative Societies Act, 1968, No. 27. Dar es Salaam: Government Printer, 1968.

Coulson, A. C. *A Simplified Political Economy of Tanzania.* Economic Research Bureau Paper 74.9. Dar es Salaam: University of Dar es Salaam, November 1973.

"Country Report." Report from the Nairobi delegation to the Nairobi Conference on Savings and Credit Societies, September 13–16, 1968.

Country Report to 5th Biennial Meeting of ACOSCA. Nairobi: Kenya Union of Savings and Credit Co-operatives, August 1978.

A Country Statement on Kenya Presented at the First General Assembly of the African Regional Agriculture Credit Association. Nairobi: Central Bank of Kenya, November 1977.

Craig, Jack. "Views of Credit Unions in Canada." Tape recording prepared for authors, Toronto, November 14, 1979.

Credit Manual for Savings and Credit Societies. Nairobi: Ministry of Co-operative Development, November 1975.

"Credit Society." *Reporter* (Dar es Salaam), September 11, 1964, p. 29.

"Credit Union Growth 'Down Under' Is Way Up." *World Reporter* 4 (November 1972): 1–3.

"Credit Union League Backs Aid Project in Tanganyika." *Regina* [*Sask.*] *Leader-Post,* December 15, 1962.

"Credit Unions Are Breaking Moneylender's Grip." *Standard* (Dar es Salaam), January 6, 1967, p. 2.

"Credit Unions Are Now This Man's Life Work." *Sunday News* (Dar es Salaam), June 14, 1964, p. 6.

"Credit Unions Get a Boost." *Tanganyika Standard,* October 16, 1964, p. 5.

Credit Unions in British Columbia. Vancouver: British Columbia Central Credit Union, 1975.

Credit Unions in Canada. Toronto: Canadian Co-operative Credit Society Ltd., 1979.

Croteau, John T., Notre Dame University. Unpublished paper of October 19, 1979, prepared for authors.

Culbreth, Harry W. Letter to Kenneth J. Marin, Oct. 16, 1969. Copy supplied to Jack Dublin.

CUNA National Member Survey Results. Madison, Wis.: CUNA International, Inc., November 1977.

Curry, Robert L., Madison, Wis. Letter to Jack Dublin, February 21, 1980.

" 'David' Nyerere Takes on IMF Goliath." *New African,* January 1980, pp. 33–35.

Davidson, Basil. *Black Mother, Africa: The Years of Trial.* London: Gollancz, 1968.

De Blij, Harm J. *Africa South.* Evanston, Ill.: Northwestern University Press, 1962.

Decentralization of Government Administration (Interim Provisions) Act 1972. Dar es Salaam: Government Printer, 1972.

"Decree to Provide for the Establishment, Regulation, and Registration of Co-operative Societies." Revolutionary Council of Zanzibar Decree No. 3 of 1979.

DeGroot, Paul. "Western Separation Movement Gaining More Support." *Seattle Times,* March 30, 1980, p. A–26.

"Detroit Credit Expert to Aid African Nation." *Michigan Catholic,* December 13, 1962, p. 6.

"The Development of Co-operative Savings and Credit Societies in Tanzania." Paper presented by manager, SCULT, to ACOSCA Eastern Regional Workshop, March 24–28, 1980.

Development Plan 1974–1978. part I. Nairobi: Government Printer, n.d.

"The Difficult Road to Socialism." *Weekly Review* (Nairobi), April 7, 1978, pp. 3–7.

Diploma Course in Management and Accountancy. Moshi: Co-operative College, n.d.

Diploma Programs in Social Leadership and Social Development, Antigonish: Coady International Institute, n.d. [June 22–December 9, 1979; June 20–December 7, 1980.]

Directors' report presented at annual convention, Credit Union League of Saskatchewan, February 20–21, 1963, Regina, Sask.

Donald, Gordon, Jr. *Credit for Small Farmers in Developing Countries.* Boulder, Colo.: Westview Press, 1976.

Downie, Leonard, Jr. "Study Group Wants Increased Sharing of World's Resources." *Capital Times* (Washington, D.C.), December 24, 1979.

Dublin, Jack. *Credit Unions: Theory and Practice.* 2nd ed. Detroit: Wayne State University Press, 1971.

———. "Foreign Assistance through Private Investment: A New Challenge to Credit Unions and Other Co-operatives." *Journal of International Law and Economics* 6, no. 1 (June 1971): 27–58. Publication of the National Law Center, George Washington University.

———. "Theoretical and Practical Issues in Weaning Process of Cooperatives." *Dynamics of Interrelations between the Agricultural Cooperatives and the Government. Proceedings of CIRCOM 3rd International Symposium, March 24–28, 1974.* Tel Aviv: International Research Centre on Rural Cooperative Communities [CIRCOM], 1976, pp. 268–84.

———. "Work Plan Report." Moshi, Tanzania, Contract No. AID/sd-236, CUNA-East Africa Regional Credit Union Development Project, November 1965, revised March 8, 1966. Internal document.

———. Letters to A. A. Bailey, Director, World Extension Division, CUNA, October 11, October 27, and November 12, 1966.

———. Letter to Bill Chambers, March 23, 1964.

———. Letters to A. P. H. D'Souza, Nairobi, October 20, 1964, October 12, 1966.

———. Letter to J. G. Kiano, Nairobi, August 15, 1963.

———. Letter to J. A. N. Kibue, Nairobi, December 3, 1964.

———. Letter to E. P. Mwasha, Regional Co-operative Office, Mbeya Region, June 6, 1969.

———. Letter to Dan J. Nyanjom, Nairobi, September 22, 1964.

———. Letter to Father Tom O Brien, Mbitini, Kenya, August 19, 1964.

———. Letter to Betty Smith, Michigan Credit Union League, April 12, 1963.

———, and Dublin, Selma M. Interview with Peter P. Podovinikoff, Vancouver, B.C., December 22, 1982.

Dumont, René. *False Start in Africa.* London: Sphere, 1968.

"East African Building Society." March 25, 1978. Internal document supplied by J. F. M. Nyaranget, branch manager of Tom Mboya branch, East African Building Society.

Economic and Financial Review 10, no. 1 (July–September 1977). Publication of the Central Bank of Kenya.

"Economy Must Be Ours." *Standard* (Dar es Salaam), March 1, 1967, p. 1.

"Education for Self-Reliance—Nyerere," *Standard* (Dar es Salaam), March 10, 1967, pp. 4, 7.

Eleventh Annual Report for Financial Year Ended 30 June 1977, Nairobi: Central Bank of Kenya, 1977.

Ellsworth, Pat. *You—The Credit Union Member.* Longview, Wash.: Key Word, 1976.

El-Namaki, M. S. S. *Problems of Management in a Developing Environment.* Amsterdam: North-Holland Publishing Co., 1979.

Employment, Incomes, and Equality: A Strategy for Increasing Productive Employment in Kenya. Geneva: International Labour Office, 1972.

Engelmann, Konrad. *Building Cooperative Movements in Developing Countries.* New York: Praeger, 1968.

"Equality Won't Obstruct Other Goals—Kibaki." *Nairobi Times,* December 4, 1977, p. 1.

Fifth African Conference on the Mobilization of Local Savings. Madison, Wis.: World Extension Division, CUNA International, Inc., n.d. Report of a conference held at Dar es Salaam, Tanzania, January 1–7, 1967.

"Final Report on the Tanganyika Project." *MCUL Foundation 1965 Annual Report.* Detroit: Michigan Credit Union League, n.d.

"Financial Crisis Hits Credit Union League." *Standard* (Dar es Salaam), June 16, 1968.

"First Credit Society Opened." *Sunday Nation* (Nairobi), August 30, 1964, p. 5.

The First Ten Years of the National Bank of Commerce. Dar es Salaam: National Bank of Commerce, 1977.

A Five Year Development Project for Credit Union Development in Africa. Madison, Wis.: CUNA International, Inc., 1968.

"Four Hundred Credit Unions Is the Target." *Nationalist* (Dar es Salaam), June 29, 1964, p. 2.

"4th International Conference on Cooperative Thrift and Credit." *Cooperative Information.* Publication of the International Labour Office. Report of a conference held in Rio de Janeiro, April 17–21, 1977.

"Fourth National Development Plan 1979–1984: Mombasa District Development Plan, Co-operatives Sector." Mombasa: Co-operative Development Department, April 1978. Final draft.

Friedland, William H., and Rosberg, Carl A., Jr., eds. *African Socialism.* Stanford, Calif.: Stanford University Press, 1967.

Gai, Yost. "Co-operative Legislation in East Africa." In *African Co-operation and Efficiency,* edited by Carl Gösta Widstrand. Uppsala, Sweden: Scandinavian Institute of African Studies, 1972.

Gannon, J. Deanne, Washington, D.C. Letter to authors, October 2, 1979.

Gershman, Carl. "The World According to Andrew Young." *Commentary* 66 (August 1978): 17–23.

Glen, A. Rod, Nanaimo, B. C. Letter to Jack Dublin, October 19, 1979.

Giles, Richard Y. *Credit for the Millions.* New York: Harper & Bros., 1951.

"Government Aims To Foster Co-ops" and "U.S. Aid to Kenya Co-ops Announced." *Daily Nation* (Nairobi), October 21, 1964, p. 3.

"Government Statement on New Co-operative Structure for Tanzania." Radio address of Prime Minister Kawawa, May 14, 1976, translated from Swahili verbatim reproduction in *Mzalendo,* May 16, 1976.

Griffith, William E. "Africa." *Survey,* January 1965.

Guide to the Member Information Pamphlet. Nairobi: Ministry of Co-operative Development, January 1976.

Gunaratne, Shelton A. "The Politics of News." *Media Asia* 5, no. 3 (1978): 171–72.

Gutting, David. "Credit Union Growth and New Economic Realities." *Missouri Courier* 19 (June 1977): 105–9.

Habib, Philip C. "U.S. Interests in Africa." *Current Policy No. 48.* Washington, D.C.: Bureau of Public Affairs, U.S. Department of State, November 1978.

Hancock, Graham, ed. *Africa Guide 1979.* Saffron Walden, England: World of Information, 1979.

Handbook for the Committeemen and Office Bearers of Co-operative Savings and Credit Societies. Nairobi: Ministry of Co-operative Development, May 1972.

"Harris Poll Finds Significant Changes in Americans." *Congressional Clearinghouse on the Future* 2, no. 6 (December 1977).

Helleiner, G. K., ed. *A World Divided.* Cambridge: Cambridge University Press, 1976.

Hellie, M. R., Boulder, Colo. Letter to authors, October 29, 1979.

Herrick, Allison Butler; Harrison, Sidney A.; John, Howard J.; MacKnight, Susan; and Skapo, Barbara. *Area Handbook for Tanzania.* Foreign Area Studies, American University. Washington, D.C.: U.S. Government Printing Office, 1968.

Hewlett, Robert, and Markie, John. "Cooperative Farming as an Instrument of Rural Development: Examples from China, Vietnam, Tanzania, and India." *Land Reform, Land Settlement, and Cooperatives.* Rome: UN Food and Agriculture Organization, 1976.

Heyming, Peter. "Opening Remarks to the 1979 Annual General Meeting." *Enterprise,* July–August 1979, pp. 14–15, 17. Publication of the British Columbia Central Credit Union.

Higgins, Marguerite. "Red Threat Spreads in Africa." *Daily Tribune* (Royal Oak, Mich.), January 21, 1965, p. 20.

Hill, A.V. *Tides of Change.* Prince Rupert, B. C.: Prince Rupert Fishermen's Co-operative Association, 1967.

Hoskyns, Catherine, "Africa's Foreign Relations: The Case of Tanzania." *Socialism in Tanzania.* Nairobi: East African Publishing House, 1972, pp. 96–105.

Howarth, Fred. "Comments on the Report of the Presidential Special Committee of Enquiry into the Co-operative Movement and Marketing Boards." Internal document of the Co-operative College, Moshi, August 1966.

Hunt, Diana. "Personal Savings in Africa: Strengthening the Institutional Framework (Commercial Banks, Post Office Savings Banks, Thrift and Credit Co-operatives, and Savings Banks Proper)." Working Paper No. 323. Nairobi: Institute for Development Studies, University of Nairobi, August 1975.

Hydén, Göran. "Can Co-ops Make It in Africa?" *Africa Report* 15, no. 9 (December 1970): 12–15.

———. "Co-operatives and Their Socio-Political Environment." *Cooperatives and Rural Development in East Africa.* New York: Africana, 1970, pp. 61–80.

———. *Efficiency vs. Distribution in East Africa Co-operatives.* Dar es Salaam: East African Literature Bureau, 1973.

———; Mutaho, A. Z.; Rutaguza, G. H. M.; Migot-Adholla, S. E.; Hanti, I. M.; Rwegoshora, A. K.; and Mwase, Ngila R. L., eds. *Co-operatives in Tanzania.* Dar es Salaam: Tanzania Publishing House, 1976.

Ibegbu, Godfrey O. *The Multi-Purpose Cooperative Society.* Madison, Wis.: International Cooperative Training Center, University of Wisconsin, 1967.

Inspection Manual, Savings and Credit Societies. Dar es Salaam: Co-operative Development Department, United Republic of Tanzania, July, 1967.

International Annual Report. Madison, Wis.: World Council of Credit Unions, 1978, 1979.

James, Daniel. *Che' Guevara.* London: Allen & Unwin, 1970.

Johnson, Byron L. "NIEO: The New International Economic Order." *Fellowship,* June 4, 1978.

Johnson, G. E. "Determinants of Individual Hourly Earnings in Kenya." Discussion Paper No. 99. Nairobi: Institute for Development Studies, University of Nairobi, 1971.

Joint Annual Conference of Regional Ujamaa and Cooperative Development Officers, Regional Management Technicians, and Related National Cooperative Organizations and Local Institutions. Iringa, April 14–19 1980. Dodoma: Office of the Prime Minister, 1980.

Joint ICA/ACOSCA Regional Seminar For Leaders of Savings and Credit Societies Programmes in the Region, Moshi, October 1–6, 1973. Moshi: International Co-operative Alliance Regional Office for East and Central Africa, 1973.

Jumba-Masagazi, A. H. K. "African Socialism: A Bibliography." Research Information Centre Information Circular No. 4, East African Academy, September 1970.

Kamau, C. M. *The Effects of Kenyanization on Personal Saving.* Working Paper No. 97. Nairobi: Institute for Development Studies, University of Nairobi, 1973.

Kaplan, Irving, ed. *Tanzania, A Country Study.* Foreign Area Studies, American University. Washington, D.C.: U.S. Government Printing Office, 1978.

———; Dobert, Margarita K.; Marvin, Barbara J.; McLaughlin, James L.; and Whitaker, Donald P. *Area Handbook for Kenya.* 2nd ed. Foreign Area Studies, American University. Washington, D.C.: U.S. Government Printing Office, 1976.

Karioki, James N. *Tanzania's Human Revolution.* University Park: Pennsylvania State University Press, 1979.

Kariuki, Josiah Mwangi. *"Mau Mau" Detainee.* New York: Oxford University Press, 1963.

Kenya: An Economic Survey. London: Barclays Bank D.C.O., 1956.

Kenya: Into the Second Decade. World Bank Country Economic Report. Baltimore: Johns Hopkins University Press, 1975.

"Kenya Leader Promises Closer Military Ties with U.S." *Seattle Times,* February 21, 1980, p. A–2.

"Kenya To Encourage Credit Societies." *Nationalist* (Nairobi), June 9, 1964, p. 8.

"Kenya's Secret South African Deal." *Newsweek,* May 5, 1980, p. 23.

Kenya Union of Savings and Credit Co-operatives Ltd. and What It Does. Nairobi: Kenya Union of Savings and Credit Cooperatives, n.d. Brochure.

Kenyon, Ron. *To the Credit of the People.* Toronto: Ontario Credit Union League Ltd., 1976.

Kibaki, Mwai. "Planning Strategy for Sustained Growth." *Weekly Review* (Nairobi), December 12, 1977, pp. 27–32.

"Kibaki's Plan to Make 'All' Kenyans Rich." *Weekly Review* (Nairobi), December 12, 1977, pp. 9–12.

Kirsch, Ottfried C. "Credit Unions to Support Rural Development Projects in Africa." Draft manuscript prepared for *CIRCOM Journal of Rural Cooperation*, May 1979.

———, and Göricke, Fred V. *Scope and Impact of the Credit Union Movement in Selected African Countries*. Institute for International Partnership, Konrad Adenauer Foundation, English Series no. 3. Mainz: Hase & Koehler, 1977.

Kissinger, Henry. *White House Years*. Boston: Little, Brown, 1979.

Knapp, John N., Nairobi. Letters to Jack Dublin, December 7, 1963, September 19, 1964.

Koenigswinter, Dubiel, ed. *Rural Cooperatives in the Federal Republic of Germany*. Bonn: Ministry of Food, Agriculture, and Forestry, 1961.

Koff, David. "Black Man's Land." Huntington Beach, Calif.: PTV Publications, 1979. Television script.

The Konrad Adenauer Foundation's Project Policy Paper for the Sector of Thrift and Loan Societies. Bonn, Germany: Institute for International Partnership, Konrad Adenauer Foundation, 1978.

Kulundu, Charles. "Details of 'Arusha Declaration' Are Announced." *Daily Nation* (Dar es Salaam), February 6, 1967, p. 3.

Kurtz, Laura S. *Historical Dictionary of Tanzania*. Metuchen, N.J.: Scarecrow Press, 1978.

KUSCCO Central Fund Scheme. Nairobi: Kenya Union of Savings and Credit Co-operatives Ltd., n.d.

Kuuya, P. Masette. *Transfer of Technology: An Overview of the Tanzania Case*. Economic Research Bureau Paper 77.3. Dar es Salaam: University of Dar es Salaam, March 1977.

Laidlaw, Alexander F. *Challenges to Co-operators: Two Provocations*. Nanaimo, B.C.: Mid-Island Consumer Services Co-op, March 1979.

———. *Co-operatives and the Poor: A Review from within the Co-op Movement*. London: International Co-operative Alliance, 1978, pp. 51–93.

———. "Co-operatives in the Third World." *Action* (1979): 8–10. Publication of the Canadian International Development Agency.

———. "Co-operatives in the Year 2000." *Agenda and Report of the International Co-operative Alliance, XXVII Congress, Moscow, October 13–16, 1980*. London: International Co-operative Alliance, 1981, pp. 107–63.

———. "I've Changed My Mind." *Co-op: The Harbinger of Economic Democracy* (Ann Arbor, Mich.), May–June 1979, pp. 43–44. Publication of North American Student Cooperative Organization.

———. "Third World Co-operatives, Government and the Poor." *New Harbinger* (Ann Arbor, Mich.) 5 (fall 1978): 22–26. Publication of North American Student Cooperative Organization.

Lapham, Lewis H. "America's Foreign Policy: A Rake's Progress." *Harper's*, March 1979, pp. 43–50, 124–26.

Legum, Colin. "Why? Nyerere Explains—And Who's Behind Him . . ." *Daily Nation* (Dar es Salaam), February 28, 1967.

———; Zartman, I. William; Langdon, Steven; and Mytelka, Lynn K. *Africa in the 1980's: A Continent in Crisis*. New York: McGraw-Hill, 1979.

Lele, Uma. *The Design of Rural Development, Lessons from Africa*. Baltimore: Johns Hopkins University Press, 1975.

Leys, Colin. *Underdevelopment in Kenya: The Political Economy of Neo-Colonialism 1964–1971*. Berkeley and Los Angeles: University of California Press, 1974.

Litvak, Lawrence; DeGrasse, Robert; and McTigue, Kathleen, eds. *United States Investment in South Africa*. Palo Alto: South Africa Catalyst Project, 1978.

Loxley, John. "Structural Change in the Monetary System of Tanzania." *Socialism in Tanzania*, Vol 2. Nairobi: East African Publishing House, 1975, pp. 102–11.

MacEoin, Gary. *Agent For Change: The Story of Harvey (Pablo) Steele*. Maryknoll, N.Y.: Orbis, 1973.

McGrath, Mary Jean, ed. *Cooperatives, Small Farmers, and Rural Development*. Madison, Wis.: University Center for Co-operatives, University of Wisconsin, December 1978.

———, ed., *International Cooperative Training Journal.* Madison, Wis.: Board for International Cooperative Training, 1965–66, vols. 1–4 (1965), vol. 2 (1966).

MacKinnon, Donald J. "Keep Purpose Constant." *Credit Union Magazine,* June 1979, pp. 67–68.

McNamara, Robert. "Address to the Board of Governors." Speech given at World Bank Meeting, Nairobi, September 24, 1973.

Madery, Ronald D. Letter to A. A. Bailey, November 15, 1966. Copy supplied to Jack Dublin.

———. Letter to Henry W. Warren, December 6, 1966. Copy supplied to Jack Dublin.

———, and Mwasha, E. P. *Travel Report, Mtwara, Ruvuma, Iringa & Mbeya Regions, October 16–29, 1966.* Dar es Salaam: CUNA/AID East Africa Regional Credit Union Development Program, 1966.

Mahuwi, T. J. *Lending Policies: Savings and Credit Societies.* Moshi: Co-operative College, 1980.

"Majority Share of National Wealth Too Small." *East Africa Standard* (Nairobi), August 31, 1964, p. 2.

Makokha, Adrian W. "Kenya a Battlefield for Foreign Aid." *East Africa Standard* (Nairobi), May 29, 1964, p. 5.

Malecela, J. S. Opening Speech at co-operative senior officers conference, Moshi, November 3–12, 1970. Dodoma: Co-operative Development Department, n.d.

Managing Committee Manual for Savings and Credit Societies. Nairobi: Ministry of Co-operative Development, November 1975.

Manyanya, I. M. *Let Us Talk About Co-operative Savings and Credit Society.* Moshi: Co-operative College, February 1977.

Marnham, Patrick. *Fantastic Invasion, Notes on Contemporary Africa.* New York: Harcourt, 1979.

"Masses Must Come First." *Standard* (Dar es Salaam), April 11, 1967, pp. 1–3.

Matoyo, Aloys Stephen. Untitled paper given at Sixth African Conference on Mobilization of Local Savings, Maseru, Lesotho, January, 1968.

———. *Report on First 10 Years' Performance of ACOSCA's Eastern Region.* Nairobi: African Co-operative Savings and Credit Association, 1978.

May, George S. "Economic Role of Credit Unions in Canada." Unpublished notes and discussion outline prepared for the authors, Toronto, February 4, 1980.

———, and Hornal, Robert J. *Report on 1976 Summer Seminars for Victoria Co-operative Credit Association, Melbourne, Australia, February 20–29, 1976.* Vancouver: British Columbia Central Credit Union, 1976.

Mazuri, Ali. "The Africanization of Socialism." *Sunday Nation* (Kenya), April 2, 1978, p. 12.

Mbilinyi, Marjorie J. *The Transition to Capitalism in Tanzania.* Economic Research Bureau Paper 74.7. Dar es Salaam: University of Dar es Salaam, 1974.

MBIONI, February 1966, December 1966, October 1967, March–April 1968, May 1968. Monthly newsletter of Kivukoni College, Tanzania.

Mbithi, Philip M., and Rasmusson, Rasmus. *Self-Reliance in Kenya: The Case of Harambee.* Uppsala, Sweden: Scandinavia Institute of African Studies, 1977.

Mboya, Tom. "Intellectuals Told: Quit Ivory Towers." *Nation* (Nairobi), n.d.

———. *Speech by the Minister for Economic Planning and Development Delivered in Parliament.* Nairobi: Kenya News Agency, Ministry of Information, Broadcasting, and Tourism. 1965.

Meier, Gerald M. *Problems of Cooperation for Development.* New York: Oxford University Press, 1974.

"Memorandum Arising out of the Co-operative Managers' Conference to Consider the Report of the Special Committee of Enquiry into the Co-operative Movement and Marketing Boards." Dar es Salaam: Office of the President, August, 1966. Internal document.

"Merger Scheme for Kenya Co-ops." *East Africa Standard* (Nairobi), June 9, 1964, p. 5.

Mfinanga, A. L. "Report to Executive and Central Committee of ICA." Dar es Salaam: Co-operative Union of Tanzania, October 14, 1977. Internal document.

Mickelwait, Donald R.; Sweet, Charles F.; and Morss, Elliott R. *New Directions in Development: A Study of U.S. AID.* Boulder, Colo.: Westview Press, 1979.

Miller, Ken. "The Credit Union Movement in Australia." Paper prepared for the authors, Sydney, Australia, October 12, 1976.

———, Sydney, Australia. Letter to the authors, January 6, 1983.

Minister for Economic Affairs and Development Planning. *A Stride Forward.* Dar es Salaam: Ministry of Information and Tourism, June 14, 1966.

Miracle, Marvin P.; Miracle, Diane S.; and Cohen, Laurie. "Informal Savings Mobilization in Africa." Department of Agricultural Economics, University of Wisconsin, November 1, 1978.

Model By-Laws of Co-operative Savings and Credit Societies. Document no. CCS–0034. Nairobi: Republic of Kenya, 1972.

Money and Banking in Kenya. Nairobi: Central Bank of Kenya, December, 1972.

Moody, J. Carroll, and Fite, Gilbert C. *The Credit Union Movement.* Lincoln: University of Nebraska Press, 1971.

Moorehead, Alan. *The White Nile.* New York: Dell, 1962.

Moose, Richard M. "The New Situation in Zimbabwe." *Current Policy No. 155.* Washington, D.C.: Bureau of Public Affairs, U.S. Department of State, 1980.

Moronda, B. E. *The Co-op Movement and Socialism in Rural Tanzania.* Political Science Paper 7. Dar es Salaam: University of East Africa, March 1970.

Msambichaka, L. A., and Mabele, Robert B. M. *Agricultural Credit and the Development of Ujamaa Villages in Tanzania.* Economic Research Bureau Paper No. 74.10. Dar es Salaam: University of Dar es Salaam, November, 1974.

Munisi, Riskiankira S. L. "Administration of Rural Credit through Co-ops in Tanzania—Relating to Ujamaa Villages." *Agricultural Economic Report.* London: Wye College, University of London, 1976.

Münkner, Hans H. "Challenges Facing ACOSCA in the Second Decade." Paper disseminated at Tenth Anniversary Education Conference and Fifth Biennial Meeting of ACOSCA, Nairobi, August 21–28, 1978.

———. "Cooperatives for the Rich or for the Poor?" *Asian Economies,* June 1976, pp 32–54.

———, ed. *Credit Union Development in Africa.* Institute for International Partnership, Konrad Adenauer Foundation, English Series no. 4. Mainz: Hase & Koehler, 1978.

Munro, J. Forbes. *Africa and the International Economy, 1800–1960.* Totowa, N.J.: Rowman & Littlefield, 1976.

Mutayoba, J. G. "Can the Credit Unions be Related to Local Savings?" Speech given at International Credit Union Conference, Dar es Salaam, January 26, 1963.

Mwasha, E. P. Letter to A. A. Bailey, Dar es Salaam, May 21, 1968. Copy to Jack Dublin.

———. Letter to Jack Dublin, July 16, 1969.

———. "A Review of Credit Union Development in the United Republic of Tanzania." *Fourth African Conference on Mobilization of Local Savings Report, Nairobi.* Madison, Wis.: World Extension Department, CUNA International, Inc., 1965, pp. 31–37.

Mwenegoha, H. A. K. *Mwalimu Julius Kambarage Nyerere: A Biobibliography.* Nairobi: Foundation Books, 1976.

National Basic Intelligence Factbook. Washington, D.C.: Office of Geographic and Cartographic Research, U.S. Central Intelligence Agency, July 1978.

Ndege, William. "A Crusading Presidency." *African Affairs,* February 1979, pp. 29–30.

Ndegwa, D. N. *The Kenya Shilling.* Nairobi: Central Bank of Kenya, October 1977.

Nelson, Anton. *The Freemen of Meru.* New York: Oxford University Press, 1967.

Newsletter on Rural Financial Market Research and Policy. Columbus: Agricultural Finance Program, Ohio State University, October–December 1979.

Newsom, David D. "Communism in Africa." *Current Policy No. 99.* Washington, D.C.: Bureau of Public Affairs, U.S. Department of State, 1979.

Ng'entu, J. N. "Objects of Credit Unions, Duties and Responsibilities of Committees, Legal Rights of Supervisory Committee." Paper delivered at First Supervisory Committee Seminar, Co-operative College of Kenya, Nairobi, March 18–19, 1977.

1978 Annual Report. Washington, D.C.: National Credit Union Administration, 1979.

Njiru, L. N. *Economic Activities of Kagaari Co-op Society and Their Social and Political Impacts.* Political Science Paper 7. Dar es Salaam: University of East Africa, 1970.

Nkwera, Sigismund Venant. *SCULT* (in Swahili). Dar es Salaam: Savings and Credit Union League of Tanganyika, 1970.

Not for Ourselves Alone: Report of the Proceedings of the Third African Conference on Mobilization of Local Savings, June 1–6, 1964, Kampala, Uganda. Madison, Wis.: World Extension Department, CUNA International, Inc., n.d.

Nyanjom, Dan J. Letter to J. A. N. Kibue, May 25, 1965. Copy supplied to authors.

Nyerere, Julius K. *The Arusha Declaration: Ten Years After.* Washington, D.C.: Embassy of the United Republic of Tanzania, February 14, 1977. Press release.

———. "The Economic Challenge: Dialogue or Confrontation." *International Development Review,* no. 1 (1976): 2–8.

———. "41 Royal Marine Commando Farewell Message." Dar es Salaam: Tanganyika Information Services, April 5, 1964. Press release.

———. *Freedom and Unity/Uhuru na Umoja.* Dar es Salaam: Oxford University Press, 1966.

———. "The Honour of Africa." Dar es Salaam: Ministry of Information and Tourism, December 14, 1965. Address to the National Assembly.

———. Remarks on ABC news program "Issues and Answers," September 26, 1976, June 25, 1978. Washington, D.C.: Tyler Business Services, 1978.

———. "McDougall Memorial Lecture on FAO." Dar es Salaam: Tanganyika Information Division, Office of the Vice-President, November 15, 1963.

———. "Mwalimu Nyerere Address to TANU Annual Conference." Dar es Salaam: Tanganyika Information Services, April 1, 1964. Press release.

———. Press statement. Dar es Salaam: Tanganyika Information Services, January 23, 1964.

———. *Principles and Development.* Dar es Salaam: Ministry of Information and Tourism, June 1966.

———. *Socialism and Rural Development.* Dar es Salaam: Government Printer, September 1967.

———. Speech delivered to the Mary-Knoll Congress, New York City, October 16, 1970.

———. Speech delivered to the Pan-African Congress, Dar es Salaam, June 19, 1974.

———. Statement issued to the *Washington Post,* January 8, 1976.

"Nyerere Names the Firms, List Now Complete." *Sunday News* (Dar es Salaam), February 12, 1967, p. 1.

"Nyerere Throws Challenge to Nation." *Nationalist* (Dar es Salaam), February 28, 1967, pp. 1, 4.

Nzioka, C. F., and Onyango, Grace. "Report on Visit to Western and Nyanza Provinces, Aug. 21–27." Nairobi: Ministry of Co-operative Development, September 29, 1977. Internal Document.

O'Brien, Conor Cruise. *To Katanga and Back: A UN Case History.* London: Hutchinson, 1962.

O Brien, Father Tom. Letter to Jack Dublin enclosing copy of progress report on Vya Co-operative Credit Society, September 7, 1965.

Odinga, Oginga. *Not Yet Uhuru.* African Writers Series, no. 38. Nairobi: Heinemann Educational Books Ltd., 1967.

Otundo, A. G. T. "Annual Report 1977, Savings and Credit Section." Co-operative Development Department, Nairobi, March 14, 1978. Internal document.

"Overseas Credit Union Funding Detailed." *Leadership Letter,* December 24, 1979. Publication of CUNA International, Inc.

Overview Analysis of the World Council of Credit Unions. Madison, Wis.: World Council of Credit Unions, February 1980.

Peterson, Henry D., Dodge City, Kans. Letter to authors, December 11, 1979.

"Plan to Strengthen Kenya Co-operative Societies." *Sunday Nation* (Nairobi), August 30, 1964, p. 5.

Podovinikoff, Peter P., Vancouver, B. C. Interview with authors, December 22, 1982.

Policy Paper. Dar es Salaam: Savings and Credit Union League of Tanganyika, June 1976.

Porter, Sylvia. "Credit Unions: Still Your Best Friend?" *Seattle Times,* December 16, 1979.

"President Hits Out at 'Colonial Attitude.' " *Tanganyika Standard,* October 16, 1964, p. 5.

"The President's Speech at the 1964 Republic Day Rally." Dar es Salaam: Information Services Division, Tanzania Ministry of Information and Tourism, 1964. Press release.

"Progress Report Covering First Six Months of Operation." Washington, D.C.: CUNA Global Projects, 1969. Internal document.

"Public Ownership in Tanzania." *Sunday News* (Dar es Salaam), February 12, 1967, pp. 1, 4.

Quarterly Report July–Sept. 1977. Dar es Salaam: Nordic Project for Co-operative Assistance to Tanzania, November 1977.

Raiffeisen, F. W. *The Credit Unions.* 8th ed. Neuwied, West Germany: Raiffeisen, 1966.

Ray, Ellen; Schaap, William; Van Meter, Karl; and Wolf, Louis, eds. *Dirty Work 2: The CIA in Africa.* Secaucus, N.J.: Lyle Stuart, 1979.

Reader, John. "Microcosm of a Continental Force: Tribalism in Kenya." *Smithsonian,* June 1979, pp. 40–51.

Report and Accounts 1975. Dar es Salaam: Tanzania Housing Bank, 1975.

Report of the Cooperative Future Directions Committee. Ottawa, Ont.: Secretariat, Cooperative Future Directions Committee, October 1978.

Report of the president of CUNA International, Inc., to the joint meeting, Indianapolis, Ind., February 11, 1954.

Report of the Presidential Special Committee of Enquiry into the Co-operative Movement and Marketing Boards. Dar es Salaam: Government Printer, 1966.

Report of the Third ACOSCA Biennial Meeting, Kabwe, Zambia, Sept. 2–8, 1974. Madison, Wis.: World Council of Credit Unions, 1974.

Report of the Working Committee on National Association of Co-operative Savings and Credit Societies in Kenya. Nairobi: Kenya National Promotion Committee, 1973.

"Report on Appraisal of Request from the Tanzanian Government for Technical Assistance from the Nordic Countries for Cooperative and Rural Development." Arusha: Nordic Co-operative Projects, DANIDA, December 1977. Internal document.

"Report on the Proposals for an Africa Programme Part II." Report from World Extension Division, CUNA International, Inc., to Michigan Credit Union League, October 10, 1962.

Report on Rural Co-operative Credit and Savings Regional Seminar, Nairobi, July 16–26, 1974. Moshi: Regional Office for East and Central Africa, International Co-operative Alliance, 1974.

Report on the Tanganyika Post Office Savings Bank. Dar es Salaam: East Africa Posts & Telecommunications Corp., 1971.

Resnick, Idrian D. Statement in "The Crisis of Development and Interdependence."

Hearings before the Subcommittee on Africa. Committee on Foreign Affairs, 93rd Cong., 1st and 2nd Sess., May 23, June 12, June 20, July 27, 1973. February 28, 1974. Washington D.C.: U.S. Government Printing Office, 1974, pp. 105–25.

"Resolutions and Recommendations." *Fourth African Conference on Mobilization of Local Savings, Nairobi.* Madison, Wis.: World Extension Division, CUNA International, Inc., 1965, pp. 137–43.

"The Restructuring of America in the Decade Ahead." *Public Affairs Forum 3,* n.d. Publication of the Society of Chartered Property and Casualty Underwriters, Malvern, Pa.

"Review and Assessment of Future Cooperative Development in Kenya of Technical Assistance Requirements." Nairobi: Kenyan-Nordic Evaluation Mission, March 1976. Internal document.

Riley, Norman, and Amit, H. R., eds. *Report of Proceedings of African Seminar, East and Central, Kitwe, Zambia, Feb. 11–28, 1974.* Antigonish: Coady International Institute, February 1974.

Rocky Mountain Poll, Survey of Attitudes toward Credit Unions. Phoenix, Ariz.: Behavior Research Center, July 1979.

Rodney, Walter. *How Europe Underdeveloped Africa.* Dar es Salaam: Tanzania Publishing House, 1976.

Runcie, Neil, ed. *Credit Unions in the South Pacific.* London: University of London Press, 1969.

———; Miller, Ken; Robinson, Les; and Elliott, Reg. "Australia Credit Union Movement." Tape recording prepared for authors, Sydney, Australia, October 10, 1979.

"Rural Development: Two-year Diploma Course." Nyegezi, Tanzania: Social Training Centre, 1977. Co-operative syllabus.

Ruttkay, Fraño. *The First Credit Cooperative Society in Europe.* Prague: Central Cooperative Council, 1970.

Ryan, J. C. *Agricultural Credit in Uganda.* Bombay, India: Agricultural Credit Department, Reserve Bank of India, 1960.

Sagay, J. O., and Wilson, D. A. *Africa: A Modern History (1800–1975).* London: Evans, 1978.

Saul, John S. "Marketing Co-operatives in a Developing Country: The Tanzania Case." *Socialism in Tanzania,* Vol. 2, Nairobi: East African Publishing House, 1975, pp. 141–52.

"Save Funds in Credit Unions, Urges Mtaki." *Standard* (Dar es Salaam), January 3, 1967, p. 3.

Savings and Credit National Seminar at Moshi, Oct. 8–13, 1973. Dodoma: Office of the Prime Minister, n.d.

A Savings and Credit Society for Your Employees. rev. ed. Nairobi: Kenya National Promotion Committee, September 1972.

"Savings Level No Longer Key to Fitness." *Leadership Letter,* February 25, 1980. Publication of CUNA, Inc.

Schille, Charles. "Africa Cooperative Savings and Credit Association Celebrates 10th Anniversary." *Atlantic Co-operator* (Manitoba), November 1978.

Schroeder, Jac K. *Credit Unions, a Self-Study Program for Credit Union Employees.* Vancouver: British Columbia Central Credit Union, 1971.

Schumacher, E. F. *Small Is Beautiful.* New York: Harper & Row, 1975.

SCULT Country Report on Savings and Credit Societies. Dar es Salaam: Savings and Credit Union League of Tanganyika, n.d. Paper disseminated at Tenth Anniversary Educational Conference and Fifth Biennial Meeting of ACOSCA, August 21–29, 1978, Nairobi.

Seibel, H. Dieter. *The Developmental Function of Traditional Cooperative Societies in Africa.* Monrovia, Liberia: n.p., 1968.

Seidman, Ann. *Comparative Development Strategies in East Africa.* Nairobi: East African Publishing House, 1972.

———. *An Economic Textbook for Africa.* London: Methuen & Co., 1969.

Shah, Ramesh M. *History of Co-operative Movement in Tanzania, A Critical Evaluation.* Moshi: Co-operative College, December 1977.

———. "Role of Foreign Aid in Developing Countries with Special Emphasis on Tanzania." Paper disseminated at Twelfth Annual Social Science Conference of East African Universities, University of Dar es Salaam, Dar es Salaam, December 20–22, 1976.

Shonfield, Andrew. "The Politics of the Mixed Economy in the International System of the 1970's." *International Affairs,* January, 1980, pp. 1–15.

Sijaona, L. Nangwanda. Speech at opening of International Credit Union Conference on Mobilization of Local Savings at Msimbazi Community Centre, Dar es Salaam, January 30, 1963.

Sillery, Anthony. *Africa: A Social Geography.* 2nd ed. New York: Wiley, 1972.

Sixth AID Cooperative Advisory Committee Meeting Summary Minutes. Washington, D.C.: Agency for International Development, January 15, 1965. Statements of Jack Dublin, pp. 66–71; Gordon Roth, pp. 71–80; Richard N. Gardner, pp. 87–91.

Slater, Montagu. *The Trial of Jomo Kenyatta.* London: Secker & Warburg, 1955.

"Socialism Is Not Racialism." *Nationalist* (Dar es Salaam), February 14, 1967.

"Some Views from the International Co-operative Alliance Regional Office for East and Central Africa on the Re-institution of Co-operative Unions in Tanzania as Submitted to the Co-operative Commission in November, 1980." Internal document of International Co-operative Alliance Regional Office for East and Central Africa, Moshi, 1980.

"A Special Report on Socialism." *Time,* March 13, 1978.

Sprudzs, Aleksandrs. *Comparative Study: Mechanisms of Assistance and Advisory Service Delivered by Established Cooperatives in Canada, Sweden, U.S.S.R. to Cooperatives in Developing Countries.* Ottawa: International Development Research Centre/Canada, 1980.

Staff Manual. Nairobi: Credit and Finance Division, Urban Credit Section, Ministry of Co-operative Development, August 1972.

"Start Savings and Credit Societies—Tanzanians Told." *Washirika UCS News* (Dar es Salaam), October 1979, pp. 6–7. Newsletter of Union of Co-operative Societies.

Streeten, Paul. "From Growth to Basic Needs." *Finance and Development* 16 (September 1979): 28–31.

Summary: Report of International Conferences in East Africa-West Africa. Madison, Wis.: World Extension Division, CUNA International, Inc., 1963.

Syllabus for the Three-Month Savings and Credit Societies and Rural Savings and Credit Schemes Specialized Course. Moshi: Co-operative College, n.d.

Syllabus for Ujamaa and Co-operative Development Assistants/Home Economists Course. Dar es Salaam: Office of the Prime Minister, 1977.

Tamarkin, M. "The Roots of Political Stability in Kenya." *African Affairs* 77 (July 1978): 297–320.

Tanganyika: An Economic Survey. London: Barclays Bank D.C.O., 1956.

Tanganyika under U.K. Administration. London: United Kingdom Colonial Office, 1960.

"Tanu's Policy of Socialism and Self-Reliance." *Standard* (Dar es Salaam), February 6, 1967, pp. 2, 3, 5.

"Tanzania Leads in Credit Societies." *Nationalist* (Dar es Salaam), January 3, 1967, p. 2.

Tanzania Rural Savings and Credit Scheme for Villages and Ujamaa Villages. Dodoma: Office of the Prime Minister, May 1975, revised, November 1975.

"Task Order #15." Internal document of CUNA International, Inc., and Agency for International Development, Contract No. AID/csd-236, Washington, D.C., July 30, 1965.

Taylor, J. Clagett. *The Political Development of Tanganyika.* Stanford, Calif.: Stanford University Press, 1963.

Temu, D. Y. "The Implication on Rural Credit of the Dissolution of the Cooperative

Societies and the Experience of the Tanzania Rural Development Bank in Financing Villages." Paper presented at the Institute of Financial Management seminar, Dar es Salaam, December 16, 1977.

Tendler, Judith. *Inside Foreign Aid.* Baltimore: Johns Hopkins University Press, 1975.

———. *Inter-Country Evaluation of Small Farmer Organizations: Lessons of the Ecuadorean Experience.* Washington, D.C.: Office of Development Programs, Latin America Bureau, Agency for International Development, 1976.

———. *Inter-Country Evaluation of Small Farmer Organizations: Lessons of the Honduran Experiment.* Washington, D.C.: Office of Development Programs, Latin America Bureau, Agency for International Development, 1976.

Tenth African Conference on Mobilization of Local Savings and Third Annual Meeting of ACOSCA, Tunis, Tunisia, Sept. 12–15, 1972. Madison, Wis.: World Council of Credit Unions, 1972.

Ten Years toward Self-Reliance. Nairobi: Africa Co-operative Savings and Credit Association, 1978.

Thiong'o, C. J. and Onyango, G. A. "Report on Tour of Inspection and Supervision of Co-operative Savings and Credit Societies in Eastern Province from 6th June–11th June 1977." Nairobi: Co-operative Development Department, 1977. Internal document.

"Thrift and Loan Societies/Uganda." Report of Co-operative Development Department, Kampala, Uganda, on 1961–64 figures.

Toffler, Alvin, ed. *Learning for Tomorrow: The Role of the Future in Education.* New York: Random House, 1974.

Topshee, G. E. *Saint Francis Xavier, Extension, and the Third World.* Antigonish, Nova Scotia: Saint Francis Xavier University, 1978. Adaptation of paper by A. Quennec, February 1974.

Towards Socialist Planning. Tanzania Studies no. 1. Dar es Salaam: Tanzania Publishing House, 1972.

Tremblay, Rosario. "Desjardins International: I. Desjardins Policy; II. African Experience." Paper prepared for the authors, Levis, Quebec, October 1979.

Turtiainen, Turto, ed. "Internal Evaluation of Mutual Activities of the Co-operative Department, the Movement and the Nordic Project during 1972–77." Kenya: Nordic Project for Co-operative Assistance, June 1977. Internal document.

"U.S. Policy toward Africa Matures, Partnership Grows." *Front Lines* 18, no. 6 (1980): 1, 3. Publication of Agency for International Development, Washington, D.C.

Urban Credit Union Movement. Nairobi: Ministry of Co-operative Development, 1976.

The Urban Wards (Administration) Act, 1976, no. 4 Bill Supp. Dar es Salaam, June 18, 1976.

Utunzaji wa Mahesabu Katika Shirika La Akiba, Bookkeeping Manual for Savings and Credit Societies. Dar es Salaam: Idara Ya Vyama vyu Ushirika, 1972.

Vail, David J. *Technology for Ujamaa Village Development in Tanzania.* Syracuse: Maxwell School of Citizenship and Public Affairs, Syracuse University, 1975.

"Vance: Aid Programs Help Counter Soviet Challenge." *Front Lines* 18, no. 6 (1980): 1, 7. Publication of Agency for International Development, Washington, D.C.

Vance, Cyrus. "America and the Developing World." *Current Policy No. 75.* Washington, D.C.: Bureau of Public Affairs, U.S. Department of State, 1979.

———. *U.S. Policy toward Africa.* Washington, D.C.: Bureau of Public Affairs, Office of Media Services, U.S. Department of State, 1977. Speech given at Annual Convention of National Association for the Advancement of Colored People, St. Louis, Mo., July 1, 1977.

"Views on the Restructuring of the Co-operative Movement in Tanzania." *Co-operative News* 13, no. 2 (1977): 5–9. Publication of Regional Office for East and Central Africa, International Co-operative Alliance, Moshi.

The Villages and Ujamaa Villages (Registration, Designation, and Administration) Act, 1975. Dar es Salaam, Aug. 12, 1975 (passed July 16, 1975).

Von Pischke, J. D. *A Penny Saved . . . : Kenya's Cooperative Savings Scheme and Some Related Aspects of Rural Finance.* Working Paper No. 204. Nairobi: Institute for Development Studies, University of Nairobi, 1975.

Voorhis, Jerry. *Credit Unions, Basic Cooperatives.* Chicago, Ill.: Cooperative League of the U.S.A., 1965.

———, Claremont, Calif. Letter to Jack Dublin, October 10, 1979.

———. "People, Our Best Investment." Address to thirty-ninth annual meeting of the Ontario Credit Union League, Toronto, March 29, 1979.

Walden, Jerrold L. "C.I.A.: A Study in the Abrogation of Administrative Powers." *George Washington Law Review* 39 (October 1970): 66–101.

Walinsky, Louis J., ed. *The Selected Papers of Wolf Ladejinsky.* New York: Oxford University Press, 1977, pp. 500–11.

Weber, George L., Mipa, Tanzania. Letter to Jack Dublin, September 6, 1963.

Wegner, Herb. "Examining the Future for Credit Unions." Undated copy of speech given as president of CUNA, sent to Jack Dublin December 13, 1979.

———, Silver Spring, Md. Letter to Jack Dublin, December 13, 1979.

Weisbord, Robert H. *African Zion.* Philadelphia; Jewish Publication Society of America, 1968.

Widstrand, Carl Gösta, ed. *African Co-operatives and Efficiency.* Uppsala, Sweden: Scandinavian Institute of African Studies, 1972.

———, ed., *Co-operatives and Rural Development in East Africa.* New York: Africana, 1970.

Williams, G. Mennen. Statement made to the Michigan Credit Union League in Washington, D.C., October 21, 1963.

"Williams Reviews Mistakes and Successes." *Credit Union Magazine,* July 1978, pp. 52–53.

Workshop on Savings and Credit Schemes Held at Co-operative College, Moshi, Nov. 4–9, 1974 (in Swahili and English). Dodoma: Ujamaa and Co-operative Development Department, Office of the Prime Minister, 1974.

"Wright Looks at Goals and Problems." *Credit Union Magazine,* July 1978, pp. 51–52.

Yudelman, Montague. "Impact of the Bank's Rural Development Lending." *Finance and Development* 16 (September 1979): 24–28.

Index

Jack Dublin is an independent credit union consultant. He has held senior positions with the U.S. Agency for International Development, the Credit Union National Association, the Bureau of Federal Credit Unions, and the Michigan Credit Union League. He has served as the U.S. delegate to international credit union and co-operatives conferences in Latin America, Africa, Asia, Europe, and Great Britain. He is a former president of Lafayette Federal Credit Union. In 1980–81 he was a senior lecturer at the Co-operative College, Tanzania. Selma M. Dublin is a former research associate of the Academy for Educational Development and former director of its Information Center on Instructional Technology.

The Dublins have been participants in the East African community since the early 1960s, mainly in Tanzania, where they lived with their four children from 1963 to 1967. *Credit Unions: Theory and Practice* (Wayne, 1966, 2nd ed., 1971), Jack Dublin's first book, grew out of his lectures at the Nyegezi Social Training Centre. In the late 1970s the Dublins returned to study the maturing Tanzanian and Kenyan credit union movements they had helped to establish. This book is the culmination of their continuing research.

Their research and consulting firm, International Technical Services, is located in Edmonds, Washington.

The manuscript was edited by Anne M. Guerrini. The book was designed by Richard Kinney. The typeface for the text is Mergenthaler's VIP Times Roman, based on a design supervised by Stanley Morison in 1931. The display face is Mergenthaler's VIP Eurostile, based on a design by A. Novarese in 1962.

The text is printed on 55-lb. IP's Glatfelter paper. The hardcover books are bound in Permalin's Buckram finish paper over binder's boards. The paperback books are bound in Riegel's Carolina Cover CIS. Manufactured in the United States of America.